PENGUIN  CLASSICS

THE NEW PENGUIN FREUD
GENERAL EDITOR: A

THE JO
TO T.

SIGMUND FREUD was bo⟶   ⟶etween the ages of
four and eighty-two his hom⟶   ⟶nna: in 1938 Hitler's invasion
of Austria forced him to seek asylum in London, where he died in the
following year. His career began with several years of brilliant work
on the anatomy and physiology of the nervous system. He was almost
thirty when, after a period of study under Charcot in Paris, his interests first turned to psychology; and after ten years of clinical work in
Vienna (at first in collaboration with Breuer, an older colleague) he
invented what was to become psychoanalysis. This began simply as a
method of treating neurotic patients through talking, but it quickly
grew into an accumulation of knowledge about the workings of the
mind in general. Freud was thus able to demonstrate the development of sexual instinct in childhood and, largely on the basis of an examination of dreams, arrived at his fundamental discovery of the
unconscious forces that influence our everyday thoughts and actions.
Freud's life was uneventful, but his ideas have shaped not only many
specialist disciplines, but also whole intellectual climate of the twentieth century.

Until her retirement, JOYCE CRICK was for many years Senior Lec-
turer in German at University College London, and is now Honorary
Special Professor in Modern Languages at the University of Notting-
ham. In the field of Germanistics she has written on Thomas and
Heinrich Mann, Christa Wolf, Günter Grass and Bertolt Brecht; in
the field of Comparative Literature she collaborated on editing the
German material for Princeton University Press's edition of Coleridge's *Notebooks*, volumes III and IV, edited his translation of
Schiller's *Wallenstein* dramas and has written on Kafka in translation
and on the German reception of Virginia Woolf. Her previous translations include selected texts for Cambridge University Press's volumes of *German Aesthetic and Literary Criticism*. In 2000 she was
awarded the Schlegel Tieck Prize for her new translation of Freud's

The Interpretation of Dreams (first edition) for Oxford University Press's Modern Classics series.

JOHN CAREY is an Emeritus Professor of English Literature at Oxford University, a Fellow of the British Academy and chief book reviewer for the *Sunday Times*. His books include critical studies of Milton, Donne, Dickens and Thackeray, *Original Copy*, a selection of his reviews and journalism, and a study of the elitism of early twentieth-century writers, *The Intellectuals and the Masses* (1992). He has also published three anthologies – of reportage, science-writing and utopias – and edited Thackerary's *Vanity Fair* for Penguin Classics. *Pure Pleasure*, his choice of the fifty most enjoyable books of the twentieth century, appeared in 2000.

ADAM PHILLIPS was formerly Principal Child Psychotherapist at Charing Cross Hospital in London. He is the author of several books on psychoanalysis including *On Kissing, Tickling and Being Bored, Darwin's Worms, Promises, Promises* and *Houdini's Box*.

SIGMUND FREUD

The Joke and Its Relation to the Unconscious

Translated by JOYCE CRICK
with an Introduction by JOHN CAREY

PENGUIN CLASSICS

PENGUIN BOOKS

Published by the Penguin Group

Penguin Group (USA) Inc., 375 Hudson Street, New York, New York 10014, U.S.A.
Penguin Group (Canada), 90 Eglinton Avenue East, Suite 700, Toronto,
Ontario, Canada M4P 2Y3 (a division of Pearson Penguin Canada Inc.)
Penguin Books Ltd, 80 Strand, London WC2R 0RL, England
Penguin Ireland, 25 St Stephen's Green, Dublin 2, Ireland (a division of Penguin Books Ltd)
Penguin Group (Australia), 250 Camberwell Road, Camberwell,
Victoria 3124, Australia (a division of Pearson Australia Group Pty Ltd)
Penguin Books India Pvt Ltd, 11 Community Centre, Panchsheel Park, New Delhi – 110 017, India
Penguin Group (NZ), 67 Apollo Drive, Rosedale, North Shore 0632, New Zealand
(a division of Pearson New Zealand Ltd)
Penguin Books (South Africa) (Pty) Ltd, 24 Sturdee Avenue, Rosebank,
Johannesburg 2196, South Africa

Penguin Books Ltd, Registered Offices: 80 Strand, London WC2R 0RL, England

First published as *Der Witz und seine Beziehung zum Unbewußten*
by Deuticke (Leipzig and Vienna) 1905
English translation published in Penguin Books (U.K.) 2002
This edition published 2003

7 9 10 8 6

Sigmund Freud's German text collected in *Gesammelte Werke (1940–52)*
copyright © Imago Publishing Co., Ltd, London, 1940
Translation and editorial matter copyright © Joyce Crick, 2002
Introduction copyright © John Carey, 2002
All rights reserved

Extracts from *The Robbers & Wallenstein* by Friedrich Schiller, translated by
F. J. Lamport (Penguin Classics, 1979), reproduced by permission of Penguin Books.
Translation copyright © F. J. Lamport, 1979.
Extract from *Back to Freud's Texts* by Ilse Grubrich-Simitis, translated by Philip Slotkin
(Yale University Press, 1996), reproduced by permission of Sigmund Freud Copyrights.

LIBRARY OF CONGRESS CATALOGING IN PUBLICATION DATA
Freud, Sigmund, 1856–1939.
[Witz und seine Beziehung zum Unbewussten. English]
The joke and its relation to the unconscious / Sigmund Freud ; translated by Joyce Crick ;
with an introduction by John Carey.
p. cm.
Includes bibliographical references.
ISBN 978-0-14-243744-5
1. Wit and humor—Psychological aspects. 2. Subconsciousness. I. Title.
PN6149.P5F6813 2003
155.2'32—dc21   2003043314

Printed in the United States of America
Set in Adobe New Caledonia

Contents

Introduction by John Carey vii
Translator's Preface xxix

A   *Analytic Part* 1
  I *Introduction* 1
 II *The Technique of the Joke* 9
III *The Tendencies of the Joke* 85

B   *Synthetic Part* 113
 IV *The Mechanism of Pleasure and the Psychological Origins of the Joke* 113
  v *The Motives for Jokes – The Joke as Social Process* 135

C   *Theoretical Part* 154
 VI *The Relation of the Joke to Dreams and to the Unconscious* 154
VII *The Joke and the Varieties of the Comic* 175

Introduction

Freud's book about jokes is even more original than his book about dreams. Many previous writers had suggested that dreams give us access to depths of our nature from which we are debarred in waking life. He is often credited with 'discovering' the unconscious in *The Interpretation of Dreams* (1900). But the existence of the unconscious had been acknowledged long before, as Lancelot Law Whyte's *The Unconscious Before Freud* (1962) has shown. By contrast the relationship Freud posits between jokes, dreams and the unconscious in the present work was quite new. Previous writers on humour, several of whom he cites, had never suspected anything of the kind. But for Freud the connection was vital. His theory of jokes grew out of his theory of dreams, because he believed that dreams use jokes as part of their disguise.

Dreams, according to Freud, express unconscious wishes. These usually relate to infantile sexuality (as, for example, the wish to copulate with one's mother, which Freud thought virtually universal among male children). However, dreams cannot express these wishes directly, because they are opposed by the part of our psychical apparatus that Freud calls the censorship (*Zensur*). The censorship's job is to prevent anxiety, and other distressing symptoms, which would ensue if the unconscious wishes became conscious. Accordingly it intercepts them and stops them entering consciousness. To get past the censorship, dreams have to adopt disguises, and this is what Freud called the 'dream-work'. The disguises they adopt include riddles, homonyms and other kinds of joke. They seem (Freud noted) to have a partiality for bad puns. For example, one of his patients dreamed that he was kissing his uncle in a car, which

Freud deciphered as a disguised reference to the word 'auto-eroticism'.

Freud's friend Wilhelm Fliess was the first to notice that the patients' dreams Freud told him about were full of jokes and puns. They seemed, he objected, too 'ingenious and witty' for sleeping people to have thought up. But Freud replied that all dreams are 'insufferably witty', and have to be, because the direct path to the expression of their wishes is barred. They must trick the censorship (which is apparently less good at spotting and decoding jokes than the unconscious is at inventing them). Pursuing this train of thought, Freud became convinced that 'The apparent wittiness of all unconscious processes is intimately related to the theory of wit and the comic.'[1]

It is easy to see how this led to the daring speculation that jokes, like dreams, come from the unconscious. If we have a hidden joker, deep in our psyches, who manufactures dreams, then the same joker may be responsible for jokes too. Laughter, after all, is involuntary, as dreams are. Further, it has always eluded – still eludes – scientific explanation. No one knows why we laugh. As we shall see, the explanation of jokes that Freud evolved proposed an answer to that intractable question as well.

How successful Freud is in likening jokes to dreams is something this Introduction must confront. But we should keep in mind throughout the purpose that he allocates to all jokes and all humour – a purpose he persistently alludes to and drives home in his closing paragraphs. All jokes and all humour, Freud maintains, are forms of economy. They represent a 'saving in expenditure' of psychical effort. In the case of what he calls 'innocuous' jokes (simple puns, for example), the saving arises because we delight in chance analogy, as children do in play, and so avoid the effort of critical, discriminatory thought. In the case of 'tendentious' (lustful or hostile) jokes, we satisfy aggressive instincts, and so economize on the effort that normally inhibits such satisfaction. In both cases, and in all other categories of humour and comedy, 'the pleasure comes from a saving' (p. 228).

We need to register how strange this is, how curiously specific and all-embracing, and how unlike our common notions of what jokes do. We are used to thinking that we joke about what normally makes us sad or afraid. The joke gives us a sense of release or relief by replacing fear or sadness with laughter. Here, for example, is a joke about death:

A cat-owner on holiday is phoned by his neighbour back home with the sad news that his cat has fallen to its death from the roof of the house. The cat-owner reprimands the neighbour for breaking the news so abruptly. 'What else could I have done?' demands the neighbour. 'Well,' says the cat-owner, 'you could have led up to it gradually. One day you could have phoned to say you had seen the cat poking around on the roof among the chimneys. Then you could say it was straying near the edge, and so on.' A week passed. Then the neighbour phoned again. 'Hi, it's me. I'm phoning to say I've seen your mother poking around on the roof among the chimneys.'

You could see this joke as an escape from the feelings that normally accompany bereavement, a sort of truancy. That is not incompatible with Freud's general approach, except that he would take the further and, he would insist, vital step of describing it in economic terms – as a saving of expenditure.

Why? In his theory of dreams the idea of economy had hardly figured at all. In explaining why the censorship, which suppresses all unconscious wishes during waking hours, allows them to enter consciousness when disguised as dreams at night, Freud speculates that it may be a kind of economy. Allowing the dream to take its course and enter consciousness may represent a saving of energy compared with holding the unconscious as tightly under control at night as in the daytime. But the question seems of little interest to him, and he concludes that 'the explanation no doubt lies in relations of energy of which we have no knowledge'.[2] There is little in his Dream book to prepare us for the key role that economy plays in his book on jokes.

As that example from the Dream book illustrates, 'economy' may signify a saving of energy as well as of money. In the first sense it was a term transferred from physics or hydraulics, and was used by a number of late nineteenth-century psychologists when referring to the build-up and release of psychical energy. Freud himself often employs it in this way in his early works. However, in the Joke book the financial meaning of 'economy' is firmly endorsed, not just in passing references such as Hamlet's joke about 'Thrift' (p. 34), but more forcefully in the long comparison between joke-condensation and business-enterprise in section V.

We may do well to allow ourselves to compare the economy of the psyche with a business concern. As long as the business turnover is very small, the main thing of course is that on the whole not much is spent and that the running costs are kept extremely low. The frugality applies to the absolute height of the expenditure. Later, when the business has expanded, the importance of running costs lessens; it no longer matters how high the amount of expenditure becomes as long as the turnover and returns can be sufficiently increased. Restraint in expenditure for running the business would be petty, indeed positively unprofitable. However, it would be wrong to assume that given the absolute amount of the expenditure there would be no more room for the tendency towards economy. The boss's thrifty-mindedness will now turn to parsimony in single items, and feel satisfied if the same activity can now be managed at a lower cost when its previous costs were higher, however small the economy may appear in comparison with the total expenditure. In a quite analogous way, economy in details remains a source of pleasure in the complicated business of our psyche . . . (p. 152)

Why was this financial analogy so important to Freud? Why did it come to dominate his theory of jokes? What effect did it have on the choice of specimen jokes that he included in his treatise? These are obviously crucial questions to ask about his theory, since the idea of economy is its crucial and distinguishing component. Towards the end of this Introduction I shall try to supply answers.

But first, some of the difficulties Freud encountered in inter-preting jokes as products of the unconscious. These difficulties need pointing out since Freud's persuasive rhetoric serves to obscure them. That is its purpose. Scientific proof is clearly impossible in such a matter, as it was in his theory of dreams, so persuasion is all-important. But unless we school ourselves to resist Freud's persuasion, a critical assessment of his theory cannot be developed.

An initial question to ask is, if jokes reflect the unconscious, as Freud claims, then whose unconscious do they reflect? On this point, Freud wavers. Sometimes he implies that he is himself an inventor of jokes, as he is a dreamer of dreams, and can offer his own experience in evidence, as he often does in his Dream book. He even lays claim to a special kind of first-hand insight into jokes, not susceptible to logical inquiry. This insight, or intuition, allows him, he says, to discriminate between true jokes, which have come from the unconscious, and false or spurious jokes, which have not. A particular 'feeling' tells him 'this is a joke, this is something you can claim is a joke' (p. 70). A similar awareness of the unconscious at work is, Freud tells us, felt by the joker in the course of a genuine joke's incubation. A joke, he claims, has 'quite outstandingly' the characteristic of being a notion that has occurred to us involuntarily.

One senses . . . something undefinable, which I would best compare with an *absence*, a sudden letting-go of intellectual tension, and then all at once the joke is there, for the most part simultaneously clad in words. (p. 164)

Freud seems here to be drawing on his own experience, as well, perhaps, as that of jocular friends whom he has consulted.

However, for most people jokes are not things they invent but things they hear, remember and retell – and Freud generally seems to accept that this is the case. Although, as we saw in the previous paragraph, he sometimes writes as if he is privy to the psychological processes involved in his (and 'our') invention of jokes, he elsewhere stipulates that few people are capable of the 'joke-work'. Joke-makers are an élite, characterized by a special personal aptitude for passing from the preconscious to the unconscious (pp. 137, 163). Since for the most part their identities are no longer known it is plainly difficult to hazard any conclusions about the state of their unconscious, as Freud concedes. A rare exception is Heinrich Heine, behind whose jokes, he believes, can be detected 'bitterly serious' feelings about his own poverty and his relatives' wealth (pp. 138–9). But Freud confesses that he knows of no other case in which such 'subjective determinants' can be convincingly demonstrated.

This is obviously, though Freud is at pains to conceal it, an enormous setback for his theory. With dreams, he was able to psychoanalyse patients for many hours, compiling extensive files on their past lives and on the free associations they made in response to his questions. With jokes, none of this vital data is available. He never finds, and psychoanalyses, a joker. Nor does he give us an example of a joke he has himself made up, together with its psychological origin, as he often does with his dreams. Yet despite his ignorance about the originators of jokes, it is the originators' experience that he is intent on recapturing. '[T]he functions the joke performs in the inner life of the person who makes it, or – the only way to put it correctly – the person it occurs to' are always for him the important thing, more important than the joke's effect on hearers or retellers (p. 130). The joke-work is 'the process of joke-formation in the first person' (p. 162).

It is easy to see why he maintains this emphasis. It is necessary for his comparison of jokes with dreams. Dreams are not heard, laughed at and retold, as jokes are. With dreams, the dreamer is the focus of the analyst's attention, and this must remain true of jokes if the joke-dream analogy is to stand. Since the original joke-makers are mostly unknown, however, nothing can with certainty be said about them. The only realistic subjects for study are the hearers and retellers. Yet to draw attention to this would be to make Freud's joke-dream analogy unworkable. Hence his tendency, noted above, to imply that we all have an inner knowledge of joke-invention, while freely contradicting such an assumption elsewhere in the book.

Since he cannot rely on psychoanalysing jokers, as his Dream book relies on psychoanalysing dreamers, Freud has to find some other method of demonstrating a correspondence between jokes and dreams. His answer is to analyse the structure of jokes and relate it to the structure of dreams. In his Dream book he had argued that the two chief principles observed by the dream-work in structuring dreams were condensation and displacement (representation of one thing by another). The main argumentative thrust of the present work is to establish that the same principles govern the structure of jokes.

There are serious objections to such a project, which Freud, understandably, does not dwell on. To start with, 'condensation' does not mean the same thing in the two cases. Dreams are 'condensed', according to Freud's theory, because a large amount of complicated psychological history, elicited by Freud in the course of psychoanalysis, can be shown to have been selected from and abbreviated in the patient's dream. With jokes, nothing of the kind is demonstrable. The psychological history that precedes them is, as we have noted, missing. The best that Freud can do to show condensation in jokes is to cite jokes that run two words into one – as in the case of Heine's joke about the lottery-collector who boasts that Baron Rothschild has treated him quite 'famillionairely' (p. 11). This, admittedly, is the kind of joke the dream-work might make use of, as the 'auto-eroticism' example (above) suggests. But the auto-eroticism dream, like all Freud's specimen dreams, condenses and illuminates a tangled history of neurosis. The 'famillionairely' joke does not – so far as we know.

Inevitably Freud meets the same difficulty with the structural feature called 'displacement'. In dreams, according to his theory, displacement is absolutely vital. It is the chief means at the disposal of the unconscious for disguising the dream's true content. For example, in dreams about copulating with one's mother, the mother's genitals will be 'displaced'. That is, they will be represented by something else – a box, a cave, or any other of a long list of symbols Freud supplies in the heavily expanded third edition of his Dream book (1911). It need not even be an actual symbol. The feeling 'I have been here before,' which many people have in dreams, is, Freud states, a cover for the same guilty wish: 'These places are inevitably the genitals of the dreamer's mother.'[3] Freud's therapeutic skill as a psychoanalyst lay in decoding these symbols and allowing the patient to confront his or her guilty wish. But with jokes none of this is possible. To talk of 'displacement' in jokes is itself questionable, for all we have is the text of the joke. What, if anything, has been 'displaced' remains speculative. It cannot be retrieved by analysis as (Freud believed) dream displacements can be.

The impression we have, reading the present work, that the examples do not quite exemplify what Freud wishes them to, is traceable to this recurrent problem. For instance, a type of displacement common, Freud believes, in dreams is 'representation by the opposite'. This often involves the replacement of a disagreeable thing by something agreeable. He claims to find the same displacement in a joke about an Irish waxworks where the effigies of the Duke of Wellington and his horse are apparently indistinguishable (p. 60–61). But this, of course, is not at all how representation by the opposite would work in a dream. There, only the opposite would appear, and the dream-interpreter would have to supply the suppressed object that it symbolized. Having both the Duke and his horse in the joke destroys the similarity to a dream. Besides, the joke depends on other factors – the young lady's naïveté, the guide's repartee – that Freud leaves out of the account. In addition, it is a joke at the expense of the Irish, a special category of English joke serving xenophobic ends, and Freud ignores this too. He believes, indeed, that all these narrative interests in jokes (everything that we normally think of as constituting a funny story) are secondary. We make the mistake, he claims, of thinking that we are amused by the 'content' of a joke. But 'the content of a joke is separate from the joke' (p. 89). What really makes us laugh is the hidden psychical mechanism (in this case 'representation by the opposite') that he has uncovered. Of course, he does not deny that the 'total impression' of a joke is of form and content together. But he insists that we 'allow ourselves to be pretty well deceived' in ascribing so much importance to content. He may be right. Such a claim is impossible to disprove – or prove. The patient's acceptance of the psychoanalyst's diagnosis, which validates – or seems to validate – Freud's interpretation of dreams, is never available in the case of jokes.

The other types of displacement Freud claims to find in jokes are equally troublesome when we relate them to his dream theory. He states that 'representation by a small or very, very small item' must occur in jokes, since it occurs in dreams. As it happens he can find almost no jokes that exemplify it, which, if he were thinking scientifically, would prompt him to re-examine his thesis. Further, the two examples he does produce do not seem to fit the category. The first is the story of the Galician Jew on the train (p. 69). In dreams a 'small item' or a 'little one' (a child) normally stands (or so Freud hypothesizes in the third edition of his Dream book) for the genitals. There is nothing of this kind in the Galician Jew joke. Presumably the 'small item' Freud takes as its essence is the Jew's travelling-companion's question about the date of Yom Kippur, which identifies him as another Jew. It could equally be argued, though, that this is inessential. Any identifying question by the travelling-companion could be substituted. What is funny (or was meant to be funny to the joke's original hearers) was that a 'gentleman in modern dress' should turn out to be a Jew. Jewish efforts at cultural assimilation are ridiculed (see Translator's Preface, p. xli). But this constitutes the kind of narrative interest that, as we have seen, Freud relegates to the secondary status of 'content'.

Freud's second example of representation by a 'small item' is the story of the Baroness in childbirth, whose doctor and husband ignore her cries of pain because they are playing cards (p. 70). This is one of the most troubling of Freud's anti-woman anecdotes. That he could ever have reckoned it a 'good' joke comes as a shock. It is even more shocking when he makes it clear that what he classifies as a 'small item' are the woman's cries of pain, and more offensive still (at least to modern sensibilities) when it emerges that this, like the Galician Jew joke, is a joke against Jewish social mobility. The Yiddish quality of the Baroness's final agonized cry, 'Ai, waih, waih' (see section II, n. 57) is meant to betray her lowly social origins, which burst through the façade of aristocratic pretension. Freud later decided it was an 'unmasking' and had no justifiable claim to be called a joke (pp. 196–7).

It may seem unnecessary to go on at such length about the apparently frequent mismatch in Freud's exposition between the specimen jokes and the 'displacement' they are meant to illustrate. Yet since Freud's argument consists very largely in relating joke-displacement to dream-displacement, examining the relationship is indispensable to a critical reading. Besides, readers of his Joke book who have been uneasily conscious of the persistent failures of understanding prompted by such mismatches are entitled to know that their stupidity is not to blame (or at any rate is shared by a fellow-reader). In reality, as we have seen, a factor that obstructs any easy understanding of the text is that the terms evolved by Freud in his analysis of dreams cannot have the same meaning when applied to jokes. But he writes as if they can.

The term 'unification', of central importance to his theory, is relevant here. The mark of unification, he explains, is that 'new and unexpected unities are being set up' (p. 57). The jokes illustrating this category are *bons mots* or clever quips, such as the epigram from Fischer, 'Experience consists of experiencing what we do not want to experience,' or Voltaire's response to a poem entitled *Ode to Posterity*, 'This poem will not reach its address' (p. 58). The second is an example of repartee, and Freud goes on to suggest that repartee always entails unification because it establishes an unexpected unity between attack and counter-attack.

When we turn to the occurrence of 'unification' in dreams, however, we find something very different. Dreams (according to Freud) unify in two respects. First, they feature composite characters, made up of two or more people, often from widely separate periods of our life. Second, the items from the latent 'dream-thoughts' that dreams select and disguise are joined up to make a narrative, often baffling and apparently absurd, of course, but nevertheless clearly a 'new and unexpected unity' in Freud's sense. What seems questionable, however, is how the jokes Freud cites meet this criterion. What new unity does the 'experience' joke establish? Or the 'posterity' jibe? Both jokes depend on clever repetition or redeployment of the same word or the same idea. But that seems quite different from the 'unexpected unities' represented by the strange, surreal narratives that we encounter in dreams. The well-established link between dreams and poetry, illustrated, for example, by Coleridge's dream-poem 'Kubla Khan', depends largely on the observation that 'new and unexpected unities' of a dream-like kind are what poetic metaphors create. Coleridge, in *Biographia Literaria* (1817), indeed, identifies the poet's peculiar gift of 'secondary imagination' as a unity-making ('esemplastic') power of the sort Freud appears to have in mind.[4] But the jokes Freud offers seem very far from creating new unities in this sense.

What they do seem to create is a particular kind of pleasure in the hearer. This is not an aspect that Freud considers, but it is arguable that an element of our enjoyment of these clever jokes is a self-congratulatory awareness of our own cleverness in enjoying them. We feel ourselves to be, as it were, in the company of clever people like ourselves, and feel joyful at the distinction it confers. We laugh in self-glorifying delight. This seems to be what Thomas Hobbes had in mind when he contended that 'those grimaces called laughter'[5] are always eventually self-congratulatory. When, as often, repartee jokes contain allusions to literature or other learned material the self-congratulatory element seems especially prominent. We delight in our membership of the closed circle to which the joke can appeal. One of the few jokes collected by Freud that still seems funny to today's readers is evidently of this kind – the Sophoclean lament 'Never to have been born would be the best for mortal kind,' to which the wits of a German comic weekly added the rider 'But that scarcely happens to one in 100,000' (p. 48).

The difficulties experienced by the reader that we have considered so far relate broadly to Freud's interpretation of his specimen jokes and the categories he places them in. Another kind of problem is raised by his distinction between jokes and the comic. In contemporary English usage the idea of a joke and of the comic virtually coincide. Jokes are comic, comics make jokes. Consequently it can be puzzling to find Freud insisting that a clear distinction is to be made between jokes and the comic, and that 'Contact with the comic certainly does not apply to all jokes, nor even to the majority' (p. 201). To some degree he is here presuming on the reader's acquaintance with discussions of 'the comic' in earlier German aesthetic theory. His own theory of the comic, and of its difference from jokes, diverges from previous authorities, however, and can be deduced from his treatise. From a modern scientific viewpoint, it is a curiosity. But it is important to grasp it, since it illustrates both

Freud's desire to find an organic basis for psychical phenomena, and his adherence to the idea that economy of expenditure underlies all humour.

The distinction between a joke and the comic in Freud's theory is that a joke is something made up or invented, while the comic is something we see or hear by chance – an ungainly person, perhaps, or an artless remark made by a child – and laugh at. To explain why such laughter occurs Freud constructs a mechanistic theory of the mind's operations. He selects as his paradigm of the comic the antics of clowns in a pantomime. The physical movements of clowns are, he explains, characteristically too large for the purposes they are designed to attain. We instinctively compare them with the smaller movements we ourselves would make to achieve the same objective. This largeness in the clown's movements is of key importance. For, Freud argues, for us to form the idea of something large requires more psychical energy than to form the idea of something small. Indeed, forming the idea of something large requires an exertion of our nervous system, as if we were striving ourselves to be that large thing.

Direct observation shows us that people habitually express dimensions of large and small in their imagined contents by means of varying expenditure in a kind of *mimicry of the imagination*. (p. 188)

Children, common people and members of 'certain races' actually make appropriate manual gestures, Freud notes, when they talk about a 'high mountain' or a 'little dwarf'. With more sophisticated people, he argues, these movements are internalized, but they still happen.

I believe . . . that this mimicry does exist, though less vigorously, quite apart from any communication, and that it also comes about when a person is imagining to himself, thinking of something vividly; and that he is then expressing the dimensions of large and small in his body, just as he does when speaking, at least by means of alterations in the innervation of his facial features and sensory organs. (p. 188)

In effect, Freud continues, when we think of something large, such as a mountain, we make inner exertions as if we were trying to put ourselves in its place and take on its proportions. So, too, with the circus clowns and with other phenomena that Freud classifies as comic.

Eyes popping, nose hooked down to the mouth, ears sticking out, humped back – it is probable that all these only have a comic effect because we are imagining the movements that might have been necessary to bring these features about . . . (p. 186)

It remains for Freud to explain why 'mimicry of the imagination' of this sort produces laughter, and here the comparison that, he believes, we instinctively make between the circus clowns' exaggerated movements and the smaller movements we should make for the same purpose is crucial. For at the very moment when we are exerting ourselves internally to imitate the clowns' movements (or, presumably, to hunch our backs or make our ears stick out) we become aware that this exertion is unnecessary. The extra psychical energy we have mobilized instantly becomes superfluous and is released, Freud states, in the form of laughter (p. 189).

The shortcomings of this theory will be obvious. The contention that to think of something big requires more psychical energy than to think of something small would lead us to assume that, for example, theorizing about subatomic particles was relatively effortless psychically compared to, say, imagining fairy-tale giants. Freud claims that his notion of 'mimicry of the imagination' is supported by physiology, which, he says, teaches that during the process of imagining 'innervations travel to the muscles'. But for the purposes of his theory it would be necessary to demonstrate that the innervations that travel to the muscles are larger when a large object is being thought of, and no such experimental findings are forthcoming. However, the truth or otherwise of the theory is less important than what it tells us about Freud's preoccupations. Its inherent unlikelihood is, indeed, an advantage from this angle, for it suggests how far Freud was prepared to sacrifice probability in order to gain certain theoretical ends. He was a scientist by training, and the idea of a physical basis for phenomena attracted him. Early in his Dream book he states:

Even when investigation shows that the primary exciting cause of a phenomenon is psychical, deeper research will one day trace the path further and discover an organic basis for the mental event.[6]

His mechanistic theory of the comic, with its image of innervations travelling to the muscles, clearly reflects this strain in his thinking. But it reflects even more forcibly the importance of the idea of economy. For the whole elaborate speculation, with its strange assumptions about quantifiable psychical movements, is introduced for the purpose of establishing that laughter results from an economy, a saving of psychical effort. We gear ourselves up, as it were, to make a big effort, and then find that we require only a small one, whereupon laughter bursts from us like unused steam from a piston engine.

An aspect of Freud's theory of the comic that may cause some confusion is its relation to children. Children, Freud stipulates, are without a feeling for the comic. For comic laughter in his theory entails, as we have seen, a comparison between the way another person, such as a pantomime clown, performs an action and the way one would perform it oneself. A child, according to Freud, would be incapable of the second part of this comparison. However, a child would, he believes, be capable of recognizing that the clown was performing the action wrongly and that he, the child, could do it better. This feeling of superiority would make the child laugh, but his laughter, Freud decides, would not contain comic feeling. It would be the laughter of 'pure pleasure' (p. 218). None of this is easy to follow, and the confusion redoubles when Freud goes on to suggest that we should regard the comic as the regained 'lost laughter of childhood' (p. 219). Since he has just asserted that a child's laughter is not comic, this is puzzling.

Besides, as he goes on, he seems to think of comic laughter not as the laughter of a child, but as laughter at a child. When we laugh at another person as comic, it is because we liken him to a child. Our thought, as we watch him perform an action, is 'he does it in the way I used to do it as a child'. Of course, this thought could not occur to a child, so it is not apparent how it can prompt the 'lost laughter of childhood'. On the contrary, it seems to be very much the laughter of an adult. Stupid people are comic, Freud concludes, in so far as they remind us of lazy children, and bad people are comic in so far as they remind us of naughty children. In general, what is 'Comic is what is not proper for adults' (p. 222). It is difficult to reconcile all this with the 'lost laughter of childhood', and, for that matter, with Freud's earlier classification of deformities – hunched backs, long noses, ears that stick out – as comic. To say that these are not proper for adults, with the implication that they are proper for children, would obviously be absurd. All told, the introduction of the child does not seem to clarify Freud's theory of the comic.

By contrast, his section on 'tendentious' jokes is one of his most clear, brilliant and convincing. Tendentious jokes, in his definition, are jokes with a purpose. With masterly directness he proposes that they can all be reduced to two kinds, hostile jokes and obscene jokes. Such jokes make possible the satisfaction of an instinct, whether aggressive or lustful, in face of an obstacle that stands in its way. This obstacle is repression, caused by civilization and education. Tendentious jokes thus allow us to return to primary sources of pleasure normally barred by our internal censorship. Developing his argument Freud refines our understanding both of the hostile and of the obscene subcategories. Hostile jokes work by making our enemy small, inferior, despicable or comic. They help us to overcome internal constraints (laughing at people with physical defects) and external constraints (laughing at people in authority). They can operate against creeds and institutions (such as marriage) as well as against people, and when they take on this larger task Freud calls them 'cynical' jokes (p. 107).

On obscene jokes he is equally illuminating and arresting. A person laughing at an obscene joke, he suggests, is laughing as if he were a spectator of an act of sexual aggression. Freud proposes a historical scenario to explain the development of obscene jokes from mere 'bawdry'. In an earlier state of society, he thinks, bawdry was a weapon of sexual aggression directed against a particular person. The desire to see another person's sex organs exposed is one of the original components of the libido, and if opposed it becomes hostile and cruel and may resort to bawdry. The woman's inflexibility thus becomes a first condition for the development of bawdry. Originally it presupposed the presence of a woman who was feeling ashamed. Among country people in inns, Freud has noticed, bawdry still begins when women enter, whereas in higher society it is confined to the company of men and is refined into obscene jokes. Whatever the historical accuracy of this account, it admirably clarifies, for Freud's purposes, the connection between obscene tendentious jokes and sexual aggression.

We saw earlier that in his main theoretical section Freud tended to dismiss the 'content of the thought' in a joke as of secondary importance when compared with a joke's hidden mechanism. The subjects of the joke-narrative – the comic Irishman, the naïve maiden – misled us into believing that they were the source of our laughter, when in fact, according to Freud, laughter arose from stratagems linked to the unconscious, such as 'representation by the opposite'. It is remarkable, then, that in this section on tendentious jokes, which is so successful and impressive, the thought-content of jokes should be of absolute primary importance. The vital consideration is always against whom or what the joke's aggression is directed. It is worth noting too that Freud seems to doubt whether the unconscious plays any part in the generation of tendentious jokes, except in the case of cynical jokes (p. 172). In other words this whole section seems to lie somewhat apart from his major thesis about the relationship between jokes and dreams.

The same is true of his brief but penetrating section on humour (VII.[F]), which includes his generous assessment of Shakespeare's Falstaff. Freud believes that humour has an 'essential affinity' with the comic, yet his treatment of it is quite free from the entanglements of his comic theory. He interprets humour as our way of obtaining pleasure in spite of distressing feelings. Its specialized role in countering feeling is what chiefly distinguishes it from the comic and from jokes, but it differs from them too in that it involves only a single person – oneself. The distressing feelings that it provides release from include pity, anger, pain and tenderness. When we resort to humour it is in situations that would prompt such feelings, but by humour we defend ourselves against them and prevent their arising. Byron, though Freud does not cite him, seems to have anticipated Freud's analysis of how humour works when he wrote: '. . . if I laugh at any mortal thing,/ 'Tis that I may not weep'.[7] Given the enormous role played by humour in human survival, it might be wished that Freud had examined it at greater length. Yet his account, though succinct, seems to contain all the essentials of the subject. The comparison with childhood, which caused such confusion in his exposition of the comic, is here perfectly clear. The exaltation of the humorous person's ego in the face of affecting circumstances could derive, Freud suggests, from a comparison with his childish self. In effect he is saying, 'I am too big . . . for such occasions to distress me.' From this perspective humour could be seen as an essential ingredient in true adulthood.

It is time now to turn to the specimen jokes that Freud selects for his treatise, and to ask what they tell us about him and the society in which he lived. In general it could be said that these jokes reflect a culture obsessed by money. Universal worship of the 'golden calf' (pp. 39–40) is openly acknowledged. Plutocrats are feared and flattered. Intellectuals, who find it hard to scrape a living, take refuge in asserting that the rich are stupid. Yet their stupidity has somehow permitted them to amass fortunes that intellectuals envy. Businessmen are known to be crooks, but are accepted in 'good society' (p. 64). Refusing to pay your debts is regarded as a clever ruse, just part of the cut-and-thrust of business life (pp. 30–31). The first joke to be analysed in the book – the poor lottery-collector's boast that the great Baron Rothschild had treated him quite 'famillionairely' – sets the tone: an 'unmistakably bitter' observation, as Freud interprets it, conveying the unpleasantness of being condescended to by the rich.

It is also a world in which women are systematically degraded. The jokes that involve women are almost without exception offensive. Old, ugly, unmarriageable women, sometimes with deformities such as hunchbacks or misshapen limbs, are routine comic butts of the marriage-broker jokes Freud selects (pp. 52–6). He seems, at one point, to feel some awkwardness about these. They operate, he admits, at the expense of inferior and powerless people, but he maintains that their real target is the 'shameful' system of marriage-brokering itself and 'the pitiful situation of girls who let themselves be married under such arrangements' (p. 103). This explanation does nothing, however, to alleviate the degradation of women in the jokes.

Marriage, in the specimen jokes, is invariably seen from the man's point of view, and as a troublesome arrangement, calculated neither to bring happiness nor to satisfy male sexuality. A doctor comes away from a lady's bedside and says, 'I don't *like the look* of your wife.' 'I haven't *liked the look of her* for a long time,' the husband hastens to agree (p. 30). A young husband punningly acknowledges to a friend that it is sad but true that he is married (p. 15). The cynical male witticism ('A wife is like an umbrella. After all, before long one takes a cab') that declares the inevitability of husbands resorting to prostitutes is commended by Freud for its truth (pp. 67, 108). A Baron and a doctor play cards outside the room in which the Baroness is in labour. On the doctor's advice they ignore her cries of pain until they become barely articulate screams, only then interrupting their game to give assistance (p. 70).

What kind of person could have thought these jokes funny? Men, evidently. They would hardly appeal to women. But it is surely plausible to suggest that these offensive and degrading jokes would not be attractive to men simply because of their gender. It seems, rather, that jokes of this kind would be more likely to attain popularity among men who were living in a ruthless and exploitative culture, where to display one's superiority to women and to any kind of tenderness was part of the struggle between males to gain acceptance and ascendancy. In this respect the jokes against women can be seen as a component of the economic circumstances that Freud's other specimen jokes imply.

Prominent among the specimen jokes are jokes about Jews. They account for a much larger proportion than would be found in a representative selection of jokes from, say, late nineteenth- or early twentieth-century England. Jokes about Jews were, in a sense, the origin of Freud's book. He told Fliess that he had already begun making a collection of Jewish jokes in June 1897. The jokes reflect both a seeming complicity with anti-Semitism and a defiance of it. The specimen jokes about Jewish beggars, for example, bespeak an attempt to show wit and resilience in the face of humiliation. The beggar who treats himself to salmon mayonnaise, despite being in debt, and then stoutly defends his self-indulgence (pp. 41-2), and the beggar who insists on a trip to Ostend for his health, on borrowed money (p. 47), are spokesmen for the victims of a materialistic society. They revenge themselves on it by being just as materialistic and unscrupulous as it is itself. Given that charity among Jews was, as Freud explains, a sacred duty, the beggars also provide an irritant that threatens to disturb the otherwise complacent money-worship. Yet the beggars are, at the same time, made absurd. They are not a serious threat. Behind their stories lie wretchedness and despair – as in the joke about the intellectual who tries to support himself by tutoring but becomes an alcoholic (p. 44). The jokes represent Jews as filthy and parsimonious – taking a bath once a year, their beards clogged with scraps of decaying food. Such stories, told about Jews by Jews, function, Freud suggests, as a kind of immunization against the culture's endemic anti-Semitism. They are, he argues, a response to the brutal jokes about Jews that circulate among foreigners and Gentiles (*Fremden*). In this respect they testify to 'the manifold and hopeless misery of the Jews' (pp. 108-9, 111).

Freud himself had always reacted to anti-Semitism with defiance. At school, in response to the anti-Semitic attitudes of his classmates, he made a hero of the Semitic general Hannibal, who fought against the Romans. When he was eleven or twelve, his father told him how, as a young man, he had been out walking one Saturday, wearing a new fur hat, when a Christian had come up and knocked it off into the mud, shouting, 'Jew! Get off the pavement.' Freud asked his father what he had done. 'I went into the roadway and picked up my cap,' was the quiet reply. This struck Freud, he recalls, as 'unheroic conduct'.[8] Hannibal would have managed things better. Jewish immigration from Eastern Europe was increasingly resented in the Vienna of Freud's youth. Between 1857 and 1880 the proportion of Jews in the city's population rose from 2 to 10 per cent. The stock-market crash of 9 May 1873 ('Black Friday') led to an orgy of anti-Semitism. Jewish bankers were blamed for the catastrophe. A rash of anti-Jewish propaganda hit the popular press, with cartoons depicting hook-nosed financiers. This was the year Freud went up to university, where he found that his Gentile fellow-students expected him 'to feel inferior'. But he refused to be ashamed of his race. Anti-Semites aroused his fury. On a train in 1883 fellow-passengers called him a 'miserable Jew' because he opened a window for fresh air, but he yelled at them and, he records, triumphed over the 'rabble'. His son remembers how at the Bavarian resort of Thumsee in 1901 a gaggle of anti-Semites shouted abuse at the family and Freud charged them with his walking stick.

Freud recognized that his defiance of anti-Semitism had become part of his unconscious. In one of his dreams two eminent colleagues in the medical faculty feature as a simpleton and a criminal. Working out why this had happened, he realized that the dream reflected his resentment at not being promoted, because he was a Jew, to the rank of *professor extraordinarius*. In his dream he had, as it were, revenged himself on the government minister responsible by usurping his office.

In mishandling my two learned and eminent colleagues because they were Jews, and in treating the one as a simpleton and the other as a criminal, I was behaving as though I were the Minister. I had put myself in the Minister's place. Turning the tables on His Excellency with a vengeance! He had refused to appoint me *professor extraordinarius* and I had retaliated in the dream by stepping into his shoes.[9]

It remains to answer the question we posed at the start. Why does Freud so insistently interpret humour in economic terms? Why is his theory of jokes constructed on an economic model? In his concluding paragraphs he is at pains to indicate how pervasive the concern with economy has been. Our pleasure in jokes arises from savings of expenditure upon inhibition; our pleasure in the comic from savings of expenditure upon ideation; our pleasure in humour from savings of expenditure upon feeling. 'In all three methods of operation in our psychical apparatus, the pleasure comes from a saving' (p. 228). As we have seen, the cultural context established by the specimen jokes Freud offers is itself predominantly economic, reflecting a ruthlessly acquisitive society in which humane and tender feelings are stifled. How should we assess this coincidence between the theory and its context?

One explanation would be that the encompassing, money-obsessed culture infiltrated Freud's mental processes to the extent of providing him with a model for his thought. But this explanation, though it is no doubt part of the truth, does not go far enough, since it leaves out of account the anti-Semitism prevalent in Freud's Vienna, and his own fierce resentment of it. If we incorporate these factors into our interpretation we can see that Freud's theory of jokes is itself a kind of joke. Like the Jewish jokes against Jews that he analyses, it represents a rejoinder, a pointed response to what he calls 'the manifold and hopeless misery of the Jews'. Since the time of Shylock, and, indeed, long before, Jews in Western culture had been traduced and ridiculed. Above all they had been laughed at for their parsimony, the cheese-paring economies involved in the accumulation of wealth. Freud's reply was to demonstrate that laughter is itself parsimony, a saving of the effort usually spent on emotions or inhibitions. Jewish economies have traditionally been the target of mockery. But that Gentile mockery, when inspected by a great Jewish intellectual, emerges as merely another economy.

Whether Freud's countermove against the mockers ('Turning the tables on His Excellency with a vengeance!') was conscious or unconscious cannot be ascertained, and to Freud the distinction would be meaningless. He derived the functions of consciousness from the dynamics of the unconscious. 'Everything conscious,' he maintained, 'has an unconscious preliminary stage.' What we call conscious thought is no more than a circuitous path to the satisfaction of an unconscious wish. The theory of jokes and the unconscious must, according to Freud's reasoning, be a satisfaction of this kind. We can safely say, too, that it was generated as much by the culture in which Freud lived as by Freud.

To return, finally, to the joke cited at the start about the cat-owner and his friend. This joke provides a useful guideline, for the very reason that it is completely unlike Freud's jokes. To consider why this is so reveals the limits he set to his investigation into joking. For his selection of specimen jokes is, of course, not random. Any selection illustrates aims present before the selection was made. The cat-owner joke reflects a reassuring community in which people keep pets, and friends try to help one another, however obtusely. Freud could easily have collected such jokes, but they were alien to his purpose. The jokes he collected, from the outset, were jokes about Jews, and though he does not restrict his treatise to these, his specimen jokes reflect a society dominated by money, resentment, disparagement, scandal, insult, cruelty, social rank and – in its figuration of Jews – offensive racial stereotypes. It is a living proof of the 'saving of expenditure on feeling' that, in his theory, underlies humour – not least anti-Jewish humour.

John Carey, 2001

Notes

1. See Translator's Preface, n. 2.
2. *The Interpretation of Dreams*, VII.D.
3. Ibid., VII.E.
4. *The Collected Works of Samuel Taylor Coleridge*, ed. J. Engell and W. Jackson Bate (London and Princeton, NJ, 1983), vol. 7:1, pp. 168–70 and 304.
5. *Leviathan*, part 1, chapter 6.
6. *The Interpretation of Dreams*, I.D.
7. *Don Juan*, canto IV, l. 25.
8. *The Interpretation of Dreams*, V.B.
9. Ibid., IV.

Translator's Preface

This is a problematic text for translators – the present version is in fact a third attempt – for it presents one face inviting great freedom, and another expecting great rigour. The one asks how to translate the jokes – both word-play dependent on the configurations of their language, and social jokes exploiting the peculiarities of their culture – and still keep them even remotely funny; and the other asks how to render the theoretical language of psychoanalysis dealing with them, as Freud's distinctive style deploys it, with his ellipses and object-for-subject syntax – a theoretical language complicated in this text by his uneasy adoption of the discourse of idealist aesthetics. These are already more than two problems, and threaten to take us far afield. But however far we wander, the path starts with the question of which words to choose for what, and will keep returning to it.

It is in many ways a pendant to *The Interpretation of Dreams* (1900), and draws on it for its intellectual framework and terminology. The hare Freud goes chasing may have been started in the course of his writing the Dream book, when his confidant Wilhelm Fliess appears to have remarked, while reading the final version, on the jokiness of so many of his friend's dreams. Freud replied:

It is certainly true that the dreamer is too witty, but that does not apply just to me, nor does it involve disapproval. All dreams are just as insufferably witty because they are in the thick of it, and the direct path is barred to them. If you think I should, I'll put in a further note to that effect.[1] The apparent wittiness of all unconscious processes is intimately related to the theory of wit and the comic.[2]

And a scribbled note survives among Freud's papers which includes the following headings:

a). Technique of joke.   Joke —— comic — riddle⎞
b). Psychogenesis of joke   ucs.   pcs — cs.   ⎟ perhaps
c). Tendency of joke.   also irony
d). Joke & comic, humor   satire
e). Joke & riddle.   etc.
f). Theory of pleasure in joke.

<u>Important aspect of characterization of diff. kinds of
pleasure gain through psychic localization.</u>

Book of riddles by <u>Mises</u>, <u>Polle</u>.—Aspects:
                    Joke lies in technique—de-joking [the joke]
                    Psych. localization.
                    Economy theory
                  Laughing with oversaturation
                  Preliminary stage of jesting.
                     a). Lifting of inhibitions.
                     b). Orig[inal] sources of pleasure.[3]

Between them, the comment to Fliess and these headings sum up much of what was to become Freud's *Der Witz und seine Beziehungen zum Unbewußten* (though one could wish he had kept his ruthless coinage *entwitzigen* ['de-joking'] instead of opting for the pseudo-chemical – or culinary? – *reduzieren* or 'reduce'). It was published in 1905 in Leipzig and Vienna by Deuticke, the same firm that had already brought out the works which were to become the founding texts of psychoanalysis: *Studies on Hysteria* (1895, in collaboration with Josef Breuer); and *The Interpretation of Dreams* (1900). *Der Witz* . . . is also contemporary with the important *Three Essays on the Theory of Sexuality* (also 1905). So one way of placing the present work might be as a minor essay among major works that were developing a new theory of psychical processes and were by then well on the way to establishing its main terms and categories.

Indeed, by the second edition of 1912,[4] a common discourse among colleagues had already developed, with journals, official societies and meetings – and a shared professional language. Another way of placing Freud's Joke book is in constellation with the big Dream book on the one hand and to the small *The Psychopathology of Everyday Life* (1901) on the other, for all three deal with minor manifestations of normal behaviour in everyday experience, relating them to unconscious processes in the psyche. But where the Dream book used dreams in order to theorize the existence of an unconscious, five years later, though still acknowledging its inferential status, the Joke book puts the theory in its title and takes it as the starting-point.

These placings have their repercussions on Freud's theoretical language in this text – and so on the translation too. For his jokes are embedded in a matrix of theory which, given the colourful subject-matter, is expressed in surprisingly fixed and narrow terms. In this respect the Joke book differs from the Dream book, where part of the adventure lay in Freud's inventiveness in finding new terms for his new observations. The Joke book just takes these terms over: two of the most important tools of analysis of the way dreams operate – conventionally rendered in English as 'condensation' and 'displacement' – are simply adopted from it and adapted to accommodate an elaborate joke-taxonomy. 'Joke-work' [*Witzarbeit*] is coined by euphonious analogy to 'dream-work' [*Traumwerk*]. Similarly, 'manifest' and 'latent', 'inhibition' and 'censorship' reappear, while the quantitative language of the psyche's dynamics – charge and release, saving and spending – provides a ready-made framework, with only the latter pair showing signs of extended use. So as far as terminology is concerned, apart from these two and the notorious 'cathexis', which I have replaced by the (not unproblematical) 'charge', I have used the English terms already – and by now ineradicably – established in professional and popular psychoanalytic usage. No adventure here. However, since the children in Freud's argument are at or beyond the stage of language acquisition, I have departed from conventional psychoanalytic usage and avoided describing them as 'infantile'.

Within these confines, the jokes, with their variety of topic, tone and diction, provide little moments of anarchic release, caged though they are by their quotation marks. But the analytic language Freud uses to categorize them is again marked by deliberate limitation. Not only jokes themselves, but the words available for naming them are diverse and picturesque – even more so in English than in German – but, in fact, Freud's analytic project restricts him to three groupings, with two subgroups, and so to five words only, labels for classes, which recur unvaried again and again. The joke, he argues, has its own evolution, which follows the maturation of *homo ludens*, and is symptomatic of the degree of immaturity or maturity in the one who makes it. His examples offer a wide and colourful psychological spectrum from childish ways of taking pleasure in jingles and nonsense (and momentary reversion to them) on the one hand, to the civilized adult's indirect means of venting hostility or frustrated sexuality on the other. But his *linguistic* span is narrow: at the one end *das Spiel* [(verbal) play], at the other, *der Witz* ['the witticism' or 'joke'], in its most advanced form the 'tendentious' witticism of good society, tendentious too in the tolerated *Zote* ['the dirty joke' or 'bawdry']; in between *der Scherz* ['the jest', 'pleasantry' or 'banter']. Eight for Freud's four, though not simply out of a yearning for motley (though I would have been glad to have found a place for 'fun' or 'funny'!). I allowed 'jest' to be edged out by 'pleasantry' because no one seems to use the word nowadays – Yorick and Mr Pickwick seem as far away as Pilate. 'Witticism' I introduced for two reasons. It is a more appropriate description than 'joke' for a great number of Freud's illustrations (Herr N.'s sneers, Lichtenberg's aphorisms, Karl Kraus's quips). And it provides a helpful means of negotiating the dual use of the German 'Witz' on its way into English. For *der Witz* is slippery: it can mean either general wit-in-the-abstract, as faculty, talent, intelligence, or specific, concrete joke – or, rather, the word contains both at the same time, and it depends on context where the weight of meaning lies. It may even slide from one sentence to the next. The problem is not really soluble in English, but 'witticism' at least provides a playful transitional form. The cognate *witzig* has an even wider range, covering not only 'witty', and 'joking', but 'ingenious' or 'clever' too. The reader should simply bear in mind that the one word *Witz* is rendered where appropriate by 'wit' or – sometimes – 'jokiness', and by 'witticism' or 'joke' in the present text; and *witzig* by 'witty' and 'joking', and even, on occasion, by 'jokey'.

This applies not only to translating Freud's use of the term, but also to translating the 'authorities' he refers to so often, particularly in his Introduction and when he comes to discuss the genre of the joke in its relation to the comic mode. Freud is entering an aesthetic discourse here, which he recognizes is not his own. He is noticeably more respectful of his literary and philosophical predecessors, particularly Lipps and Kuno Fischer (see notes throughout) than he was of his authorities on dreams in the Dream book. His avowals of incompetence are not merely the rhetoric of modesty: at many points where one wishes he would carry his comments further to other forms of art he stops short. But on this unfamiliar ground his writing is not sovereign. There are signs of insecurity. He takes over aesthetic categories and concepts (the naïve, the sublime, caricature, small-for-big, etc.), which have their own tradition (and even, as he observes, their own canonical jokes!), adapting them not always happily to his own. He is uneasy with the difference between genre and mode, indeed he never uses the term 'mode', and for 'genre' [*Gattung*, which he uses only once] he substitutes his natural scientist's 'species' or 'variety' [*Art*] – which I have sometimes diluted to 'kind'; this leads him to an occasional blurring of *das Komische* [the comic (mode)] with its manifestations in *die Komik* (that is, specific kinds of comedy, for example: the comedy of expectation, of contrast, of exaggeration, of situation, of superiority, etc., all terms taken – and taken for granted without explication – from his sources). He recognizes that *aesthetically* the jokiness of a joke is inextricably bound up with its form of expression – hence his note 'Joke lies in technique' and his elaborate taxonomy of its possible forms – but when he shifts his ground to the *psychology* of jokes, he re-categorizes and re-formulates that inextricability as 'the principle of confusion of sources of pleasure': our enjoyment of the form acts as the cover for a deeper pleasure. His reductive method of 'de-joking' is a move in this argument, radically separating the subject-matter from its form. This is apparent in his running metaphor for the form of expression as 'clothing' [*einkleiden*] the subject-matter – and in his habit of subsuming the organicist term *Gehalt*, that is, 'content as already shaped' – which is how his authorities use it – into *Gedankeninhalt*, that is, 'content as contained', as, in his own comparison, the mechanism of a clock is in its case.

In two important linguistic habits, however, Freud is at one with his authorities, and both cause problems for the English translator. There is, endemically, the ease with which German can turn an adjective into an abstract noun, constructing out of an accidental attribute in the empirical world a platonic world of ideas to think with – and perhaps even credit with existence. So naïve behaviour generates the naïve, comical behaviour the comic and unconscious behaviour the unconscious. In German, that is. Grammar shapes thinking, and certain kinds of thought are more easily thought in German. I have kept these formulations although they sit uncomfortably in English. And on account of the hidden danger of accepting that because there is a word for it, the thing must exist, I have gone to some lengths to avoid that frequent resort of the translator of German when faced with certain noun-clause constructions: expanding a 'that' into 'the fact that', as, uncontentiously, on p. 102: 'If we bear in mind [the fact] that the tendentious joke is so well suited to attacking the great . . .'; or, more trickily, when a preposition is involved, rendering a formulation such as . . . *unterscheiden sich darin, daß* . . . by the expedient 'are distinguished by the fact that . . .' In this case, I have put instead: '. . . *the only difference between* cases of external and internal obstacles *is that* in the latter an inhibition which already existed is lifted, while . . .' (p. 116). For the difference in question is not, in fact, strictly a fact, but a theoretical construct dependent upon Freud's preceding assumptions. Cumulatively, translators' recourse to 'facts' can undermine the speculative nature of much of Freud's thinking and make it seem even more positivistic than he claimed. So readers can be assured that when the word 'fact' occurs (not a few times) it is – with one insoluble exception – Freud's own, and not thrust on him out of translator's convenience. The cost, unfortunately, is sometimes syntactical awkwardness.

The other linguistic habit Freud shares with his authorities is not intrinsic to the language, but is characteristic of nineteenth-century idealism: the tendency to think in terms of ideal types – in the discourse of aesthetics and literary classifications, this means in terms of the definitive exemplar of the genre: the Novelle, the Tragedy – and the Joke. Modes too are identified in their abstract purity: the Sublime, the Tragic – the Comic. This produces some uneasiness. On the one hand he declares that definitions are a matter of convention and can be altered, and his own analyses tend to circumscribe and describe rather than define. But he is interested in borderline cases, while his *language* is the language of definition: addressing the nature of the joke, he hovers between the descriptive [*Charakter*] and the essentialist [*Wesen*]. So the translator's problems begin with the first words of the title. There are ways of adapting them to the English cast of mind and language, which does not abstract so readily, by particularizing to 'a joke', or by particularizing and generalizing at the same time with 'jokes'. I have done both, but I have also frequently used the singular of the ideal type as a reminder of the latent idealism of Freud's adopted discourse, signally in the title. (The same habit is already present in the Dream book, but less problematically, as genre is not an issue there.)

When Freud is writing on his own psychoanalytic ground, there are two aspects of his writing I found raised peculiar problems needing solutions, or at least decisions: one peculiar to his syntax, and one raised by an important and characteristic metaphor.

Syntactically, the agent of the action in his sentences is frequently the movement of the psyche, the feeling, the joke, the laughter, the inhibition, etc., not the persons who feel, laugh, are inhibited. These occur *to* them, happen *to* them. They are the objects, not the agents of what is going on in the psyche. At its simplest, the psychical agent is the subject of an active verb: a pleasurable mood will 'lift the inhibiting effect of critical judgement'; pleasurable effects will 'encourage children in the habit of playing' (p. 125). But it is also to be understood in this way in more complex sentence-structures, for example, when Freud writes of 'the unreliability of a joke's success when *ideas with a strong and arousing effect are called up in the listener by the thoughts expressed in it*, for then whether *his attention remains with the joking process or withdraws from it* depends on the compatibility or disparity between the tendency of the joke and *the train of thought controlling the listener*' (p. 148). Even if one cannot match Freud's syntactical forms exactly, it is important, I think, to try to render the grammatical agency of his psychical forces, for that is what expresses his dynamic conception of the psyche. It does, however, entail occasional obscurities in Freud's own language, and certainly some contortion in my attempts to render it.

It has become a commonplace to draw attention to Freud's overt use of metaphor to elucidate the activity of the psyche. The way he exploits latent metaphor, to my mind, is as important, so that the search for the source [*Quelle*, *Ursprung*] implies springs implies water implies flow implies . . . and so on, all the way to damming-up (I have borrowed Strachey's term for *Stauung*) and discharge. Metaphor becomes terminology, and the dismantling and rebuilding process of translation gives the opportunity to make this more apparent. So in this text what has engaged me more than Heine's wicked analogy of Catholic and Protestant clergy with wholesale employees and independent retailers, more even than Freud's own use of the outlay of small and large business concerns to explicate the small amount of effort in making a joke spent on mere brevity and the much greater on lifting inhibition, is his handling of the overriding figure to which both are related. For this text is pervaded by one powerful analogy to express a concept of psychical energy that is both quantitative and dynamic, entailing movement, giving out, withholding, distribution and exchange: the metaphor is money. (For a fuller critical comment on its moral and cultural implications, see John Carey's Introduction.) Indeed, it dominates the theoretical exposition so fully that it sets the actual economic terms of the argument. Like 'source', it is one of those metaphors that have become part of the worn coinage of everyday figurative speech: as we use it – in German as in English – we scarcely notice that we are saving or sparing [*sparen, ersparen*] ourselves an effort we would otherwise be spending [*Aufwand*] on what? – restoring them to their full metaphoric quality, perhaps. Spending in German is trickier than saving on account of Freud's – or the German language's – preference for nouns over verbs. For *Aufwand* is another slippery word, sliding in context from the more abstract 'expenditure' to 'expense' to 'effort spent', sometimes with the implication of 'wasted', even to the more concrete 'expensive display', and loosely to 'trouble taken'. So in trying to make the metaphor more apparent, I have used 'effort spent' and 'effort saved' frequently, certainly as much as the systematic abstractions of 'expenditure' and 'economy' and their cognates.

But what of the jokes? There is a built-in doubleness about the language of this work. Its theoretical range, I have suggested, is narrow – not much fun, in fact. But that, I suspect, may be part of the overall strategy. If Freud's argument requires the joke to be nonsense unbound, then there has to be a binding context for his jokes to cast off and bound out of. Or, one might say, he builds the serious theoretical framework as an excuse and opportunity for release in telling his favourite jokes. Either way, in this respect the text is doing what it says.

For it is the jokes that provide the colour and variety: anecdotes, puns, versified spoonerisms, satirical *bons mots*, snappy back-answers, witty aphorisms, extended disrespectful comparisons, verbal doodlings from the leisure of distinguished professors (they too!). Freud has a special weakness for all kinds of word-play, giving far more examples of them than the theory requires to make its point, and he is circumspect in his examples of dirty jokes, giving too few. He draws his witticisms from a range of sources. He takes up the canonical jokes of his authorities (from Heine's 'famillionairely' to Lichtenberg's knife without a blade that lacks a handle and countless more). But he makes a point of extending the canon vastly by adding to these from miscellaneous sources: from the current comic papers *Simplizissimus* and *Fliegende Blätter*, from contemporary wits (Herr N., Karl Kraus); he slips in little jokes of his own; above all he augments from his own collection of Jewish jokes. Here is abundance. And they have all become more than jokes (and some of them less). Like his dreams, they are permeated by the culture of their time, when a joke, he tells us, had almost the same effect as an event of the widest interest, passed on from one to another like the news of the latest victory. Contrariwise, if news of the latest victory was passed on like a new joke, the situation in Freud's imperial Austria was indeed desperate but not serious.

But how far have they survived their time? And how far can they survive the mismatch of translation? There are two possible strategies to deal with the problem. One is to recognize from the start that verbal jokes are untranslatable and can only be rendered exactly by rare accident, and that social jokes are funniest within one's own society. The bold thing to do, then, would be to substitute equivalents which make Freud's point for him in English and which we too could laugh at.[5] This is what the pioneering translator A. A. Brill did in *Wit and Its Relation to the Unconscious* (New York, 1916), with the help of one Mr Horatio Winslow. Successfully too, particularly in finding alternative verbal jokes – as Freud appreciated. But in another way, Brill was too drastic, for where he could find no equivalent, he simply left an item out – Schleiermacher's unpleasant pleasantry about jealousy is a case in point – with the consequence that the argument attached to it was weakened. And despite his inventiveness in domesticating the jokes (and he certainly has the art of pointing them!), his language for the surrounding theoretical text is both over-literal and too often plain wrong. Time has caught up with Brill's engaging version in different ways. He was translating early in the story of Freud-in-transport, when the English language of psychoanalysis was not yet fixed, but his own solutions ('foreconscious', 'investing energy', 'occupation energy', for example) lost out to Ernest Jones's normative project of making a vocabulary for psychoanalysis in English. And just as Freud's jokes bear the mark of their time and place, so now do Brill's. Their disregard of cultural authenticity is no longer an advantage. Getting to Monticello by six in the morning may be suited to a gag from a minstrel show, but the horse that could get to Pressburg in that time was carrying a different historical load.

So a new translation with a different strategy was called for. It was provided as *Jokes and Their Relation to the Unconscious* in vol. VIII of the English *Standard Edition* (London, 1960) by James Strachey. This, the fruit of Jones's great memorializing project, was also used for vol. VI of the Penguin Freud Library. Strachey's main concern was to translate the text correctly into the standardized language of what had become mainstream professional English and American psychoanalysis. As a code identifying the adepts of a mystery, it excludes – and that sits ill with the inviting jokes that provide this book's material. For the disjunction between jokes and surrounding text, between play and strenuous thinking, already present in Freud's German, is even sharper here, mitigated only by Freud's rhetorical 'we' as he invites the reader to join him in the progress of his argument and share the pleasure of his jokes. It is Strachey's language too, even more than Freud's, that pushes 'economy' and 'expenditure' into becoming entities. As for translating the jokes, he takes a more straightforward way than Brill. They are subject-matter. He wisely makes no attempt at domesticating them, on the whole lets the anecdotes and aphorisms through to make their own point. He explains the excessive and untranslatable word-play, giving some English illustrations by way of explanation where possible, and an Appendix of Brentano's riddles. Informative, but rather dull.

I have dwelt on these predecessors because their ways of dealing with the two large problems presented by this text – how to deal with the theoretical language and how to deal with the jokes – were different, and in their different ways bear the marks of their time and purposes, something more easily seen now than then. It is the excuse for the present attempt. Unlike Strachey, I am not a professional analyst. Unlike Brill, I am not an amateur joker. But as a Germanist of a certain generation, I have breathed in what John Forrester has called 'the psychoanalytic culture', and I have read this text as something on the brink of a wider aesthetic theory. My own aims in translating it, as far as I can see them, tend both to bring the text closer to the present-day common reader and to move it away, attempting on the one hand to mitigate the exclusiveness of Strachey's diction, and on the other to expose the historicity, intellectual and social, of the work. I have tried to make its theoretical language to some small degree less technical (this *can* only be a matter of degree for, as I have pointed out, Freud is writing within two theoretical discourses, both highly specialized), partly by making the tools of logical argument more colloquial (rather than the formal 'hence', 'thus', 'nevertheless' and so on, I have tried out a 'so', 'in this way', 'all the same'), partly by drawing to the surface the metaphorical basis for some of the theoretical propositions.

As for the jokes, I have taken Strachey's way. Explanations of the verbal jokes either sneak into square brackets in the text or fall, alas, with a dull thud into notes; only a few have found English equivalents ('Two heal and two howl' works; but 'a bit on the side' shows strain). Anecdotes and aphorisms transfer without too much loss. I have made no attempt at naturalizing, for that cannot but entail moderniz-ing, and though I have tried to some extent to accommodate the diction to present-day usage, it is not so far as to remove the jokes from the back numbers of *Simplizissimus*, where Freud found them when they were still current. Some may have become no longer all that funny: time has intervened with the tellers and political correctness with the listeners, but as documents of a certain quite complex historical taste they remain fascinating.

Most of the Jewish jokes have not faded – neither as jokes nor as Jewish jokes – though they now carry even heavier social and histori-cal freight than when Freud first made his collection. For the world of the Galician Jews is lost, and so is the world of the educated Viennese Jews who laughed at them. All the same, the wise and witty *The Joys of Yiddish* (New York, 1970) by Leo Rosten – to whom I am deeply and happily indebted – is witness to the successful emigration of many of these jokes into American-English – even the marriage-brokers (in 1970, at least) made it, though it seems the Pressburg horse did not. In translating Freud's examples, I have tried discreetly to echo Yiddish speech-patterns, as Freud's text does. He certainly took pleasure in them. But there are also two anecdotes that he tells close together, each with a Yiddish excla-mation as its indispensable pay-off line, in which something more profound and painful is in play than pleasure in the 'argot' [*Jargon*], as he called it, and than his analyses would at first sight suggest. They are the one about the Baroness in labour, and the one about the 'gentleman in modern dress' and the Eastern Jew in the railway carriage (pp. 69–70). Later Freud revised his description of the first story from a 'joke' to an 'unmasking': what it unmasked, he claimed, was 'original nature breaking through the layers of education': True – but sociologically that original nature had a very specific cultural voice, which was 'unmistakable' to his readers. The joke is, I would suggest, over and above Freud's universalizing interpretation, a wry debunking of Jewish social and cultural assimilation – in the Baroness's case into the impoverished minor aristocracy, in the gentleman's case into the professional bourgeoisie – to which Freud himself belonged. Between them, these two jokes identify the great social and cultural shift in which Freud and his family took part as something deeply precarious. Neither Brill nor Strachey takes the Yiddish quality of the pay-off lines into account in their renderings, in the gentleman's case reinforcing Freud's democratic blurring of sociological differences within European Jewry, in the Baroness's case reinforcing Freud's universalizing – and highly misogynistic – reading.[6] But an entire historical world is present in her cry.

There is one last problem of usage which did not worry Brill or Strachey in their translating, but has become visible today: the gender of generics. 'He' can no longer embrace 'she' as 'he' did without second thoughts in their versions. Gender in German is a grammatical convention: *der Mensch* [human being] is masculine, *die Person* [person] is feminine, and *das Kind* [child] is neuter, all requiring the corresponding pronouns and adjectives. Freud is of course correct in his use of them. But these instances alone indicate that grammar is not wholly neutral. We are more aware now of its silent pre-judgements, and modern usage looks for strategies that avoid the more crass forms of masculine universality. This is particularly necessary in translating into English, where gender is empirical. Plurals are a great help: humans, people, children have their corresponding 'they', 'them' and 'theirs', but they cannot help in all cases. Identifiable individual children (such as Mädi, the little girl who took her medicine) can be 'she' (or 'he') as appropriate, but when forced into a generic singular – what pronoun to use to match 'the child' in Freud's generalizations if a plural will not work? – the problem surfaces again. As Freud usually thinks of the generic child as a little boy, I have used the universal 'he', though not without some qualms. The raconteur is always 'he'. But in one instance (p. 216) I decided from context that an occurrence of the grammatical feminine gender [*die Person*] does indeed refer to a person of the female sex. Bathsheba was a woman. Curious – but simply to see this issue as a problem historicizes the present, latest, text too.

Notes

1. He did. See *The Interpretation of Dreams*, VI.A.
2. *The Complete Letters of Sigmund Freud to Wilhelm Fliess, 1887–1904*, tr. and ed. Jeffrey Masson (Cambridge, MA, and London, 1985), p. 371. The translation here is my own, and follows *Briefe an Wilhelm Fliess, 1887–1904*, ed. Jeffrey Masson and Michael Schröter (Frankfurt am Main, 1986).
3. Ilse Grubrich-Simitis, *Back to Freud's Texts: Making Silent Documents Speak*, tr. Philip Slotkin (New Haven, CT, and London, 1996), p. 114.
4. (Leipzig and Vienna). This was unchanged from the first, except for a few additional examples of jokes from English and Latin, mainly borrowed from an article by the book's first translator, A. A. Brill. This edition is used as the basis of the present translation on the grounds that these few further illustrations may help to clarify for the English reader the kind of word-play Freud had in mind.
5. The translations of the *Astérix* series for the Brockhampton Press by Anthea Bell and Derek Hockridge are brilliant in this respect.
6. Sara Kofman has made this joke the occasion of her attack on Freud's universalizing tendency, as well as on his misogyny. See her *Pourquoi rit-on? Freud et le Mot d'Esprit* (Paris, 1986).

A Analytic Part

I Introduction

Anyone who has had occasion to consult the literature of aesthetics and psychology for the light it can cast on the nature of the joke and its connections will surely have to admit that it has not received nearly as much philosophical attention as it deserves, given the part jokes play in our mental life. One can name only a very small number of thinkers who have gone more deeply into its problems. However, among those who have dealt with it, we find the brilliant names of the novelist Jean Paul (Friedrich Richter) and the philosophers Theodor Vischer, Kuno Fischer and Theodor Lipps.[1] But even in the work of these authors, the joke as a topic lies in the background, while the main interest of their investigations is devoted to the more comprehensive and more attractive problems of the comic.

The first impression we get from the literature suggests that dealing with the joke would be quite unworkable except in relation to the comic.

According to Lipps (*Komik und Humor*, 1898),[2] the joke is 'the utterly subjective [variety of] comedy', that is, the variety 'which we [as subject] produce, which attaches to our activity as such, where our position is entirely that of superior subject, never of object, not even of voluntary object' (p. 80). By way of further explanation, the comment: the joke is in general 'that conscious and adroit production of a comic effect, whether it is the comedy of observation or of situation' (p. 78).

Kuno Fischer clarifies the relationship of jokes to the comic by recourse to caricature, which, as he presents it, he places as an intermediary between them. The subject-matter of comedy is what is ugly in any of its manifestations: 'Where it is hidden, it must be revealed in the light of the comic gaze, where it is noticed but little or scarcely at all, it must be brought out and exposed in such a way that it stands open to the light of day . . . This is how caricature comes about' (p. 45). – 'Our entire mental world, the intellectual realm of our thoughts and ideas, does not unfold itself before the gaze of external observation; nor can it be directly imagined in visual and concrete representations, and yet it contains inhibitions, frailties and deformities, ridiculous and comic contrasts in plenty. To highlight these and make them accessible to aesthetic contemplation, some power will be necessary which is capable not merely of imagining objects directly, but of reflecting on these representations itself and of clarifying them: a power illuminating our thought. The only power that does this is *judgement*. The judgement that produces a comic contrast is *the joke*. It has already played its silent part in caricature, but it is only in judgement that it attains its distinctive form and the free field of its unfolding' (p. 49).

As we see, Lipps shifts the feature distinguishing the joke within the comic to the activation, the active attitude, of the subject, whereas Kuno Fischer characterizes the joke in terms of its relation to its object, that is, to those ugly aspects concealed in the world of our thoughts. We cannot test these definitions of the joke for their soundness, indeed we can hardly understand them, if we do not put them into the context from which they have been torn in appearing here. That being the case, we should have to work our way right through the authorities' accounts of the comic to learn anything from them about jokes. On the other hand, we become aware from other passages that these same authorities are also able to indicate essential and generally applicable features of the joke as well, quite apart from considering its relation to the comic.

The description of the joke in Kuno Fischer's work that seems to satisfy its author best runs thus: the joke is a *playful* judgement (p. 51). To elucidate this expression, we are referred to the analogy: 'as aesthetic freedom consisted in the playful contemplation of things' (p. 50). Elsewhere (p. 20), the aesthetic attitude towards the object is characterized by the requirement that we desire nothing of this object, particularly no satisfaction of our serious needs, but are content with enjoying its contemplation. The aesthetic attitude is *playful* in contrast to work. – 'It may be that out of aesthetic freedom there also arises a kind of judging detached from the usual restrictions and directives, which, on account of its origin, I shall call *"the playful judgement"*, and that this concept contains the prime requirement, if not the whole formula, that will solve our problem. "Freedom gives wit [*Witz*] and wit gives freedom," says Jean Paul. "Wit is mere play with ideas" '[3] (p. 24).

Writers have long been fond of defining wit [*Witz*] as the knack of discovering similarities between dissimilars, that is, of finding hidden similarities. Jean Paul put this idea wittily himself: 'Wit is the priest in disguise joining every couple in marriage.' Theodor Vischer fills this out by adding: 'The couples he most enjoys marrying are those whose relations disapprove of the wedding.' However, Vischer raises the objection that there are witticisms where comparison, and hence the discovery of similarity, is not an issue. So, departing slightly from Jean Paul, he defines wit as the knack of combining several ideas into a unity with surprising speed, even though, in respect of both their internal import and the context they belong to, they are entirely alien to one another. Kuno Fischer then points out that what we find in very many witty judgements are not similarities, but differences, while Lipps draws our attention to the fact that these definitions refer to the wit that the witty man *possesses*, and not to the joke or witticism that he *makes*.

Other views in some way related to one another that have been quoted in the conceptual definition or description of the joke are *'contrast of ideas'*, *'sense in nonsense'*, *'bafflement and light dawning'* [*Verblüffung und Erleuchtung*].

Definitions such as Kraepelin's put the emphasis on the contrast of ideas. The joke, he argues, is 'the arbitrary union or combination of two ideas which contrast in some way, mostly by means of verbal association'. A critic like Lipps has no difficulty in exposing the utter inadequacy of this formulation, but he himself does not exclude the factor of contrast, only displaces it elsewhere. 'A contrast remains, but it is not the contrast, however it is put, between the ideas attached to the words, but rather the contrast or contradiction

3

between the meaning or meaninglessness of the words' (p. 87). Examples clarify how this last is to be understood. 'A contrast only arises . . . when we have granted its words a meaning which then after all we are not able to grant them' (p. 90).

If this last condition is developed further, the contrast between 'sense and nonsense' becomes significant. 'What we take for a moment to have sense, confronts us with no sense at all! That is what, in this case, comprises the comic process' (pp. 85ff.). A remark appears witty when we impute a psychologically necessary significance to it, but even as we are doing so, promptly deny it. In this process, various things can be understood by significance. We lend a remark a certain *sense*, knowing that it cannot in logic belong to it. We discover a *truth* in it, which then again, going by the laws of experience or the general habits of our thought, it is impossible for us to discover in it. We grant it logical or practical consequences over and above its true content, only to deny these very consequences as soon as we have realized the nature of the remark. In each case the psychological process that provokes the witty remark in us and is the basis for our feeling of comedy consists in our immediate transition from lending sense, accepting as true, granting meaning, to our consciousness or impression of relative nothingness.'

However forceful this argument may sound, we would still like to raise the question here whether the contrast between meaning and meaninglessness, which is the basis for our sense of comedy, also contributes to the concept of the joke, in so far as it is distinct from the comic.

The factor of 'bafflement and light dawning' also leads deep into the problem of the relation of jokes to the comic. Kant says of the comic in general that it has the remarkable peculiarity of being able to deceive us only for a moment.[4] Heymans (*Zeitschrift für Psychologie* XI, 1896) explains how the effect of a joke comes about by the sequence first of bafflement and then of light dawning. He glosses his view with a splendid joke of Heine's,[5] who has one of his figures, the poor lottery-collector Hirsch-Hyacinth, boast that the great Baron Rothschild treated him as his equal, quite *famillionairely*.

Here, Heymans argues, the word that is the vehicle for the joke appears at first to be a faulty word-formation, something incomprehensible, unintelligible, puzzling. That is what makes it baffling. The comic effect arises from the solution to the bafflement, from understanding the word. Lipps adds that this first stage of light dawning, when the baffling word might mean any old thing, is followed by a second stage, when we realize that this senseless word has baffled us and then yielded its true meaning. Only this second dawning, he argues, the insight that the whole thing is down to a word which in ordinary usage makes no sense, only this dissolving into nothingness produces the comic effect (p. 95).

Whichever of these two views may appear more plausible to us, these discussions of bafflement and light dawning have brought us closer to one particular insight. For if the comic effect of Heine's *famillionairely* depends on solving the apparently senseless word, then the 'joke' is surely to be shifted to the formation of this word and to the characteristics of the word thus formed.

Quite unconnected with the views just discussed, there is another peculiarity of jokes and witticisms which all the authorities recognize as essential. 'Brevity is the body and the soul of wit, indeed it is wit itself,'[6] says Jean Paul (*Vorschule der Ästhetik*, I, IX, para. 45), only modifying as he does so some lines of the old windbag Polonius in Shakespeare's *Hamlet* (Act II, scene ii, 90–92):

> Therefore, since brevity is the soul of wit,
> And tediousness the limbs and outward flourishes,
> I will be brief.

Lipps's description of this brevity then becomes significant (p. 90). 'The joke says what it says, not always in a few, but always in too few words, that is, in words which in strict logic or in the ordinary way of thinking and speaking are not sufficient to say it. It is ultimately able to say it outright, by not saying it at all.'

'That the joke must bring out something hidden or concealed' (Kuno Fischer, p. 51), is something we already learned when the joke was compared with caricature. I emphasize this determinant

5

once again because this too has more to do with the nature of the joke than with its being a variety of the comic.

I am fully aware that the foregoing meagre extracts from the works of our authorities on the joke cannot do justice to their value. On account of the difficulties facing an error-free rendering of such complicated and finely nuanced arguments, I cannot spare those readers who thirst after knowledge the labour of seeking their desired instruction at the original source. But I do not know whether they will return fully satisfied. The criteria for jokes and their characteristics as given by the authorities and put together on the previous pages – the activity [of the subject], the relation to the content of our thinking, their character as playful judgement, the coupling of dissimilars, the contrast of ideas, the 'sense in nonsense', the sequence of bafflement and light dawning, bringing to light what is hidden, and the particular kind of brevity in the joke – admittedly, these appear at first glance to be so very accurate and so easily demonstrable from examples, that we are in no danger of underestimating the value of such insights. But they are *disjecta membra* which we would wish to see integrated into an organic whole. Ultimately they contribute no more to our knowledge of the joke than a string of anecdotes might to the characterization of a great personality, when we are justified in expecting his biography. We are wholly without insight into the interrelations we may assume among the individual determinants, such as what the brevity of jokes or witticisms can have to do with their character as a playful judgement; we also need to have explained whether a joke has to fulfil all these conditions to be a proper joke, or only some of them, or which can then be replaced by others and which are indispensable. An arrangement and classification of jokes on the basis of those features agreed to be essential would also be desirable. The classification we find in the authorities is based on the one hand on the joke's technical devices, on the other on the use of jokes in speech (punning, word-play – the caricaturing, characterizing joke, the witty put-down).

So we would not be at a loss to indicate what should be the aims of any further attempts at throwing light on the joke. To count on success, we would either have to introduce fresh aspects into the work or heighten our attention and intensify our interest as we attempt to go deeper. We can promise that at least we will not go short in this last respect. Still, it is striking how few examples of jokes acknowledged to be such are sufficient for our authorities' investigations, and how each of them takes over the same ones from his predecessors. We must not avoid the obligation of analysing the same examples, but apart from these we intend to turn to new material in order to obtain a broader basis for our conclusions. If we do that, it seems reasonable to take as the objects of our investigation examples of jokes that have made the greatest impression on us in our life and made us laugh the most heartily.

We may ask whether the topic of jokes is worth such trouble? As I see it, there is no doubt about it. Quite apart from the personal motives which urge me to acquire insight into the problems of the joke, and which will come to light in the course of these studies, I can call on the fact of the intimate interconnections between everything that goes on in the psyche. This ensures that a psychological insight even from a remote field will have an unpredictable value for other fields. Let us also bear in mind the peculiar, indeed fascinating, attraction jokes exercise in our society. A new joke has almost the same effect as an event of the widest interest; it is passed on from one to another like the news of the latest victory. Even great men who think it worth their while to tell us of their education, what cities and lands they have seen, and what outstanding people they have met, do not scorn to include in their memoirs the fact that they have heard this or that excellent joke.[7]

Notes

1. [Jean Paul Friedrich Richter (1763–1825): known as Jean Paul, prolific and popular novelist, whose wayward *ars poetica* is to be found in his *Vorschule der Ästhetik*, 2 vols (Hamburg, 1804–13); *Sämtliche Werke* 33 vols (Weimar, 1927–64), I (1937). Its section IX 'On Wit' was lastingly

influential. The work has been translated by Margaret Hale, *The Horn of Oberon: Jean Paul's School for Aesthetics* (Detroit, 1973).

Friedrich Theodor Vischer (1807–87): Hegelian philosopher, particularly of art; his first work was *Über das Erhabene und Komische* (1837). Freud appears to be using the first volume of his *Ästhetik oder Wissenschaft des Schönen*, 3 vols (Leipzig and Stuttgart, 1846–57).

Kuno Fischer (1824–1907): Professor of History of Philosophy in Heidelberg, and authority on the German literary classics. Freud takes issue with the broadly Kantian position of the two lectures Fischer published as *Über die Entstehung und Entwicklungsformen des Witzes* (Heidelberg, 1871).

Theodor Lipps (1851–1914): Professor of Psychology in Munich, with wide-ranging philosophical-aesthetic interests. Freud depends on Lipps for key terms and concepts: 'damming-up' of psychic energy, 'empathy' as the appreciation of another's reaction by feeling oneself into the other, while artistic appreciation depends on a similar self-projection into the object – these as they are presented in *Komik und Humor, eine psychologisch-ästhetische Untersuchung* (Hamburg and Leipzig, 1898), *Beiträge zur Ästhetik*, VI. At an earlier stage, when Freud was first exploring ideas that were to become specifically psychoanalytical, he was much encouraged by Lipps's assumption of an unconscious in his *Grundtatsachen des Seelenlebens* (Bonn, 1883). As Freud's own argument about jokes proceeds, Fischer and Lipps become his main authorities – Fischer to be argued against, Lipps to be embraced as mentor.]

2. *Beiträge zur Ästhetik*, edited by von Theodor Lipps and Richard Maria Werner. VI. – A book to which I am indebted for giving me the courage to undertake this essay and for making it possible for me to do so.

3. [Freud's source, Kuno Fischer, truncates Jean Paul's observation here (p. 12). The full aphorism runs: 'Here now an old but harmless world-cycle eternally recurs. Freedom gives wit (and equality too), and wit gives freedom' (Hale, op. cit., p. 143). Neither Jean Paul, nor Fischer, nor Freud is referring to jokes [*Witze*] at this point, but to the 'wit [*Witz*] that one *has*'.]

4. [*Kritik der Urteilskraft*, Pt. I, section I, para. 54, quoted by Lipps, p. 24.]

5. [Heinrich (Harry) Heine (b. Düsseldorf 1797–d. Paris 1856): poet and satirist and a favourite of Freud's. For his family background, see pp. 138–9). Hirsch-Hyacinth is a figure from 'Die Bäder von Lucca', in the third collection of Heine's *Reisebilder* (1830). The *famillionairely* joke occurs in chapter VIII.]

6. [Quoted by Kuno Fischer, p. 37.]

7. J. v. Falke, *Lebenserinnerungen*, 1897.

II *The Technique of the Joke*

[A]

Let us follow a hint from chance and take up the first example of a joke we met in the previous section.

In the part of his *Reisebilder* entitled 'Die Bäder von Lucca', Heinrich Heine introduces the delightful figure of the lottery-collector and corn-remover Hirsch-Hyacinth, who boasts to the poet of his connections with the rich Baron Rothschild and finally says: 'And as truly as God will grant me his blessings, Doctor Heine, I was sitting next to Salomon Rothschild and he treated me just like his equal, quite *famillionairely*.'

This example, acknowledged to be an excellent one and very amusing, was used by Heymans and Lipps to explain how the comic effect of a joke derives from 'bafflement and light dawning' (see above). We, on the other hand, will leave this question to one side and raise a different one: what is it, then, that makes Hirsch-Hyacinth's words into a joke? It could only be one of two things; either the thought expressed in his remark is intrinsically witty, or the witticism is bound up with the way in which his remark has formulated the thought. Whichever of these aspects of its character the joke turns towards us, let us follow and try to capture it.

In general, of course, a thought can be expressed in various linguistic forms – that is, in words – which may render it in equally apt terms. Now in Hirsch-Hyacinth's words we are confronted with one specific form of expression, and, as we sense, a particularly odd one, not the easiest to understand. Let us try to express the same thought as closely as possible in other words. Lipps has already done

9

so, and to some extent elucidated the poet's version. He says (p. 87): 'we understand Heine's meaning to be that Hirsch's reception was familiar, that is, of the sort you know which does not usually taste any more agreeable in coming from a millionaire'. We are not altering this sense in any way if we adopt a different version, which perhaps fits Hirsch-Hyacinth's words better: 'Rothschild treated me just like his equal, quite *familiarly*, that is, as far as a *millionaire* is able to.' 'The condescension of a rich man,' we would also add, 'always has something disagreeable about it for the person at the receiving end.'[1]

Whether we keep to this textual rendering of the thought or to another just as valid, we see that the question we have asked ourselves is already decided. The characteristic in this example that makes it a joke, its jokiness [*Witzcharacter*], is not attached to the thought. The observation Heine puts into his Hirsch-Hyacinth's mouth is a true one, shrewd, unmistakably bitter, and easily understandable in a poor man confronted with such great wealth, but we would not venture to call it witty. Now if someone hearing the translation cannot get the memory of the poet's version out of his head and so maintains that all the same the *thought* in itself is witty, we can easily point to a sure criterion for what gives our example the character of a joke, its jokiness, which has been lost in the translation. Hirsch-Hyacinth's words made us laugh aloud; the close paraphrase of their meaning – in Lipps's version or in ours – may please us, may give us to think, but it is quite unable to make us laugh.

But if what gives our example the character of a joke is not attached to the thought, then we must look for it in the form, in the wording in which it is expressed. We have only to study the peculiarity of this mode of expression to understand what we may call the linguistic or expressive technique of this joke, which must be intimately related to its essential nature, for its jokiness and its effect vanish when its wording is replaced by something different. By the way, we are in full agreement with the authorities in attaching such great importance to the linguistic form of a joke. As Kuno Fischer says (p. 72), for example: 'It is first and foremost the sheer form that turns the judgement into a joke, and we are reminded in this respect of a remark of Jean Paul's, which both elucidates and demonstrates the nature of the joke in this respect: "Victory owes so much to sheer position, whether in marshalling soldiers or sentences." '[2]

Now what makes up the 'technique' of Heine's joke? What has been happening to the thought – in our version, say – to turn it into the joke that makes us laugh so heartily? Two things, as we learn from comparing our version with the poet's text. First, a considerable *abbreviation* has taken place. To express the thought contained in the joke fully, we had to add to the words '*R. treated me just like his equal, quite familiarly*,' a further sentence, which, reduced to its shortest form, ran: *that is, as far as a millionaire is able to*. And even then, we still felt we needed a further sentence by way of explanation.[3] The poet puts it far more briefly:

'*R. treated me just like his equal, quite **famillionairely**.*' The entire qualification added by our second sentence to the first, the one establishing Hirsch's familiar treatment [by the Baron], is missing from the joke.

But even so, we are not left entirely without a substitute enabling us to reconstruct the qualification. For a second change has also taken place. The word '*familiar*' in the unjoking expression of the thought, has been transformed in the text of the joke into '*famillionaire*', and without doubt what makes this joke a joke and has the effect of making us laugh depends on just this very word-formation. The beginning of the newly coined word is identical with the 'familiarly' of the first sentence, and its final syllables are identical with the 'millionaire' of the second sentence. It stands in, as it were, for the component 'millionaire' from the second sentence, and consequently for the entire second sentence, and in this way puts us in a position to guess the second sentence omitted in the text of the joke. It is to be described as a composite formation made up of the two elements 'familiar' and 'millionaire', and it might be tempting to illustrate in print how it was created from these two words:[4]

FAMILI AR
MILLIONAIRE
FAMILLIONAIRE

However, the process that transposed the thought into the joke can be represented in the following way, which may seem quite fanciful at first, but all the same does provide us with the actual result we have here:

'R treated me quite familiarly,

that is, as far as a   millionaire is able to.'

Now let us imagine some concentrating force at work on these sentences, and assume that the second sentence is for some reason the less resistant. If so, this latter would be made to fade away, while its most important component, the word 'millionaire', which is able to resist the suppression, is as it were squeezed up against the first sentence and fused with the element in this sentence, 'familiar', which is so very like it; it is this very possibility, given by accident, of salvaging the essential item in the second sentence that favours the disappearance of the other, less important, components. In this way the joke then comes into being: 'R. treated me quite famillionairely.'

(milli) (airely)

Apart from some such concentrating force, which of course is unknown to us, we can describe the process of joke-formation in this case, that is, the joke-technique in this example, as one of *condensation with substitute-formation*, that is, in our example, the formation of a substitute consists of producing a *composite word*. Now this composite word, **'famillionairely'**, is incomprehensible in itself, but it is immediately understood and recognized as being meaningful in the context where it occurs. This word is the vehicle for the joke's effect, compelling our laughter – although, it is true, discovering the technique of the joke has by no means brought us any closer to its mechanism. How far can a process of linguistic condensation together with the formation of a substitute by means of a composite word give us pleasure and make us laugh? We note that this is a different problem, and we may postpone dealing with it until we have found a way of approaching it. For the present, we shall remain with jokes and their technique.

Our expectation that the technique of jokes cannot be irrelevant to understanding their nature leads us to inquire first of all whether there are any other examples of jokes constructed like Heine's 'famillionairely'. Now there are not very many of them, but still enough to create a small group characterized by the formation of a composite word. Heine himself has milked the word 'millionaire' for a second joke, copying himself as it were, when he speaks of a '**Millionarr**' ('Ideen',[5] chapter XIV), which is a transparent contraction of *Millionär* and *Narr* [fool] and, just like the first example, gives expression to a suppressed ulterior thought.

Other examples that have come my way: there is a certain fountain [*Brunnen*] in Berlin which on its erection brought Oberbürgermeister *Forckenbeck* into great disfavour. The Berliners call it the '**Forckenbecken**' and there is no denying the wit in this description, even if the word 'Brunnen' first had to be transformed into the rarely used 'Becken' [also 'fountain'] for it to coincide in an element common with the name. – The malicious wit of Europe once changed the name of a potentate called Leopold into **Cleopold** on account of his relations with a lady whose first name was *Cléo*, an undoubted feat of condensation, which constantly keeps a galling allusion alive at the cost of one single letter. – Proper names in general easily fall victim to this treatment by the joke-technique: in Vienna there were two brothers called *Salinger*, one of whom was a stockbroker [*Sensal*]. This offered the lever for calling the one brother **Sensalinger**, while to distinguish him the other received the unkind label of **Scheusalinger** [*Scheusal*: 'monster']. It was neat, and certainly witty; I do not know whether it was justified. Witticisms do not usually raise that question.

I was told the following condensation joke: after a long absence, a young man who up till then had been living a wild life abroad visited a friend here, who was surprised to notice a wedding-ring [*Ehering*] on his visitor's hand. 'What?' he cried. 'You're married?' 'Yes,' came the reply. '*Trauring* [*traurig*: 'sad'], but true.' It is an excellent joke; the two components coincide in the word '**Trauring**': [the synonymous] *Ehering* changed into *Trauring* and the saying '*Traurig, aber wahr*.'

In this case it does not spoil the effect of the joke that the composite word is not actually an incomprehensible, non-existent word like 'famillionairely', but is perfectly identical with one of the two condensed elements.

There is one witticism, again analogous to 'famillionairely', for which I myself once provided the material in conversation, quite unintentionally. I was telling a lady of the great merits of a scientist whom I consider is unjustly underestimated. 'But the man deserves a monument,' she declared. 'It's possible that he will get one one day,' I replied, 'but for the moment, he has very little success.' '*Monument*' and '*moment*' are opposites. The lady now unites the opposites: 'Then let us wish him **monumomentary** success.'

There is an excellent treatment of the same theme in English (A. A. Brill, 'Freud's Theory of Wit', *Journal of Abnormal Psychology*, 1911) to which I am indebted for some examples in a foreign language showing the same mechanism of condensation as our 'famillionairely'.

The English writer de Quincey, Brill tells us, observed somewhere that old people are inclined to fall into '**anecdotage**'. The word is fused from the two partially overlapping anec *dote* and

dotage.

In an anonymous short story Brill once found Christmas described as '**the alcoholidays**'. The same fusion of alco*hol* and

holidays.

When Flaubert published his famous novel *Salammbô*, set in ancient Carthage, Sainte-Beuve mocked it as **Carthaginoiserie** on account of the finicky detail of its descriptions: Cartha*ginois*

*chinois*erie.

The most splendid witticism in this group has for its originator one of the first men of Austria; after an important career in scholarship and public affairs, he now occupies one of the highest offices of state. I have taken the liberty of using the witticisms ascribed to this person – which in fact all bear the same stamp – as material for this inquiry,[6] above all because it would have been very hard to find better.

One day Herr N.'s[7] attention is drawn to the person of a writer who became well known on account of a number of exceedingly boring essays that he published in a Viennese daily paper. They all deal with minor episodes in Napoleon I's relations with Austria. The writer has red hair. As soon as he has heard the name, Herr N. asks: *Isn't that the boring red thread [**roter Fadian**] that runs through the history of Napoleon's exploits?*

To discover the technique of this witticism, we will have to submit it to that reductive procedure which eliminates the joke by altering its mode of expression, restoring instead the full original meaning, which can always be safely guessed from a good joke. Herr N.'s witticism about the 'roter Fadian' arises from two components, a dismissive judgement on the writer and the recollection of the famous metaphor with which Goethe introduces the extracts from 'Ottilie's Journal' in his novel *Die Wahlverwandschaften* [*Elective Affinities*, 1809]. 'We understand that the English navy has a certain arrangement by which every rope in the royal fleet, from the stoutest to the finest, is spun in such a fashion that a red thread runs through it which cannot be extracted without unravelling the whole rope, so that even the smallest piece of the rope can be recognized as belonging to the Crown. Similarly, there runs through Ottilie's journal a thread of affection and inclination that binds everything together and characterizes the whole.'[8] The unkind criticism may have run: So that's the fellow who can write nothing but boring articles about Napoleon in Austria for ever and a day! Now this remark is not witty in the least. Neither is Goethe's lovely analogy, and it is quite certainly not apt to make us laugh. Only when the two are brought into relationship and undergo the distinctive process of condensation and fusion will a joke come into being, and in this case a first-class one.[9]

The connection between the disparaging judgement on the boring historian and Goethe's lovely metaphor in *Die Wahlverwand-schaften* must have been produced along less simple lines than in many similar instances, though at this point I am not yet in a position to explain its causes. I shall try to replace the process that probably ensued by the following construction. At first the element of constant recurrence of the same topic may have roused a slight recollection in Herr N. of the well-known passage in *Die Wahlverwandschaften*, which, indeed, is usually quoted wrongly as 'it runs like a red thread'. The red thread of the simile affected the wording of the first sentence, altering it, on account of the fortuitous circumstance that the writer thus slandered was also *red*, that is, *red-haired*. It may have run: *So this is the red fellow who writes those boring articles about Napoleon*. Then the process aiming to condense both parts sets to work. Under pressure from this process, which had found its first point of support in the similarity of the '*red*' element, the '*boring*' was assimilated into '*Faden* [thread]' and was transformed into '*fad* [boring]', and then the two components were able to fuse into the wording of the joke, and this time the quotation had almost a greater share in it than the disparaging judgement, which was certainly the only factor present originally.

'So this is the *roter* [red] fellow who wrote the *fad* [boring] stuff about N.'

The *roter*   *Faden* [thread]

that runs through everything.

Isn't that the **roter Fadian** [boring fellow], *who runs through the history of N?*

I shall offer a justification of this account – but also an adjustment to it – in a later section, when I shall analyse this joke from other aspects than merely formal ones. But whatever might be doubtful about this account, there can be no doubting the fact that a process of condensation has taken place here. The outcome of the condensation on the one hand is again a considerable abbreviation; on the other, instead of the formation of a striking composite word, rather an interpenetration of the elements of both constituents. '*Roter Fadian*' would be viable as a mere insult anyway; in our instance it is certainly the product of condensation.

Now if at this point my reader were to get indignant at a way of treating the joke which threatens to spoil his pleasure in it without even explaining to him the source of this pleasure, I would first of all beg him to be patient. We are dealing only with the technique of jokes here, and our investigation into it does indeed promise to be most informative, once we have taken it far enough.

The analysis of the previous example has prepared us to encounter the process of condensation in other examples still, where the substitute for what has been suppressed can be rendered not by the formation of a composite word but by some other change in expression. What this other kind of substitute might consist of is something we may learn from other witticisms of Herr N.'s.

'I travelled **tête-à-bête** with him.' There can be nothing easier than reducing this witticism [to its elements]. Obviously it can only mean: I travelled *tête-à-tête* with X., and X. is a stupid *ass*.

Neither of these two sentences is witty. Nor if they are combined into one sentence: *I travelled tête-à-tête with that stupid ass X.* – which is just as unfunny. The witticism only comes into existence when the *'stupid ass'* is left out and, as a substitute, the **t** of one *tête* is transformed into a **b** instead; with this tiny modification, the suppressed 'ass' still gets itself expressed. We can describe the technique of this group of witticisms as *condensation with slight modification*, and we sense that the slighter the modification in the substitute, the better the witticism.

The technique of another witticism is quite similar, though not without its complications. In conversation about a person of many virtues and many faults, Herr N. says: *Yes, vanity is one of his four Achilles' heels.*[10] The slight modification here occurs in asserting that instead of *one Achilles' heel*, which has to be conceded even in the case of the hero, there are *four*. But the only creatures to have four heels, and so four feet, are the beasts. In this way the two thoughts condensed in the witticism ran:

'Apart from his vanity, Y. is an outstanding human being; but I still don't like him; he is an ass rather than a human being.'[11]

Here is another witticism, similar, only much simpler, which I got to hear in a family circle *in statu nascendi* [as it was being born]. There were two brothers, schoolboys at the *Gymnasium*, one of whom was an excellent student, the other pretty mediocre. Now the model student too did badly on one occasion, which caused his mother to say, as an expression of her concern, this could mean the beginning of a permanent downturn. The boy, who had till then been overshadowed by his brother, made eager use of the occasion. Yes, he said, *Karl is going backwards on all fours*.

The modification here consists of an addition to the assurance that in his judgement too his brother is going backwards. However, this modification represents and replaces a passionate plea in his own favour: 'You really mustn't believe that he is so much cleverer than I am just because he is more successful at school. He is only a stupid ass after all, that is, much more stupid than I am.'

Another very well-known witticism of Herr N.'s offers a beautiful example of condensation with modification. He remarked of a person in public life that *he had a great future behind him*. The butt of this witticism was quite a young man who seemed to be called by birth, education and personal qualities to take over the leadership of a great political party one day and assume governmental power at its head. But the times changed; the party was regarded as unsuitable for government, and it was to be foreseen that the man predestined to be its leader would get nowhere. The shortest reductive version that could replace this witticism would run: *This man had a great future before him, but things are over with him now*. Instead of 'had' and the supplementary sentence, we have the small alteration to the main sentence so that 'before' is succeeded by its opposite, 'behind'.[12]

Herr N. made use of almost the same modification in the case of a gentleman who had become Minister of Agriculture without any other qualification than that he was in farming himself. Public opinion had occasion to discover that he was the least talented minister ever to be entrusted with this office. However, when he gave up this office and withdrew to his farming interests, Herr N. said of him:

*Like Cincinnatus he has returned to his place **before** the plough.*

The Roman who had been called away from his farm to assume office resumed his place *behind* the plough. The place *before* the plough, then as now, was taken only by – the *ox* [*Ochs*: German diatribe equivalent for 'ass'].

We also have a clever case of condensation with slight modification when Karl Kraus[13] reports that a certain journalist for a scandal-sheet travelled to one of the Balkan states by *Orient* Erpress train. Assuredly, this word is the meeting-place of two others: '*Orient Express train*' and '*Erpressung* [blackmail]'; the element 'Erpressung' only makes its presence felt as a modification of the 'Orient Express train' required by the verb. This witticism also has a further interest for us, as it looks deceptively like a typographical error.

We could easily add to the number of these examples, but I do not think we need any fresh instances to have a secure grasp of the technical characteristics in this second group, condensation with modification. If we now compare the second group with the first, where the technique consisted of condensation with the formation of a composite word, we will easily see that the distinctions between the two are not essential ones, and the transitions [between them] fluid. Both the formation of a composite word and modification are subordinate to the concept of substitute-formation, and, if we wish, we can also describe the composite formation as a modification of the basic word by the second element.

[B]

However, this is where we may pause for the first time and ask ourselves: with which of the factors known from the literature [on the subject] does the first result of our own reflections tally? Obviously, with the factor of brevity, which Jean Paul calls the soul of wit (see above, p. 7). Now brevity is not in itself witty, otherwise every pithy remark would be a witticism. The brevity of witticisms must be of a particular kind. We recall that Lipps attempted to describe the particular mode of brevity in witticisms more closely (p. 7). That was where our own inquiry took off, demonstrating that the brevity of a witticism is often the result of a particular process which leaves a second trace – the formation of a substitute – in the wording of the witticism. However, proceeding by way of reduction, which aims to reverse the peculiar condensation-process, we also find that the joke lies only in the linguistic expression produced by the process of condensation. Naturally, our full interest now turns towards this strange process, which has gone almost unappreciated until now. And as yet we have no notion at all of how everything we value in a joke, the gain in pleasure it brings us, can come about.

Have processes similar to those we have described as the technique of jokes already been discovered in any other field of the psyche's activity? Indeed they have – in one sole, and seemingly very remote – field. In 1900 I published a book which, as its title (*Die Traumdeutung* [*The Interpretation of Dreams*]) indicates, attempts to explain the enigmatic nature of dreams and establish that they are the issue of normal psychical activity. I have occasion there to contrast the *manifest*, and often strange, *dream-content* with the *latent dream-thought* – with its own perfectly good rationale [*korrekt*] – from which it derives; and I go on to investigate the processes that turn the latent dream-thoughts into the dream, as well as the psychical forces involved in this transformation. The processes of transformation as a whole I call the *dream-work*, and as part of this dream-work I described a process of condensation which shows the greatest similarity to the technique of jokes in the way the latter leads to greater brevity and creates substitute-formations of the same nature. From our own memories of our dreams, we will all be familiar with composite formations of persons and of objects too, which make their appearance in our dreams; indeed, dreams will also form composites of words of the kind that can be taken apart in the course of analysis (e.g., *Autodidasker* = *Autodidact* + *Lasker*) (*Die Traumdeutung*, chapter VI). On other occasions, much more frequently in fact, the work of condensation in a dream will not produce composite formations, but images fully resembling a person or an object – except for one addition or alteration coming from another source – modifications, that is, just like those in Herr N.'s witticisms. There is no doubt that we are faced here, as we were there, with the same psychical process, which we are able to recognize from the identical ways of functioning in both. Such a far-reaching analogy between the technique of jokes and the dream-work will certainly increase our interest in theformer, and rouse our expectation that a comparison of jokes and dreams will contribute a great deal towards an explanation of jokes. But we will refrain from pursuing this line of work, telling ourselves that we have so far studied their technique in only a very small number of jokes, so that we cannot know whether the analogy we are relying on for guidance will continue to hold good. So let us turn away from our comparison with dreams and return to the technique of jokes; let us leave, as it were, a loose end dangling at this place in our investigation, which we shall perhaps take up again later.

[C]

The first thing we want to find out is whether the process of condensation with substitute-formation can be demonstrated in all jokes, so that it can be identified as *the* universal characteristic of their technique.

I recall a joke that has stayed in my memory on account of a particular circumstance. One of the great teachers of my youth, whom we thought incapable of appreciating a joke, just as we had never heard him make a joke himself, came into the Institute one day full of laughter, and, more readily than usual, told us what had occasioned his light-hearted mood. 'I've just been reading an excellent joke. A young man was introduced into a Paris salon; he was supposed to be a relative of the great J. J. Rousseau, and did have the same name. He was, also, red-haired. But his behaviour was so gauche that the lady of the house commented in criticism to the gentleman who had introduced him: "Vous m'avez fait connaître un jeune homme *roux* [red] *et sot* [silly], mais non pas un *Rousseau*." ' And he laughed afresh.

This, according to the authorities' classification, is a joke dependent upon sound, a near-pun of low quality, playing on the proper name, rather like the jokes in the Capuchin friar's tirade in [Schiller's] *Wallensteins Lager*[14] [*Wallenstein's Camp*, scene 8], which, it is well known, is modelled on the manner of Abraham a Santa Clara:

> *Läßt sich nennen den* Wallenstein,
> *ja freilich ist er uns allen ein* Stein.
> *des Anstoßes und Ärgernisses.*[15]

[And he calls himself Prince *Wallenstein*./ A *stony wall*, a *stain* on us *all*,]

But what is the technique of this joke?

It turns out that the characteristic which we hoped perhaps to demonstrate was universal fails us in our very first new case. There is no omission, scarcely an abbreviation, present here. In her joke, the lady states outright almost all we can ascribe to her thoughts. 'You made me look forward to someone of *J. J. Rousseau*'s kin, perhaps a kindred spirit, and lo and behold! a silly young man with red hair, one *roux et sot*.' It is true I have been able to add something, insert something into it, but my attempt at reducing it does not spoil the joke. It still holds good, and is attached to the identity of sound between *Rousseau*

and *roux sot*

This has demonstrated that condensation with substitute-formation has no part in bringing this joke about.

But what else has? Further attempts at reduction are able to tell me that the joke will continue to be resistant – up to the point where the name *Rousseau* is replaced by another. For example, if I put *Racine* in its stead, the lady's criticism, which remains just as feasible as it did before, has lost all trace of wit. Now I know where I have to look to find the technique of this joke, though I may still hesitate about how to formulate it. I shall try the following: the technique of this joke lies in the feature that one and the same word – the name – is used in two different ways, once as a whole and then broken down into its syllables, as in the game of charades.

I can offer a few examples identical to this in technique.

Making a joke relying on this technique of double use, an Italian lady is said to have taken her revenge for a tactless remark of Napoleon's. He observed to her at a court ball, referring to her fellow-countrymen: 'Tutti gli Italiani danzano si male [All Italian men dance so badly],' and she replied with ready wit: 'Non tutti, *ma buona parte* [Not all, but a *bonny part*]' (Brill, loc. cit.).

(According to Theodor Vischer and Kuno Fischer.) A performance of *Antigone* was once being given in Berlin, but in the opinion of the critics, the production lacked any sense of the antique world. Berlin wit made this criticism its own in the following way: '*Antik? O nee* [Antique? Oh nay].'

A similar joke breaking up the word is current among medical men. If one questioned a young patient as to whether he has ever masturbated, the only answer one would get would be: '*O na, nie* [lit: 'Oh no, never'; *Onanie*: 'masturbation'].'

In all three examples, which are sufficient to establish the category, [we see] the same technique in the jokes. A noun is used twice in them, once as a whole, the other time broken up into its syllables; and, thus broken up, the syllables yield a different meaning.[16]

The multiple use of the same word, once as a whole and then broken up into its syllables, has been the first instance we have encountered of a technique diverging from condensation. But, after brief reflection, we are bound to suspect from the sheer quantity of examples pouring in on us that the newly discovered technique can scarcely be confined to this one device. There is obviously an – at first – immeasurable number of possibilities as to how the same word or the same linguistic material can be exploited for multiple use. Are all these possibilities to present themselves to us as technical devices of the joke? It seems to be the case; the following examples will demonstrate it.

D. Spitzer (*Wiener Spaziergänge*, vol. II, p. 42):

'Mr and Mrs X. have a pretty lavish lifestyle. According to one view, the husband is supposed to have *earned a lot* and so put a *bit on one side*, according to another, the wife is supposed to have been a *bit on the side* and *so to have earned a lot*.'

A positively devilish good joke! And how slight the means that have gone to make it! Earned a lot – put a bit on one side, been a bit on the side – earned a lot; it is actually no more than the exchange of these two phrases that distinguishes what is stated about the husband from what is hinted about the wife. All the same, this does not make up the entire joke-technique here either.[17]

Joke-technique acquires a wide field of play if we extend the '*multiple use of the same material*' to the point where the word – or words – carrying the joke may be used once unchanged, and then *with a slight modification*.

For example, another witticism from Herr N.:

He hears a malicious remark about the Jews from a gentleman who was himself born Jewish. 'Herr Hofrat,' he says, 'your *ante-Semitism* was well known to me, but your *anti-Semitism* is new.'

In this instance only one single letter has been altered, and in casual speech its modification is scarcely noticed. This example reminds us of the other witticisms of Herr N. effected by modification (see p. 19), but unlike them it has no condensation: everything that has to be said is said in the witticism itself. 'I know that you yourself were once a Jew; so I'm surprised that you of all people should insult the Jews.'

The well-known exclamation: *Traduttore – Traditore!* [Translator – traitor!] is also an excellent example of a modification-witticism of this kind.

The similarity, almost identity, of the two words yields a most telling sketch of the straits that cause translators to sin against their authors.[18]

The range and variety of slight modifications is so great in these jokes that not one of them is entirely like another.

Here is a joke that is supposed to have really been made at a law examination! The candidate has to translate a passage from the *Corpus Juris*. '"*Labeo ait . . . I fall*," he said . . . "*You fail*," I say,' replies the examiner, and the examination is over. Anyone mistaking the name of the great jurist [*Labeo ait*: 'Labeo says'] for an item of vocabulary [*labeor*: 'I fall'], and, what is more, one incorrectly remembered, certainly deserves no better. But the technique of this joke lies in the examiner's use of almost the selfsame words that testified to the candidate's ignorance to punish him. This joke is, in addition, an example of 'quick-wittedness', the technique of which, as will emerge, is not far from that explained here.

Words are malleable material, allowing all kinds of things to be done to them. There are words which, used in certain ways, have lost their original full meaning, though in another context they still enjoy it. One witticism of Lichtenberg's[19] selects those very circumstances where the faded words are bound to recover their full meaning.

'*How's it going?*' the blind man asks *the lame man*. 'As you *see*,' the lame man answers *the blind man*.

There are also words in German that can be taken in a different sense, in more than one, in fact, depending on whether they are *full* or *empty*. For it is possible for two different derivatives from the same stem to have developed, the one into a word with a full meaning, the other into a faded final or pendant syllable, and for both still to have the same sound. The similarity of sound between a full word and a faded syllable may also be accidental. In both cases, the technique of jokes can benefit from conditions of this kind in the linguistic material.

For example, a witticism attributed to Schleiermacher,[20] which is important for us as an almost pure example of this kind of technical device: '*Eifersucht* ist eine *Leidenschaft*, die mit *Eifer sucht*, was *Leiden schafft* [lit: 'Jealousy is a passion that with zeal searches out what creates suffering'].'

This is undeniably witty, although as a joke not particularly forceful. A number of factors are absent here, which could put us on the wrong path in analysing other witticisms if we examine each factor separately. The thought expressed in the wording is paltry; in any case, it offers a very unsatisfactory definition of jealousy; there is no question of 'sense in nonsense', 'hidden meaning' or 'bafflement and light dawning'. We do not find any contrast of ideas, not even if we try; we find a contrast between the words and what they mean only with great effort. There is no sign of any abbreviation; on the contrary, the wording makes an impression of prolixity. And yet it *is* a witticism, in fact a very accomplished one. Its one striking characteristic is at the same time the feature whose removal would destroy the joke, that is, that the same words are put to multiple use in it. So we now have the choice of ascribing this joke to that subgroup in which a word is used once as a whole and then broken up (like *Rousseau, Antigone*), or to that other subgroup, where the multiple use is produced by the full and the faded meaning of a word's components. Apart from this, there is only one other factor worth noting with regard to joke-technique. An unusual connection is set up here, a kind of *unification* undertaken, as 'Eifersucht' is defined by means of its own name, by means of itself, as it were. This too, as we shall learn, is a technique of jokes. These two factors, then, must in themselves be sufficient to give a remark the character of a joke that we are looking for.

If we pursue the variety of 'multiple use' of the same word further, all at once we shall see that we are faced with forms of 'double meaning' or 'play on words', which have long been generally known and appreciated as a technique of jokes. Why have we put ourselves to the trouble of discovering something afresh when we could have taken it from the most banal treatise on jokes? In justification, we can at first only point out that we have nevertheless emphasized a different side of the same phenomenon of linguistic expression. In the works of the authorities, what is meant to demonstrate the 'playful' nature of jokes, in our investigation comes under the aspect of 'multiple use'.

The further instances of multiple use, which can also be brought together into a new, third group, that of *double meaning*, easily lend themselves to subgroupings, though these are not distinguished from one another by any essential differences, nor is the entire third group from the second. There are first of all *a)* cases of the double meaning of a *name* and its *signification as a thing*, for example, 'Discharge yourself of our company, Pistol' (in Shakespeare; 2 *Hen IV*, II.iv.145).

'Mehr *Hof* als *Freiung* [More courting than wooing],' said a witty Viennese with reference to several pretty girls who had been admired for years, but had still not found husbands. 'Hof' [court] and 'Freiung' [here, 'wooing'] are two neighbouring squares in the city centre of Vienna.

Heine: 'It is not vile Macbeth who rules here in Hambrug, but Banko (Banquo [lit: 'the bank's money']).'

Where the name cannot be used without alteration – one might say: cannot be misused – it is possible to exploit it for a double meaning by means of one of the little modifications familiar to us.

'Why did the French reject *Lohengrin?*' is a question asked in times now well behind us. The answer ran: 'For Elsa's (Elsaß [Alsace]) sake.'[21]

b) The double meaning of the literal and metaphorical signification of a word, which is a rich source for the technique of jokes. I shall quote only one example: A medical colleague known to be a joker once said to the dramatist Arthur Schnitzler: 'I'm not surprised that you have become a great writer. After all, your father held a *mirror* up to his contemporaries.' The mirror wielded by the dramatist's father, the famous physician Dr Schnitzler, was a laryngoscope [*Kehlkopfspiegel*; lit: 'larynx-mirror']; according to a well-known speech of Hamlet's, it is the aim of the drama, and so also of the dramatist who creates it, 'to hold, as 'twere, the mirror up to nature; to show virtue her own feature, scorn her own image, and the very age and body of the time his form and pressure' (III.ii.25–8).

c) True double meaning, or *play on words*, the ideal case of multiple use, as it were; in these instances, no violence is done to the word, it is not broken down into its syllabic components, it does not need to submit to any modification, nor exchange its appropriate sphere, as a proper noun, for instance, for another; just as it is, and just as it stands in the framework of the sentence, thanks to certain favourable circumstances, it can voice two meanings.

There are ample examples at our disposal.

(From Kuno Fischer.) One of the first acts of Napoleon III on coming to power was, as we know, to confiscate the estates of the Duc d'Orléans. An excellent play on words of the time said: 'C'est le premier *vol* de l'aigle.' 'Vol' means *flight*, but it also means *theft*.

Louis XV, hearing of the wit of one of his courtiers, desired to put his talent to the test; at the first opportunity, he commanded the chevalier to make a joke about himself; he himself, the King, desired to be the 'sujet' of the witticism. The courtier replied with the adroit *bon mot*: 'Le roi n'est pas *sujet*.' 'Sujet', of course, also means 'subject' in the sense of *vassal*.

A physician, leaving a wife's sickbed, shakes his head and says to her husband accompanying him: 'I don't *like the look* of your wife.' 'I haven't *liked the look of her* for a long time,' the husband hastens to agree.

Of course, the physician is referring to the woman's state of health, but he has expressed his concern for his patient in words of a kind that enable the husband to find in them the confirmation of his own antipathy to his marriage.

Heine remarked of a satirical comedy: 'This would not have been such a *biting* satire if the writer had more to *bite*.' This joke is an example of literal and metaphorical double meaning, rather than a proper play on words – but where is the point in clinging to such sharp distinctions here?

Another good play on words has been given by the authorities (Heymans, Lipps) told in a form that acts as an obstacle to understanding it.[22] I found the correct version and wording not long ago in a collection of jokes which otherwise was not much use.[23]

'Saphir once met up with Rothschild. They had hardly been chatting a while when Saphir said: "Listen, Rothschild, my funds are very low. You could lend me 100 ducats." "Well, now," replied Rothschild, "that's fine by me, but only on condition that you tell a joke." "That's fine by me too," answered Saphir. "Good, then come to my office tomorrow." Saphir presents himself punctually. "Ah," said Rothschild, as he saw him enter, "*Sie kommen um Ihre 100 Dukaten* [lit: 'You've come about your 100 ducats']." "No," replied

Saphir, "*Sie kommen um Ihre 100 Dukaten* [lit: 'You've lost your 100 ducats'], for I wouldn't dream of repaying them, not till the trump of doom."'

'What do these statues [*re*]present [*vorstellen*: 'represent' or 'put forward'?]' a stranger asks a native Berliner of a line of monuments in a public square. 'Well, now,' comes the reply, '*either the right leg or the left leg*.'[24]

Heine in 'Die Harzreise':[25] 'At this moment I cannot recall all the students' *names*, and among the professors there are many who have not yet made a *name*.'

We shall perhaps have some practice in diagnostic differentiation if we add another widely known joke about professors at this point. 'The difference between *ordinary* [*ordentlich*: (here) 'tenured'] and *extraordinary* [*außerordentlich*: (here) 'untenured'] professors lies in the fact that the *ordinary* ones don't achieve anything extraordinary, and the *extraordinary* ones don't achieve anything ordinary [*ordentlich*: (here) 'competent'].' That is certainly a play with the two meanings of the words *ordentlich* and *außerordentlich*, in and outside the Ordo (the official body) of professors on the one hand, and competent, possibly outstanding, on the other. However, the congruence of this joke with other examples we have met reminds us that in this case multiple use is much more striking than double meaning. Indeed, all one hears in the sentence is the constantly recurring *ordentlich*, sometimes as itself, sometimes modified by the negative (compare p. 26). Apart from that, the trick of defining a concept by its sound has been accomplished here too (compare 'Eifersucht ist eine Leidenschaft, etc.'), more exactly, the trick of defining two correlative concepts by means of each other, albeit negatively, producing a clever chiasmus. Finally, one can also highlight the aspect of unification, which sets up a closer connection between the elements of the statement than their nature might allow us to expect.

Heine in 'Die Harzreise': 'S. the beadle greeted me like a colleague, for he too is a writer, and has often mentioned me in his half-yearly writings; and, besides that, he has often *cited* me, and if he did not find me at home, he was always kind enough to write the *citation* with chalk on my study door' [a joke based on double meaning: *zitieren*: 'to quote' but also 'to summon to a disciplinary hearing'].

The 'Viennese Stroller' D. Spitzer invented a pithy, and certainly very witty, description of a career:

'*Eiserne* Stirne – *eiserne* Kasse – *eiserne* Krone[26] [lit: '*Iron* front – *iron* cash-box – *Iron* Crown'].' An absolutely first-class unification, everything, as it were, made of iron! The different, but discreetly contrasting, meanings of the descriptive 'iron' are what make these 'multiple uses' possible.

Another play on words may smooth the transition for us to a fresh subspecies of the technique of double meaning. This witticism at the time of the Dreyfus[27] affair is due to the witty colleague mentioned on p. 29):

'This girl puts me in mind of Dreyfus. The army does not believe in her *innocence*.'

In the one context, the word 'innocence', whose double meaning forms the basis of the joke, has the customary sense, with its opposite in 'guilt' or 'crime', but in the other it has a sexual sense whose opposite is sexual experience. Now there are very many examples of this kind of double meaning, and in them all the effect of the joke particularly depends on the sexual sense. For this group we may reserve the designation *double entendre* [*Zweideutigkeit*].

An excellent example of this kind of *double entendre* is the one told by D. Spitzer on p. 26:

'According to one view, the husband is supposed to have *earned a lot* and so put *a bit on one side*, according to another, the wife is supposed to have been *a bit on the side* and *so to have earned a lot*.'

But if we compare this *double entendre* with other examples of double meaning, we are struck by a difference which is not entirely unimportant for technique. In the 'innocence' joke, the one sense of the word was just as accessible to our understanding as the other; it would really be difficult for us to tell whether the sexual or the non-sexual meaning of the word was the more current and familiar. It is a different matter in the example from Spitzer; here, the one, banal, sense of the words 'a bit on one side', the infinitely more prominent sense, as it were, cloaks and conceals the sexual sense, which the guileless listener might even miss. Let us contrast this sharply with another example of double meaning which dispenses with concealing such sexual meaning, e.g., Heine's description of an obliging lady: 'She could make [here: *abschlagen*, which also means 'refuse'] nothing but her water.' This sounds like an obscenity; the impression of wit scarcely makes itself felt.[28] Now the peculiarity that the two senses of the double meaning do not come to mind with equal readiness also occurs in jokes which have no sexual reference, whether because the one sense is the more current one, or because it is foregrounded by its connection with the other parts of the sentence (e.g., 'c'est le premier *vol* de l'aigle'); I propose to call all these cases *double meaning with allusion*.

[D]

We have already met such a large number of different joke-techniques that I fear we might lose track of them. So let us try to put them in order:

I. Condensation:
   a) with the formation of composite words,
   b) with modification.
II. Use of the same material:
   c) as a whole and in parts,
   d) rearrangement,
   e) slight modification,
   f) the same words full and empty.
III. Double meaning:
   g) as a name and as a thing,
   h) metaphorical and literal,
   i) true double meaning (play on words),
   j) double entendre,
   k) double meaning with allusion.

This variety is confusing. It might put us out that we have been devoting our attention specifically to the technical devices of jokes, and might make us suspect that even so we have still overestimated their importance for the essential thing about jokes. If only our relief at such a conjecture were not blocked by the irrefutable fact that a joke is always spoiled the moment we remove the operation of these devices from its expression! So the indications still point us towards looking for the unity in this diversity. It must be possible to bring all these devices under one heading! It is not difficult to combine the second and third groups, as we have already said. Double meaning, play on words, is after all the ideal case of use of the same material. The latter is obviously the more comprehensive concept. The examples of break-down into parts, rearrangement of the same material, multiple use with slight modification (*c, d, e*) could not be brought under the concept of double meaning without forcing them. But what common ground is there between the technique of the first group – condensation with substitute-formation – and the technique of the other two – multiple use of the same material?

Well, a very simple and clear one, I should think. Use of the same material, after all, is only a special case of condensation; play on words is nothing but condensation *without* substitute-formation; condensation is still the overriding category. A tendency to condensation, or, more correctly, to parsimony, predominates in all these techniques. Everything seems to be a matter of economy, as Hamlet says ('Thrift, thrift, Horatio!'; I.ii.180).

Let us test the individual examples against this thrift. 'C'est le premier vol de l'aigle.' That is the eagle's first flight. True – but it is a predatory flight. Fortunately for the existence of this joke, *vol* means 'flight' as well as 'theft'. Has nothing been condensed and economized in this? The entire second thought, for certain, and in fact it has been omitted without any substitute. The double meaning of the word *vol* makes such a substitute superfluous, or, to put it just as correctly: the word *vol* contains the substitute for the suppressed thought, without any need to alter or add to the first sentence. The benefit of the double meaning is just that.

Another example: 'Iron front – iron cash-box – Iron Crown.' What extraordinary economy in comparison with an exposition of the thought where the expression did not make use of that '*iron*'! 'With the necessary effrontery and unscrupulousness, it is not difficult to amass great wealth, and as a reward for such merit, of course, it only requires ennoblement.'

Indeed, in these examples the condensation, and hence the economy, is unmistakable. But it should be possible to demonstrate it in all jokes. Where is the economy in jokes such as '*Rousseau – roux et sot* [pp. 23–4], '*Antigone – Antique? Oh nay*' [p. 25], where we first noticed the absence of condensation, and which mainly moved us to propose the technique of multiple use of the same material? It is true, we would not get by with condensation in these cases, but if we exchange this concept for the overriding one of 'economy', there is no difficulty. It is easy to tell where we are economizing in the examples of Rousseau, Antigone, etc. We are saving ourselves the statement of our criticism, the expression of our judgement, for both are already given in the name itself. In the example 'Eifersucht – Leidenschaft' we are sparing ourselves the labour of putting a definition together: 'Eifersucht, Leidenschaft – Eifer sucht, Leiden schafft' [p. 27]; put in the filler words and the definition is complete. Where the least economy is made, as in Saphir's play on words 'Sie kommen um Ihre 100 Dukaten' [pp. 30–31], at least it saves giving a new form to the wording of the reply. The words used for the question are sufficient for the reply. It is minimal, but it is solely in this minimum that the joke lies. The multiple use of the same words in address as well as in reply certainly goes with 'economizing'. Just as Hamlet interprets the rapid sequence of his father's death and his mother's marriage:

> The funeral baked meats
> Did coldly furnish forth the marriage tables. (I.ii.180–81)

But before we take the 'tendency towards economy' to be the most general feature of the technique of jokes and raise the questions of where it comes from, what it signifies, and how it is that the gain in pleasure we get from a joke should have its origin there, let us give an airing to a doubt which has a right to be heard. It may well be that every technique used in jokes shows a tendency to economize in expression. This does not mean that every economy in expression, every abbreviation, is also witty. We have been here before, at the stage when we were still hoping to demonstrate the process of condensation at work in every joke, and then we chided ourselves justifiably that a pithy saying is still not a joke. So it would have to be a particular kind of abbreviation and economy on which the jokey nature of the joke would depend, and as long as we do not know what this is, discovering the common factor in the technique of jokes brings us no nearer to solving our problem. Besides, we are brave enough to admit that the savings made by the technique of jokes are not very impressive. They remind us perhaps of the way some housewives economize when they expend time and money on the journey to go to a distant market because the vegetables are to be had for a few pence cheaper there. What does the joke save itself by its technique? Putting together a few fresh words, which would mostly have come of themselves without any trouble; instead of this, it has to go to the trouble of looking for the one word that will express both thoughts; indeed, it often has to recast the expression of the one thought into an unusual form for it to offer a foothold enabling it to combine with the second thought. Would it not have been simpler, easier and actually thriftier to express the two thoughts just as they happened, even if it meant that no shared overlap in their expression came about? Is not the economy in words expressed more than cancelled by the expense of intellectual effort? And who is being so thrifty? Who benefits from it?

We can evade these doubts for the present, if we shift the doubt itself to another place. Have we in fact already met all the kinds of joke-technique? It will certainly be more prudent to collect fresh examples and submit them to analysis.

[E]

In fact, there is a large, perhaps the most numerous, group of jokes which we have not so far considered. Perhaps we have allowed ourselves to be influenced by the low opinion in which they have been held. They are the ones that are commonly called *Kalauer*[29] (calembourgs) and are regarded as the lowest kind of dwelling-place [for wit], probably because they are the 'cheapest' and can be made with very little trouble. And really they make the smallest demands on joke-technique, just as true play on words makes the highest. In the latter, the two meanings should be expressed by the identical word, which is why it is said only once, while in the *Kalauer* it is sufficient that the two words for the two meanings should recall each other by some quite random similarity, whether it be some general similarity in structure, such as a similarity of sound in rhyme or alliteration, etc. A quantity of these 'jokes based on sound', as they are – not quite accurately – called, can be found in the Capuchin friar's sermon in [Schiller's] *Wallensteins Lager* [*Wallenstein's Camp*, scene 8]:

> *Kümmert sich mehr um den* Krug *als den* Krieg,
> *Wetzt lieber den* Schnabel *als den* Sabel

[Would rather wet its *whistle* than prime its *pistol*,/ Cares rather for *whoring* than for *warring*,]

> *Frißt den* Ochsen *lieber als den* Ochsenstirn

[It would rather roast *oxen* than *Oxenstiern*]

> *Der* Rheinstrom *ist geworden zu einem* Peinstrom,
> *Die* Klöster *sind ausgenommene* Nester,
> *Die* Bistümer *sind verwandelt in* Wüsttümer,

[The *River Rhine* is a river of *pain*,/ Every *abbey* is stripped and *shabby*,/
The *dioceses* are ravaged with *diseases*,]

> *Und alle die gesegneten deutschen* Länder
> *Sind verkehrt worden in* Elender.

[And the blessed lands of *Germany*/ Filled far and wide with *misery* –][30]

This [kind of] joke is particularly fond of modifying one of the
vowels of a word, e.g., Hevesi (Almanaccando, *Reisen in Italien*,
p. 87) observes of an Italian poet who was against the [Holy Roman]
Empire, but was still compelled to praise a German Emperor in
hexameters: 'If he cannot abolish the *Caesars*, at least he removes
the *caesuras*.'

Given the wealth of *Kalauer* at our disposal, there may perhaps
be a particular interest in drawing attention to a really poor example
to be laid at Heine's door. After long pretending to his lady that he
was an 'Indian Prince', he then throws off the mask and admits:
'Madam! I have been lying to you . . . I have no more been in *Calcutta*
than the *calcutta*-fowl I ate roasted yesterday noon.' Obviously this
joke is flawed because the two similar words are not simply similar,
but actually identical. The bird he ate roasted gets its name because
it comes – or is supposed to come – from that same Calcutta itself.

Kuno Fischer has devoted a great deal of attention to this form of
joke, and would have it sharply distinguished from the play on words
(p. 78). 'The *calembour* is a bad play on words, for it plays with the
word not as a proper word, but as a sound.' True play on words,
however, 'passes from the sound of the word into the word itself'.
On the other hand, he also counts such jokes as 'famillionaire'
[p. 11], Antigone ('Antique? Oh nay') [p. 25] among the jokes based
on sound. I see no necessity to follow him in this respect. In the
true play on words as well, the word is for us only a sound-image to
which this or that meaning is attached. But here too, linguistic
usage does not distinguish sharply, and if it treats the *Kalauer* with
scorn and the true 'play on words' with a certain respect, these
value-judgements seem to be determined by concerns other than

technical ones. We have only to notice the nature of the jokes that reach us under the name of *Kalauer*. There are some persons who, when they are in high spirits, have the gift of answering any remark made to them with a *Kalauer*. Take one of my friends: otherwise the model of modesty, if discussion turns to his serious scientific achievements, he will usually boast of his skill in such punning as well. Once, when the gathering he was entertaining in this way expressed astonishment at how he could carry on, he said: 'Yes, I'm lurking here "auf der *Ka-Lauer*",' and when they finally begged him to stop, he agreed on condition that they should declare him Poet *Ka-Laureate*. But both are splendid condensation jokes with the formation of compound words. (I am lurking here in wait [*auf der Lauer*] to make *Kalauer*.)

But in any case we gather from the disputes over the distinction between *Kalauer* and play on words that the former cannot help us towards any knowledge of a completely new joke-technique. Even though the *Kalauer* makes no pretension to using the *same* material in several senses, the emphasis still falls on the rediscovery of familiar material, on the correspondence of the two words employed in it – all of which makes the *Kalauer* only a subcategory of the group that reaches its highest point in the true play on words.

[F]

But there are in fact jokes whose technique shows almost no connection with the technique of the groups we have looked at so far.

There is a story told of Heine, who found himself one evening in a Paris salon conversing with the poet Soulié.[31] Into the room comes one of those Paris plutocrats who are compared with Midas not just on account of their money; before long he is surrounded by a crowd which treats him with great deference. 'Look,' says Soulié to Heine, 'there you see how the nineteenth century worships the golden calf.' With a glance at the object of their admiration, Heine replies, as if to correct him: '*Oh, he must be older than that*' (Kuno Fischer, p. 82).

Now where does the technique of this excellent joke lie? According to Fischer, in a play on words: 'In this way, for example, the words "golden calf" can signify both Mammon and idolatry; in the first case, the main thing is the gold, in the second, the animal statue. It can also serve as a – not exactly flattering – reference to someone who has a great deal of money and not much intelligence' (p. 82). If we make the experiment of removing the term 'golden calf', we shall, it is true, also spoil the joke. We make Soulié say: 'You see how people are flocking around the stupid fellow just because he is rich,' and that is certainly no longer a joke. It also makes Heine's reply impossible.

But let us bear in mind that what is at issue is not the witty-enough comparison on Soulié's part, but Heine's reply, which is certainly far wittier. In that case, we have no right to tamper with the phrase about the golden calf; this has to remain as the premiss for Heine's words, and our reduction should apply only to these. If we extend these words, 'Oh, he must be older than that,' we can only replace them more or less like this: 'Oh, that's not a calf any more, that's already a fully-grown ox [*Ochs*: 'ass'].' For Heine's joke, then, he needs to take the 'golden calf' no longer metaphorically, but *ad hominem*, referring it to the money-man himself. Indeed, this double meaning might already have been contained in Soulié's remark.

But hold on! It now occurs to us that this reduction has not entirely killed Heine's joke, but rather left its essentials untouched. It now runs: Soulié says: 'There you see how the nineteenth century worships the golden calf!' and Heine's reply is: 'Oh, that's no longer a calf, that's already an ox.' And in this reduced version it is still a joke. But no other reduction of Heine's words is possible.

It is a pity that this splendid example contains such complicated technical requirements. It will not help us to clarify matters, so we shall leave it and look for another where we think we can sense an inner affinity with the previous one.

Let us choose one of the 'bath jokes' dealing with the Galician Jews' aversion to bathing. For we do not require any patent of nobility of our examples, we do not ask where they come from, but only whether they do their job, whether they are able to make us laugh and whether they deserve our theoretical interest. But Jewish jokes are the very ones that answer these requirements best.

'Two Jews meet in the neighbourhood of the bath-house. "*So have you taken a bath already?*" asks the one. "*How come?*" asks the other in reply. "*Is there one missing?*"'

When we are laughing really heartily at a joke, we are not exactly in the most suitable state of mind to inquire into its technique. That is why we have some difficulties in getting into these analyses. 'That's a comical misunderstanding' comes promptly to mind. – Fine, but what about the technique of this joke? Obviously it lies in the use of the word 'take' in two senses. For the one speaker, 'taken' is a faded auxiliary; for the other, a verb with unattenuated meaning. So we have a case of taking the same word as 'full' and as 'empty' (Group II, *f*). If we replace 'taken a bath' by the simpler equivalent 'bathed', there is no joke. The reply no longer fits. So again, the joke is attached to the expression 'taken a bath'.

Quite right – but it seems that in this case too the reduction has been brought to bear on the wrong place. The joke does not lie in the question, but in the reply, in the riposte: 'How come? Is there one missing?' And there is no removing the joke from this reply by any expansion or alteration, as long as its sense is left untouched. We also have the impression that, in the second Jew's reply, his disregarding the bath is more significant than his misunderstanding the word 'take'. But we are still not seeing clearly here either, so we shall look for a third example.

Again a Jewish joke, but one where only the accessories are Jewish, and the heart of the matter universally human. It is true, this example too has its unwelcome complications, but fortunately not those that have so far been getting in the way of our seeing clearly.

'An impoverished man borrowed 25 florins from a well-to-do acquaintance, assuring him at some length of his distress. On the very same day, his patron comes upon him in a restaurant with a plate of salmon with mayonnaise before him. He reproaches him: "What, you borrow money from me, and then you go and order salmon with mayonnaise. That's what you used my money for?" "I don't get it," answers the accused, "when I've got no money I *can't* eat salmon with mayonnaise; when I've got money, I *mustn't* eat salmon with mayonnaise. *So tell me, when **can** I eat salmon with mayonnaise?*" '

Here at last there is no longer any double meaning to be discovered. Nor can the joke-technique lie in the repetition of 'salmon with mayonnaise', because this is not a 'multiple use' of the same material, but a real repetition of the identical phrase as the content requires. This analysis might put us at a loss for a while, and we might try to avoid the issue by denying that the anecdote that made us laugh has the character of a joke at all.

What else worth remarking can be said about the impoverished man's reply? That, quite noticeably, it has the character of a logical argument. Wrongly, though, for the reply is in fact illogical. The man is defending himself against the accusation that he has spent the money lent to him on a delicacy, and he asks with some appearance of justice – *when* he might actually eat salmon. But that is not the right answer at all; his benefactor is not rebuking him for indulging in the salmon on the very day that he borrowed the money, but reminding him that in his circumstances he has no right *at all* to think of such a delicacy. The impoverished *bon viveur* ignores this, the only possible meaning of the rebuke, and replies, as if he had misunderstood it, to something else.

Now what if the technique of this joke were to lie in just this *diversion* by the reply from the meaning of the rebuke? It might then perhaps be possible to demonstrate a similar shift in the point of view, a displacement of psychological emphasis in the two earlier examples we felt were related as well.

And lo! it is easy to demonstrate it successfully, and in fact it does uncover the technique of these examples. Soulié draws Heine's attention to how society in the nineteenth century worships the 'golden calf', just as the Children of Israel once did in the wilderness. A suitable reply to this from Heine would be something like: 'Yes, that's human nature for you; nothing has changed in all those thousands of years' – or some other words of agreement. But in his reply, Heine diverts from the thoughts roused by Soulié's remark;

he does not reply to it at all; he makes use of the double meaning that the phrase 'golden calf' is capable of yielding to take a byway, picks up the one element in the phrase, the 'calf', and replies as if this is where the emphasis in Soulié's remark had fallen: 'Oh, that's no longer a calf, etc.'[32]

The diversion in the bath joke is even clearer. This example is asking for representation by means of typeface.

The first [speaker] asks: 'So have you taken a **bath**?' The emphasis falls on the element 'bath'.

The second replies as if the question had run: 'Have you *taken* a bath?'

The wording 'taken a bath' is intended only to enable this shift of emphasis. If it ran: 'Have you bathed?' any shift would be impossible. The reply, not a joke, would then be: 'Bathed? What do you mean? I don't know what that is.' The technique of the joke, however, lies in its shift of emphasis from 'bathing' to 'taking'.[33]

Let us return to the 'salmon with mayonnaise' example, as the purest. What is new about it will engage our interest along many different lines. First of all we must find a name for what we have discovered here. I suggest we describe it as *displacement*, because the essential thing about it is its diversion of the train of thought, its displacement of the psychological emphasis to a different theme from the one first broached. Then we are obliged to investigate what the relationship of the technique of displacement is to the expression of the joke. From our example (salmon with mayonnaise) we have seen that a displacement joke is to a large extent independent of its linguistic expression. It does not depend on the words, but on the train of thought. To get rid of this, there is no point in substituting other words while maintaining the sense of the reply. The reduction is possible only if we alter the train of thought and have the gourmet reply directly to the rebuke, which he has avoided in the joke's version. 'What I enjoy eating I can't deny myself, and where I get the money from to pay for it is all the same to me. You want to know why I'm eating salmon with mayonnaise today? the very day you've lent me money? There's your explanation.' But that would not be a joke; it would be an instance of *cynicism*.

It is instructive to compare this joke with one that is very close to it as far as sense is concerned.

A man much given to drink earns his living in a little town by coaching pupils. But gradually his vice gets to be known and as a result he loses most of his students. A friend is given the task of urging him to improve his ways. 'Look, you could get the best coaching jobs in town if you gave up drinking. So do it.' – 'Who do you think you are?' comes the indignant answer. '*I coach so that I can drink; am I supposed to give up drinking so that I can get coaching* [German: as well as 'coaching', *Lektion* also means 'a telling-off']!'

This joke too has the appearance of logic that struck us in 'salmon with mayonnaise', but it stops short of being a displacement joke. The reply is direct. The cynicism, which is hidden in the first joke, is openly admitted in this one. – 'Of course, for me, drinking is the most important thing.' The technique of this joke is in fact quite thin and cannot be the explanation of its effect; its technique lies only in the reordering of the same material, more strictly, in the reversal of the relation of ends and means between the drinking and the coaching. As soon as my reduction no longer emphasizes this factor in the expression, I have wiped out the joke, rather along these lines: 'What kind of crazy demand is that? You know drinking is the most important thing for me, not coaching. For me coaching is after all only the means to be able to go on drinking.' So the joke *is* in fact attached to the expression.

In the bath joke, the dependence of the joke on the wording ('So have you taken a bath?') is unmistakable, and changing the words also entails doing away with the joke. For the technique here is more complicated, a combination of double meaning (of the subcategory *f*) and displacement. The wording of the question admits of a double meaning, and the joke comes about because the reply connects not with the sense intended by the questioner, but with the secondary one. We are accordingly in a position to find a reduction which preserves the double meaning in the expression, but still does away with the joke by merely removing [*rückgängig . . . machen*] the displacement:

'So have you taken a bath?' – 'What am I supposed to have taken?

A bath? What is that?' But that is no longer a joke, but an exaggeration that is either nasty or jocular.

Double meaning plays a very similar part in Heine's 'golden calf' joke. It makes it possible for the reply to make that diversion away from the intended train of thought, which in the 'salmon with mayonnaise' joke takes place without such dependence on the wording. In its reduction, Soulié's remark and Heine's reply would run something like this: 'Really, I am reminded vividly of the worship of the golden calf by the way society swarms around the man merely because he is so rich.' And Heine: 'Making a fuss of him like that on account of his wealth is not the worst thing, in my opinion. But for my judgement you don't emphasize sufficiently how people forgive his stupidity on account of his wealth.' Although this would preserve the double meaning, it would do away with the displacement joke.

At this point we should be prepared for the objection that these tricky distinctions are attempting to tear apart what after all belongs together. Does not every double meaning offer an occasion for displacement, for diverting the train of thought from one sense to another? And we are expected to consent to the argument that 'double meaning' and 'displacement' represent two quite different types of joke-technique? Now this relation between double meaning and displacement certainly exists, but it has nothing to do with our distinction between kinds of joke-technique. In double meaning, the joke contains nothing but a word capable of yielding several interpretations, so allowing the listener to find the passage from one thought to another, a process which one can – forcing it a little – equate with displacement. But in a displacement joke, the joke itself contains a train of thought in which a displacement is carried out; in this kind of joke, the displacement here is made by the work that has produced the joke, and not by the work needed to understand it. If this distinction is not clear to us, our experiments in reduction are an unfailing way of bringing them tangibly before us. But there is one valuable point in that objection which we would not dispute. It has made us aware that we should not confuse the psychical processes involved in forming the joke (the joke-work) with the psychical processes involved in its reception (the work of under-standing). Only the former is the object of our present investigation.[34, 35]

Are there other examples of the displacement-technique? They are not easy to find. The following joke, which even lacks the over-exaggerated logic of our model, is a very pure example:

A horse-dealer is recommending a mount to a client: 'If you take this horse and set off at 4 in the morning, you'll be in Pressburg[36] at half-past 6.' – 'And what am I supposed to be doing in Pressburg at half-past 6 in the morning?'

The displacement here is flagrant. Obviously, the dealer mentions the early arrival in the little town only to give a proof of what the horse can do. The client disregards the horse's performance, raising no further doubts about it, and dwells merely on the details of the example chosen as the proof. The reduction of this joke is then not difficult to make.

More difficulties are presented by another example which is quite opaque in technique, but which still can be resolved into double meaning with displacement. The joke tells of the excuse made by a *Schadchen* (a Jewish marriage-broker), so it belongs to a group that will occupy us frequently.

The *Schadchen* has assured the suitor that the girl's father is no longer living. After the engagement it emerges that the father is still alive – and serving a term in prison. The suitor then accuses the *Schadchen*. 'So?' says the *Schadchen*. 'What did I tell you? That you call *living*?'

The double meaning lies in the word 'living', and the displacement is made because the *Schadchen* diverts from the usual sense of the word as the opposite of 'dead' and seizes on the sense it has in the phrase: 'That's not living.' In doing so he is retrospectively declaring that his earlier statement had a double meaning, although in this case particularly this multiple sense was very remote. To that extent the technique would be similar to that of the 'golden calf' joke and the bath joke. But there is another factor to be noted here, which strikes us as so prominent that it interferes with our understanding of the technique. One might say that this is a 'characterizing' joke;

it is concerned to illustrate that mixture of brazen dishonesty and quick wit characteristic of the marriage-broker. We shall learn that this is only the joke's outside, its façade; its meaning, that is, its intention, is something else. We shall also postpone attempting a reduction of it.[37]

After these examples, complicated and difficult to analyse as they are, it will be gratifying to recognize an instance of a completely plain and transparent model of a 'displacement joke'. A *Schnorrer* [Jewish beggar][38] presents the rich Baron with a request for support for his journey to Ostend; the doctors, he claims, have recommended sea-bathing to restore his health. 'Fine, I'll give you something towards it,' says the rich man; 'but does it have to be Ostend you go to, the most expensive of all the seaside resorts?' – 'Herr Baron,' comes the answer in rebuke, 'for my health nothing is too expensive.' – Certainly a proper standpoint, but just not proper for the supplicant. The answer is made from the standpoint of a rich man. The *Schnorrer* is behaving as if it were his own money he is to sacrifice for his health, as if money and health applied to the same person.

[G]

Let us take up that most instructive example of 'salmon with mayonnaise' afresh. Like the *Schadchen* joke, it too turned its outer side towards us, noticeable for a striking display of logic-chopping; we learned from our analysis of it that the task of this logic was to cover up a flaw in thinking, namely, the displacement of the train of thought. This may remind us, if only by way of association by contrast, of other jokes which, quite to the contrary, openly put some absurdity, some nonsense, some foolishness on view. We are curious to see what may comprise the technique of these jokes.

I shall put the most forceful and at the same time the plainest example of the group at the head. Again, it is a Jewish joke.

Issy [German: *Itzig*, comic, potentially anti-Semitic, name for a Jew] has been declared fit for the artillery. He is obviously an intelligent fellow, but stroppy and with no interest in army service. One of his superiors, who wishes him well, takes him aside and says: 'Issy, you're no good for us. I'll give you some advice: *Buy yourself a cannon and make yourself independent.*'

The advice, which makes us laugh heartily, is patent nonsense. After all, cannons are not for sale, and it is impossible for one individual to make himself independent as a military power, 'set up on his own', as it were. But we do not doubt for a moment that this advice is not mere nonsense, but witty nonsense, an excellent joke. So by what means does the nonsense become a joke?

We do not need to reflect for very long. From the authorities' discussions touched on in our Introduction, we may surmise that there is sense hiding in this nonsense, and that it is this sense in the nonsense that makes the nonsense a joke. The sense in our example is easy to find. The officer who gives Issy the artillerist the nonsensical advice is only pretending to be foolish in order to show Issy how foolish he is being himself. He is imitating Issy. 'I'll give you some advice now that is just as foolish as you are.' He picks up on Issy's foolishness and gets him to see sense by making it the basis of a suggestion which is bound to answer Issy's wishes, for if Issy owned his own cannon and ran the trade of war on his own account, with his intelligence and his ambition, how well he would do! How well he would look after it and how closely he would familiarize himself with its mechanism so as to meet the competition of other cannon-owners!

I shall interrupt the analysis of this example to demonstrate the same sense in nonsense in a shorter and simpler, but no less glaring, instance of a nonsense joke.

'*Never to have been born would be the best for mortal kind.*'[39] '*But,*' add the philosophers of the *Fliegende Blätter*,[40] '*that scarcely happens to one in 100,000.*'

The modern supplement to the ancient saying is plain nonsense, becoming even more foolish by the addition of the apparently cautious 'scarcely'. But it is linked to the first sentence as an indisputably correct qualification, and so it can open our eyes to the realization that the piece of wisdom we have listened to with awe is not much better than nonsense either. Anyone who was never born is not a member of mortal kind at all; for them there is no good and no best. So in this case the nonsense in the joke serves to expose and demonstrate another instance of nonsense – as it did in the example of Issy the artillerist.

At this point I can add a third example, which from its content would scarcely deserve the detailed account it requires, but which is again a particularly clear illustration of the use of nonsense in a joke to demonstrate another instance of nonsense.

A man who has to go away on a journey entrusts his daughter to a friend, requesting him to keep an eye on her virtue during his absence. After months he comes back and discovers she has been made pregnant. Naturally, he reproaches his friend. The friend alleges he cannot explain the misfortune. 'Where did she sleep then?' the father finally asks. – 'In my son's room.' – 'But how can you let her sleep in the same room with your son, when I begged you to look after her?' – 'But there was a screen between them. There was your daughter's bed, and there was my son's bed, and the screen between them.' – 'And what if he'd gone round the screen?' – '*I didn't think of that,*' said the other thoughtfully. '*It could have been managed that way.*'

It is very easy to arrive at a reduction of this otherwise rather poor joke. It would obviously run: You have no right to blame me. How can *you* be so *foolish* as to hand your daughter over to a house where she has to live in the constant company of a young man? As if it were possible for a stranger to be responsible for a girl's virtue under such circumstances! So here too the ostensible foolishness of the friend is only the mirror-image of the foolishness of the father. Our reduction has done away with the foolishness in the joke, but it has also done away with the joke. We are not rid of the element of 'foolishness'; it has found a different place in the context of the sentence that reduced the joke to its underlying sense.

Now we are able to attempt a reduction of the cannon joke as well. The officer would have to say: 'Issy, I know you are an intelligent businessman. But I tell you, it is *very foolish of you* if you don't see that it is impossible to carry on in the same way in the army as in business life, where everyone works for himself and against the others. In the army the word is subordination and co-operation.'

So the technique of the nonsense jokes we have dealt with so far in fact consists in the introduction of something foolish, nonsensical, whose underlying meaning is the illustration, the demonstration, of something else foolish and nonsensical.

Does the use of absurdity in the technique of jokes always have this significance? Here is another example which answers in the affirmative:

Once, when Phokion was applauded after making a speech, turning to his friends he asked: '*Have I said something foolish?*'

This question sounds absurd. But we understand what it means at once. 'What have I said that could please these foolish people so much? I really should be ashamed of their applause; if it pleased the foolish, it can't have been very clever itself.'

But we learn from other examples that absurdity is very often used in the technique of jokes without the purpose of demonstrating another instance of nonsense.

A well-known university teacher, who was in the habit of spicing his not very attractive specialism with jokes, is congratulated on the birth of his youngest child, granted him when he was of an already advanced age. 'Yes,' he replied to his well-wishers, 'it is remarkable *what human hand can do.*' – This reply appears quite particularly senseless and inappropriate. After all, we call children a blessing from God, quite the opposite of the work of human hand. But it soon occurs to us that this reply does have a meaning, and an obscene one at that. It is out of the question that the happy father is pretending to be foolish in order to label something or someone else as foolish. The apparently senseless reply has a startling effect on us, 'baffling', as we and our authorities would put it. We have heard that they derive the entire effect of such jokes from the alternation of 'bafflement and light dawning'. We will attempt to form our own judgement on this later; for the moment we are content to emphasize that the technique of this joke consists in the introduction of such baffling, nonsensical elements.

A joke of Lichtenberg's assumes a very special position among these stupidity jokes.

He wonders *that cats should have two holes cut in their fur in the very place where they have eyes*. But to wonder at something self-evident, at something which is actually only the statement of an identity, is certainly foolish. It reminds me of a seriously intended exclamation of Michelet's (*Das Weib*),[41] which, as I recall, runs something like this: How beautifully Nature has arranged things, so that as soon as a child comes into the world it finds a mother ready to take it to her! Michelet's statement is a real foolishness, but Lichtenberg's is a joke which makes use of foolishness for some purpose, and which has something hidden behind it. But what? At this moment, it is true, that is something we cannot tell.

[H]

We have now already learned from two groups of examples that the joke-work makes use of departures from normal thinking, of *displacement* and *absurdity*, as technical devices for creating jokes. We would certainly be justified in expecting that other kinds of faulty thinking might also be put to the same use. And in fact it is possible to offer some examples of this kind:

A gentleman goes into a pastrycook's and orders a cake; but he soon brings it back and asks for a glass of liqueur instead. He drinks this up and makes to go off without paying. The shopkeeper detains him. 'What do you want of me?' – 'To pay for the liqueur.' – 'But I gave you the cake for it.' – 'You didn't pay for that either.' – '*But I didn't eat it.*'

This little story too displays that appearance of logic which is already familiar to us as the façade appropriate to a flaw in thinking. The flaw obviously lies in the – non-existent – connection the cunning customer has drawn between returning the cake and taking the liqueur for it instead. It is rather that the situation breaks down into two transactions which for the vendor are independent of each other, but for the customer's purposes can be substituted for each other. He took the cake first and returned it, so he does not owe anything for it, then he takes the liqueur, and that he should pay for. We might say that the customer is using the term of exchange 'for it' with a double meaning; more correctly, that by means of a double meaning he is setting up a connection which as far as the facts of the matter are concerned does not hold water.[42]

Now this is the opportunity to make a – not unimportant – confession. We are engaged here in an inquiry into joke-technique based on examples, so we should be sure that the examples we have chosen really are proper jokes. But it looks as if in a number of instances we have been hesitating as to whether the example in question can be called a joke or not. Indeed, we do not have a criterion at our command until our investigation has yielded one; linguistic usage is unreliable, and itself requires scrutiny; in deciding, all we have to lean on is a certain 'feeling', which we may interpret to the effect that, in judging, our decision is being made according to certain criteria that are not yet accessible to our knowledge. For us to appeal to this 'feeling' will not be admissible as a sufficient explanation. In the last example, we are bound to be doubtful now whether we can call it a joke, a sophistical joke, perhaps, or whether it is just a sophistry pure and simple. We simply do not yet know what goes to make the character of a joke.

By contrast, there is no doubt that the next example, which demonstrates the complementary flaw in thinking, as it were, is a joke. Again, it is a story of a marriage-broker.

The *Schadchen* is defending the girl he has proposed in face of the young man's objections. 'I don't like the mother-in-law,' the young man says. 'She is a malicious, stupid person.' – 'You're not marrying the mother-in-law, you're marrying the daughter.' – 'Yes, but she's no longer so young, and she's not exactly pretty either.' – 'That doesn't matter. If she's not young and pretty, she'll be all the more faithful to you.' – 'There's not much money going, either.' – 'Who's talking about money? Are you marrying the money? It's a wife you want.' – 'But she's got a hump-back as well.' – 'Now what *are* you after? *So she's not to have one single fault?*'

So in reality it is all about a girl who is no longer young, not pretty, with a very small dowry, who has a repulsive mother, and on top of everything a terrible disfigurement. Not very inviting circumstances to contract a marriage, for sure. But for every one of these blemishes, the marriage-broker knows what angle to take to reconcile the young man to it; the unforgivable hump he then claims is the one fault that should be granted every person. Again there is the appearance of logic characteristic of sophistry and meant to hide the flaw in the thinking. The girl has obviously nothing but defects, several that could be overlooked, and one that is impossible to ignore; she is simply unmarriageable. The go-between behaves as if his excuses did away with all her defects one by one, when in fact some fall in her value is left over from each to be added to the next. He insists on dealing with each factor separately, and refuses to add them up into a total sum.

The same omission is the heart of another piece of sophistry which has given rise to a great deal of laughter, though one might have doubts about how justified its claim to be called a joke might be.

A. borrowed a copper kettle from B., and after its return is accused by B. because the kettle now has a huge hole in it, making it useless. His defence runs: '*In the first place, I didn't borrow a kettle from B. at all; in the second, the kettle had a hole in it already when I took it over from B.; in the third, I gave it back to him all in one piece.*' Each single objection is sound in itself, but taken together they exclude one another. A. treats in isolation what has to be considered in connection in just the same way as the marriage-broker deals with the bride's shortcomings. We could also say: A. puts an 'and' in the place where only an 'either – or' is possible.

We encounter a different sophistry in the following marriage-broker story.

The suitor has complained that the bride has one leg shorter than the other and limps. The *Schadchen* contradicts him. 'You've got it wrong. What if you went and married a woman with sound, straight limbs? Where's the benefit? You won't have a day's rest, worrying that she doesn't fall down. Then she breaks her leg. And then she's lame for the rest of her life. And then the pain, the hassle, the doctor's bill! But if you take *this one*, it won't happen to you; you've got it all *ready-made*.'

The appearance of logic is pretty thin here, and nobody would want to give a 'ready-made misfortune' any preference over one that was merely possible. The flaw in the train of thought will be easier to demonstrate from a second example, a story I cannot entirely strip of its argot.

In the temple at Cracow the great Rabbi N. is sitting and praying with his disciples. All of a sudden he utters a cry and, when asked by his anxious disciples, pronounces: 'The great Rabbi L. in Lemberg has at this moment just died.' The congregation goes into mourning for the departed. In the course of the next days anyone arriving from Lemberg is asked how the Rabbi died, what was the matter with him, but they know nothing about it, they left him in the best of health. It is finally established quite certainly that Rabbi L. in Lemberg did not die on the hour in which Rabbi N. had a telepathic sense of his death, for he is still alive. A stranger takes the opportunity to mock a disciple of the Cracow Rabbi. 'Your Rabbi did make a fool of himself, didn't he, that time he saw the Rabbi L. in Lemberg die? The man is still alive.' 'No matter,' replied the disciple, 'it was wonderful of him to gaze [*Kück*][43] all the way from Cracow to Lemberg anyhow.'

The flaw in thinking shared by both these last examples is openly admitted here. The figments of fantasy are raised disproportionately in value by contrast to reality, possibility put almost on a par with actuality. The rabbi's distant gaze across the sweep of land separating Cracow from Lemberg would be an impressive feat of telepathy if something true had come of it, but that is not the important thing for the disciple. After all, it *might* have been possible that the Rabbi of Lemberg *could* have died in the same moment as the Cracow Rabbi announced his death, and for the disciple the emphasis is displaced from the *circumstance* that makes his master's feat so remarkable on to his unqualified admiration for the feat. 'In magnis rebus voluisse sat est [In great things it is enough to have wished]'[44] testifies to a similar point of view. Just as in this example reality is disregarded in favour of possibility, in the previous one the marriage-broker expects the suitor to consider the possibility that a wife might be crippled by an accident as by far the more important thing, so that in comparison the question of whether she is really crippled or not should fade completely into the background.

This group of *sophistical* flaws in thinking is joined by another interesting one, where the flaw may be described as *automatic*. It is perhaps only a whim of chance[45] that all the examples I shall offer from this fresh group again belong to the *Schadchen* stories:

'For the discussion about the bride, a *Schadchen* has brought along an assistant to support him in what he has to say of her. She's built like a fir-tree, says the *Schadchen*. – Like a fir-tree, repeats the echo. – And what eyes she has, you have to see them. – And eyes she has, confirms the echo. – And for education, there's nobody like her. – And education! – But it's true, there is one thing, the broker concedes, she has a little hump. – *But such a hump!* confirms the echo again.' The other stories are quite analogous, though they have more sense.

'The bridegroom is very unpleasantly surprised when the bride is introduced to him, and draws the broker to one side to whisper his objections. "What have you brought me here for?" he upbraids him. "She is ugly and old, she squints, and she's got bad teeth and watery eyes . . ." – "You can say it out loud," interjects the broker, *"she's deaf as well."* '

'Together with the broker, the bridegroom pays his first visit to the bride's house and, while they are waiting in the parlour for the family to appear, the broker draws attention to a glass cabinet in which the finest silver objects are displayed. "Look at that, you can tell from these things how rich these people are." – "But," asks the mistrustful young man, "mightn't it be possible that these fine things are borrowed for the occasion to give an impression of wealth?" – "What are you thinking of?" the broker rebuffs him. *"Who would lend these people anything!"* '

In all three cases the same thing occurs. A person who has reacted in the same way several times in succession continues this way of speaking on the next occasion too, where it becomes incongruous and contradicts their intentions. They are failing to adapt to the requirements of the situation, succumbing to automatic habit. Thus the assistant in the first story forgets that he was taken along to dispose the suitor in favour of the proposed bride, and since he had done his job properly up till then by underlining the bride's alleged good points in his repetitions, he now emphasizes the discreetly admitted hump as well, when he should have played it down. The broker of the second story becomes so fascinated by the enumeration of the bride's flaws and frailties that he completes the list out of his own knowledge of her, though that is certainly not his office, nor his intention. Finally, in the third story, he lets himself get so carried away by his eagerness to convince the young man of the family's wealth that, just to stay in the right on the one point that proves it, he comes out with something that is bound to upset all his efforts. In all cases the automatic reaction wins out over adapting his thought and speech to suit the situation.

That is easy to see, of course, but it is bound to be confusing when we notice that these three examples could be described as 'comic stories' with the same right as we have referred to them as 'jokes'. The exposure of psychic automatism belongs to the technique of the comic, as every [act of] unmasking or self-betrayal does. At this point we find ourselves suddenly faced with the problem of the relation of the joke to comedy which we had tried to avoid. (See the Introduction.) Are these only 'comic stories', perhaps, and not 'jokes'? Is comedy operating here with the same means as the joke? And again, what goes to make the peculiar joking character of jokes?

We must keep in mind that the technique of the jokes just studied consists only of the inclusion of 'flawed thinking', but we are compelled to admit that so far our investigation of them has led us more into the dark than to knowledge. Still, we shall not give up our expectation that a fuller knowledge of joke-techniques will enable us to reach a result that may become the starting-point for further insights.

[I]

The next examples of jokes with which we shall continue our investigation are not such hard work. Their technique reminds us above all of what we already know.

A witticism of Lichtenberg's, for instance:

'January is the month when we offer our dear friends [our good] *wishes, and the others are the months in which they are not fulfilled.'*

As these witticisms are to be called refined rather than coarse, and work with slight and unobtrusive means, let us first reinforce the impression they make by dint of accumulation.

'Human life falls into two halves, in the first, we wish for the second to arrive, in the second, we wish for the first to return.'

'Experience consists of experiencing what we do not want to experience.' (Both in Kuno Fischer.)

It is inevitable that these examples should remind us of a group we dealt with earlier, which were distinguished by 'multiple use of the same material'. The last example in particular will make us ask why we did not include it there instead of introducing it here in a fresh context. Experience is again described by its own wording, just as previously jealousy was (cf. p. 27). Nor would I object very much to assigning it there. But in the other two examples, which do indeed have a similar character, another factor, I think, is more striking and more important than the multiple use of the same words, which in their case lacks any trace of double meaning. For I would like to emphasize that in these witticisms new and unexpected unities are being set up, ideas are being related to one another and definitions made by reference to one another or to a common third element. I would like to call this process *unification*; it is clearly analogous to condensation by concentration into the same words. In this way the two halves of human life are described by the reciprocal relations discovered between them; in the first, one wishes for the second to arrive, in the second, for the first to return. More precisely, they are two very similar reciprocal relations which were chosen to be described. The similarity of the relations is then matched by the similarity of the words – which is just what might remind us of the multiple use of the same material (wish – to arrive)/(wish – to return). In Lichtenberg's witticism, January and the months contrasted with it are characterized by setting up a relation, modified in turn, to a third element; that is, the good wishes which are received in the one month and not fulfilled in the others. The difference from multiple use of the same material, which does indeed approach double meaning, is very clear here.[46]

The following is a fine example of a unification joke, needing no explanation:

The French poet J. B. Rousseau once wrote an Ode to Posterity; in Voltaire's opinion, the poem was not at all worthy of going down to posterity, and he remarked wittily: '*This poem will not reach its address.*' (In Kuno Fischer.)

From the last example we may note that unification is essentially what lies at the basis of what we call quick-witted jokes. Indeed, the quick-wittedness consists in the defence's engagement with the aggression, in 'turning the tables', in 'repaying in the same coin', that is, in creating an unexpected unity between attack and counter-attack.

For example: baker to landlord, who has a sore on his finger: '*I suppose you dipped it in your beer?*' Landlord: '*No, but one of your rolls got under my nail.*' (In Überhorst, *Das Komische*, II, 1900.)

His Majesty is travelling through his provinces and notices among the crowd a man who looks remarkably like his own sublime personage. He beckons to him to ask him: '*Was your mother once in service at the palace, perhaps?*' – 'No, Your Highness,' came the reply, '*but my father was.*'[47]

On one occasion when he was riding out, Duke Karl of Württemberg happened to meet a dyer who was busied with his trade. '*Can you dye my white horse blue?*' the Duke calls out to him, and gets this answer in return: '*Certainly, Your Highness, if he can stand boiling.*'

In this excellent riposte – which answers a nonsensical question with an equally impossible condition – there is another technical factor also at work which would have been missing if the dyer's reply had run: 'No, Your Highness, I'm afraid the horse won't stand boiling.'

Unification has another, particularly interesting, technical device at its command: putting things together as a series with the conjunction *and*. A series of this kind signifies relationship; we never understand it otherwise. For example, when Heine in his *Harzreise* [chapter 1] tells us of the town of Göttingen: '*In general, the inhabitants of Göttingen are divided into students, professors, philistines and swine,*' we understand this sequence in precisely the sense which is further underlined when Heine adds: 'although these four estates are anything but sharply distinguished'. Or, when he speaks of the school where he had to put up with '*so much Latin, Flogging and Geography*', this series, which is made more than clear by the middle position given to flogging between the two school subjects, means to tell us that we should certainly extend the schoolboy's opinion, unmistakably indicated by the flogging, to Latin and Geography as well.

Among Lipps's examples of 'witty enumeration' ('coordination'), we find, quoted as closely related to Heine's 'students, professors, philistines and swine', the line of verse: '*Mit einer Gabel und mit Müh' zog ihn die Mutter aus der Brüh* [With a fork and effort too his mother pulled him from the stew]';[48] as if the effort were an instrument like the fork, Lipps adds by way of explanation. But our impression of the line is that it is not at all witty, though very comical, while Heine's sequence is undoubtedly a witticism. We shall perhaps remember these examples later when we no longer need to avoid the problem of the relation between the comic and jokes.

[J]

We noticed from the example of the Duke and the dyer that it would still be a unification joke if the dyer were to answer: '*No*, I'm afraid the horse would not stand boiling.' But in fact his answer ran: '*Yes*, Your Highness, if he can stand boiling.' In the replacement of the properly appropriate 'no' by a 'yes', there is a new technical device for jokes; we shall pursue its use in other examples.

A joke close to the one just mentioned, to be found in Kuno Fischer, is simpler: Frederick the Great hears of a preacher in Silesia who has the reputation of consorting with spirits; he sends for the man and greets him with the question: '*You can call up spirits?*' The reply was: '*At Your command, Your Majesty, but they don't come.*' It is quite obvious here that the device used by the joke consisted of nothing but the replacement of the only possible 'no' by its opposite. To carry out this replacement, the 'yes' had to have a 'but' added on to it, so that 'yes' and 'but' in meaning are tantamount to 'no'.

This *representation by the opposite*, as we shall call it, serves the joke-work in various ways. In the following two examples it occurs almost pure: Heine: '*In many respects this woman resembles the Venus de Milo: she too is extraordinarily old, likewise she has no teeth, and on the yellowish surface of her body she has some white spots.*'

A representation of ugliness by means of its points of congruity with the most beautiful; though admittedly these congruities can consist only in characteristics expressed in terms with a double meaning or in unimportant items. The latter applies to the second example:

Lichtenberg: *The Great Mind.*

'*He had united in himself the characteristics of the greatest men: like Alexander he carried his head lop-sided, like Caesar always had something braided into his hair, like Leibnitz he could drink coffee and, once he was sitting comfortably in his armchair, like Newton he would forget to eat and drink, and like him would have to be woken up; he wore his wig like Dr Johnson, and he always left a button of his breeches undone like Cervantes.*'

A particularly fine example of representation by the opposite, which dispenses entirely with using words of double meaning, was brought back by J. v. Falke from a journey to Ireland. 'The scene: a waxworks,' let us say Madame Tussaud's. Also present: a guide, accompanying a group of old and young with his explanations from one figure to the next. [In Freud's English] '*This is the Duke of*

Wellington and his horse,' whereupon a young lady asks the question: *'Which is the Duke of Wellington and which is his horse?' 'Just as you like, my pretty child,'* comes the reply, *'you pay your money and you have your choice.' (Lebenserinnerungen* [1879], p. 271.)

The reduction of this Irish joke would run: 'The barefaced nerve – what these waxwork people presume to offer the public! You can't tell the difference between horse and rider. (Joking exaggeration.) And that's what we pay good money for!' This indignant exclamation is now dramatized, based on a little episode; the place of the public in general is taken by one lady; the figure of the rider is given individuality; it has to be the Duke of Wellington, who is so very popular in Ireland. But the effrontery of the owner or guide who pockets the visitors' money and offers them nothing for it is represented by its opposite, by words in which he stresses what a conscientious businessman he is, whose dearest concern is to respect the rights due to the public on account of the money they have paid. We also see now that the technique of this joke is not an entirely simple one. As the swindler finds a way to assert his conscientiousness, the joke is an instance of representation by the opposite; but he does so when the occasion requires something quite different of him, so that when something about the similarity of the figures is expected, he replies as a respectable businessman, the joke is an example of displacement. The technique of this joke lies in the combination of the two devices.

From this example it is not far to a small group which may be called going-one-better jokes. In these, the 'yes' that would be appropriate in the reduction is replaced by a 'no', but on account of its content this is the equivalent of an even stronger 'yes', and vice versa. For example, Lessing's epigram:[49]

> *Die gute Galathee! Man sagt, sie schwärz' ihr Haar;*
> *Da doch ihr Haar schon schwarz, als sie es kaufte, war.*

[Good Galatea dyes her hair, 'tis cried,/ Tho' when she bought it, 'twas already dyed.]

Or Lichtenberg's malicious mock-defence of scholastic philosophy:

'There are more things in heaven and earth than are dreamt of in your philosophy,' said Prince Hamlet scornfully [I.v.166–7]. Lichtenberg knows that this judgement is not nearly sharp enough, for it does not take into account everything that could be said against philosophy. So he adds what is missing: 'But there is also much in philosophy that can be found neither in heaven nor on earth.' True, his version does emphasize the compensations of philosophy for the shortcomings Hamlet censures, but in these compensations there lies a second and even greater criticism.

Two Jewish jokes are more transparent, being free of any trace of displacement, though rather coarse-grained.

Two Jews are talking about bathing. '*I take a bath every year*,' says the one, '*whether I need it or not*.'

It is clear that by such boastful assurance of his cleanliness he is convicting himself all the more of uncleanliness.

One Jew notices the remains of food in the other's beard. '*I can tell you what you ate yesterday. – Tell me then. – Lentils. – Wrong, the day before yesterday!*'

The following is also a splendid going-one-better joke, which is easy to derive from representation by the opposite:

The King in his condescension is visiting the surgical clinic and he comes upon the professor about to amputate a leg; he accompanies the stages of the amputation with loud expressions of his royal satisfaction. '*Bravo, bravo, my dear Geheimrat*.' After the operation is completed, the professor approaches him and asks, bowing deeply: '*Does His Majesty command the other leg too?*'

What the professor may have thought during the royal applause can certainly not have been put without some alteration: 'That must give the impression that I am removing the poor devil's damaged leg by royal commission and just for royal approval. I really do have other reasons for this operation.' But then he goes before the King and says: 'I have no other reasons for an operation than Your Majesty's commission. The approval bestowed on me has filled me with such rapture, that I am only awaiting Your Majesty's command to amputate the sound leg as well.' He succeeds in making himself understood by saying the opposite of what he is privately thinking and has to keep to himself. This is an opposite that goes one better, and as such expects us to disbelieve it.

Representation by the opposite is, as we have seen, a frequently used and powerful device of the joke-technique. But there is something else we should not overlook: this technique is by no means only confined to jokes. After Mark Antony's long speech in the forum has retuned the mood of his listeners around Caesar's corpse, when he finally flings the words at them once again:

'For Brutus is an *honourable* man –' he knows that the people around him will shout the true meaning of his words back at him:

'They are *traitors*: honourable men!' [*Julius Caesar*, III.ii.88 and 159.]

Or when *Simplizissimus*[50] publishes a collection of unbelievably brutal and cynical remarks under the title: '*Men of feeling*', that is also a representation by the opposite. But this we call 'irony', no longer a joke. Irony is characterized by no other device than representation by the opposite. What is more, we read and hear of the *ironic joke*. So there is no longer any doubt that technique alone is not sufficient to characterize the joke. Something else must be added which we have not so far discovered. On the other hand, nothing has yet belied the fact that when the technique is dismantled [*Rückbildung*], the joke is spoiled. For the moment we may find it difficult to combine the two firm points we have reached in the elucidation of jokes.

[K]

If representation by the opposite is among the technical devices of the joke, then we might expect that the joke could also make use of its contrary, representation by what is *similar* or related. As we continue our investigation we do in fact learn that this is the technique of a new and particularly large group of intellectual jokes [*Gedankenwitze*].[51] We shall describe the nature of this technique far more accurately if we say representation 'by what is belonging or connected' instead of 'by what is related'. Let us even make a start with this feature and elucidate it straight away with an example.

An American anecdote runs: by a number of pretty risky enterprises, two less-than-scrupulous businessmen succeeded in amassing a great fortune, and then devoted their efforts to entering good society. One means to this end, it seemed to them, was to have their portraits done by the most exclusive and expensive painter in town, whose pictures were regarded as great occasions. The precious pictures were first shown at a grand reception, and the two hosts themselves led the most influential connoisseur and critic to the salon wall where the two portraits were hanging side by side, to lure him into giving an appreciative judgement. He gazed at the pictures for a long time, then shook his head as if he were missing something, merely asking as he pointed to the space between the two pictures: [Freud's English] *'And where is the Saviour?'* (that is, where is the picture of the Saviour?).

The meaning of this remark is clear. Again it is a question of representing something that cannot be expressed directly. How is this *'indirect representation'* brought about? Let us follow a series of readily available associations and inferences and take the path that leads backwards from the representation of the joke.

The question: 'Where is the Saviour, the picture of the Saviour?' allows us to surmise that the speaker has been reminded by the sight of the two pictures of a similar sight, as familiar to him as it is to us, but showing an element that is missing here, the picture of the Saviour between two other pictures. There is only one instance of this kind: Christ hanging between the two thieves. So what the critic wanted to say and could not was: 'You're a couple of rogues'; more fully: 'What do I care about your pictures? You're a couple of rogues, I know.' And in the end, by way of some associations and inferences, he did say it, via a route which we would describe as *allusion*.

We recall at once that we have already encountered allusion. In double meaning, that is; in cases where two meanings can be expressed in the same word, and where the more frequent and more current one is so strongly foregrounded that it is bound to occur to us first of all, while the other, more remote, meaning takes second place, we decided to call this *double meaning with allusion*. In a large number of the examples we had examined up to that point, we had observed that their technique was not a simple one, and now we recognize that the complicating factor in them is allusion (see for example the joke dependent on a switch of phrases about the woman who had been a bit on the side and earned a lot, or the professor's absurd joke on being congratulated on his latest child, that it was remarkable what human hand could do, p. 50).

In the American anecdote we now have before us a case of allusion free of double meaning, and we discover that its distinctive character is substitution by something connected conceptually. It is easy to surmise that the usable connection can be of more than one sort. So that we do not get lost in sheer profusion, let us discuss only the most distinct varieties, and these only in a few examples.

The connection used for the substitution may be a mere similarity in sound, such that this subspecies is analogous to the pun among the verbal jokes. But it is not the similarity of two words to one another, but of whole sentences,[52] or characteristic word-combinations and the like.

For example, Lichtenberg coined the saying: '*Neue Bäder heilen gut* [lit: 'New spas cure well']', reminding us at once of the proverb: '*Neue Besen kehren gut* [equiv: 'New brooms sweep clean']', as they share the first word-and-a-bit, the last word, and the sentence-structure as a whole. And it certainly originated in the witty philosopher's mind as an imitation of the well-known proverb. In this way Lichtenberg's saying becomes an allusion to the proverb. By means of this allusion, something is hinted that cannot be said outright: that in the success of a spa, there are other factors involved besides the constant of thermal waters.

Another witticism or joke of Lichtenberg's can be analysed technically in a similar way: '*Ein Mädchen, kaum zwölf Moden alt* [lit: 'A girl scarce twelve fashions old'].' That sounds like the expression of time '*zwölf Monden* [twelve moons]' (i.e., *Monate* [months]), and might perhaps have been a slip of the pen in writing down the second expression, admissible in poetic diction. But it makes good sense to use the changing fashions instead of the changing moon to indicate the age of a female person.

The connection may consist of similarity up to one single *slight modification*. Again, this technique parallels a verbal technique. Both kinds of joke produce almost the same impression, but, to go by the processes operating in the joke-work, they are better kept distinct from each other.

An example of a verbal joke or pun of this kind: the great singer *Marie Wilt*, famous for more than the compass of her voice, was offended when the title of a play based on Jules Verne's well-known novel was used as an allusion to her figure: '*Around the Wilt* [*Welt*: 'world'] *in eighty Days.*'

Or, of a well-born and over-lifesize lady: '*Every yard a queen*', a modification of Shakespeare's well-known '*Every inch a king*', and an allusion to this quotation. There would really be no serious objection if anyone would rather locate this joke as a substitute-formation among the condensations with modification (p. 19) (cf. *tête-à-bête*).

Of a person who was ambitious, but obdurate in pursuit of his aims, a friend said: '*Er hat ein Ideal vor dem Kopf* [lit: 'He has an ideal in front of his head', i.e., 'He can't see beyond his ideal']'. '*Ein Brett vor dem Kopf haben* [lit: 'To have a board in front of one's head', i.e., 'He can't see beyond his nose', 'He is stupid']' is the current phrase which this modification is playing upon, also claiming its meaning for itself. Here too we can describe its technique as condensation with modification.

Allusion by means of modification and condensation with substitute-formation are almost indistinguishable when the modification is limited to an alteration of the letters, e.g., artritis.[53] The allusion to the scourge of arthritis suggests that the practice of poetry by those without a vocation is also a public danger.

Negative prefixes enable very fine allusions to be made at a cost of very small alterations:

'My fellow-*un*believer Spinoza,' says Heine. 'We, by the *dis*grace of God, day-labourers, serfs, negroes and bondmen ...' is how Lichtenberg begins a manifesto – going no further – for these unfortunates, who at least have more right to such titles than kings and princely personages have to its unmodified form.

Finally, *omission* is also one form of allusion, comparable to condensation without substitute-formation. In fact, in every allusion something is being omitted, that is, the train of thought leading to the allusion. It depends only on which is the more obvious – the gap in the wording of the allusion or the substitute which partially fills the gap. In this way we might be brought by way of a series of examples from glaring omission back to allusion proper.

Omission without substitution is to be found in the following example: in Vienna there lives a witty and belligerent writer,[54] whose biting invective has repeatedly drawn physical assaults from his victims. Once, when a fresh misdeed of one of his habitual opponents was being discussed, a third party observed: '*If X. hears that, he will get another box on the ear.*' It is part of the technique of this joke that we are baffled at first by the apparent illogicality, for to have one's ears boxed as the direct consequence of having heard something does not strike us as plausible in the least. The illogicality vanishes if we fill the gap with: '*then he will write such a caustic article against the person concerned that, etc.*'. Allusion by means of omission and illogicality, then, are the technical devices of this joke.

Heine: '*He praises himself so highly that fumigating-candles are going up in price.*' This gap is easy to fill. What has been left out is replaced by a conclusion that leads back to it as an allusion. Self-praise stinks! [German proverb.]

Now once again the two Jews outside the bath-house!

'*Another year gone by already!*' sighs one of them.

These examples surely dismiss any doubts that omission belongs to allusion.

A persistent and striking gap is to be found in the next example, which is still a true and proper allusion-based joke. Following a bohemian celebration in Vienna, a joke book was published in which, among others, the following most remarkable aphorism was recorded:

'*A wife is like an umbrella. After all, before long one takes a cab.*'

An umbrella does not give sufficient protection from the rain.

That 'after all, before long' can only mean: if it is raining really hard, and a cab is a public vehicle. But since we have to do with a kind of comparison here, let us postpone a fuller investigation of this joke until later.

Heine's 'Die Bäder von Lucca' contains a real wasps' nest of the most stinging allusions, making the most inventive use of this form of witticism for polemical ends (against Count Platen[55]). Much earlier, before this use dawns on the reader, a certain theme, particularly unsuitable for direct representation, has been introduced by allusions drawn from the most varied material, e.g., in Hirsch-Hyacinth's malapropisms: 'You are too corpulent and I am too lean, you have a great deal of imagination and I have all the more business-sense, I am a practical man and you are *a diarrhetical man*, in short, you are my anti*podex*.' – 'Venus *Urinia*' – 'fat Gudel of *Dreckwall* [lit: "Turd Bank"] in Hamburg', and the like. Then events as the poet describes them take a turn which at first only seems to demonstrate the poet's mischievous ill-nature, but soon reveals its symbolic relation to his polemical aim, and also declares its allusive nature. Finally, the attack on Platen breaks out and allusions to the theme already announced – the Count's homosexuality – now come fizzing and flowing from every sentence Heine aims at the talent and character of his enemy. For example: 'Even if the Muses are not kind to him, he still has the genius of language in his power, or rather he knows how to assault him; for he does not have the free love of this genius; he has to keep running after this boy too, and he is only able to capture the outward forms, which despite their lovely curves have no nobility of expression.'

'And then he is like the ostrich, which believes it is sufficiently hidden if it buries its head in the sand, so that only its backside is visible. Our noble bird would have done better if he had hidden his backside in the sand and shown us his head.'

Among the joke's devices, allusion is perhaps the most frequent and the easiest to use; it lies at the basis of most of the short-lived jokes we habitually include in our conversations, which cannot survive removal from their native soil or being preserved on their own. But the case of allusion in particular reminds us of that circumstance which began to throw us off course in our assessment of joke-technique. For allusion too does not in itself have the character of a joke or witticism; there are correctly formed allusions that have no claim to this description. Only the 'witty' allusion is a witticism – so that the feature identifying jokes and witticisms, which we have been pursuing into the field of their technique, eludes us there again.

I have occasionally referred to allusion as '*indirect representation*', and I see now that we might very well gather the various kinds of allusion together with representation by the opposite and with the techniques referred to below into one single large group for which '*indirect representation*' might be the most comprehensive name. *Faulty thinking – unification – indirect representation*, then, are names for the aspects under which the techniques we have met belonging to the intellectual joke could be grouped.

As we investigate our material further, we think we recognize a new subclass of indirect representation, which can be described very exactly, but illustrated by only a few examples. This is representation by *a small or very, very small item* which solves its task of giving full expression to an entire character by expressing it by some minute detail. Placing this group under allusion becomes feasible if we consider that this tiny item does indeed have a connection with what is to be represented, as something that can be concluded from it. For example: 'A Galician Jew is travelling on the railway and has made himself very comfortable, unbuttoned his coat, put his feet up on the bench. Then a gentleman in modern dress enters the carriage. At once the Jew pulls himself together, takes up an unobtrusive position in his seat. The stranger turns the pages of a notebook, makes some calculations, thinks, and suddenly turns to the Jew with the question: "Excuse me, when is Yom Kippur?" (Day of Atonement.) "*Ai-ai-ai*,"[56] says the Jew, and puts his feet up on the bench again before replying.'

It is undeniable that this representation by something small is linked to the tendency to economy which we retained, after our inquiry into the technique of verbal jokes, as their ultimate common factor.

The following is a very similar example: the doctor who has been requested to attend the Baroness at her confinement declares that the moment has not yet arrived, and suggests to the Baron that meantime they play a game of cards in the next room. After a while the Frau Baronin's cry of pain reaches the ears of the two men: '*Ah mon Dieu, que je souffre.*' The husband leaps up, but the doctor detains him: 'It's nothing. Let's carry on playing.' A while later they hear her crying out in labour: '*Mein Gott, mein Gott, was für Schmerzen!* [lit: 'My God, my God, how it hurts!']' – 'Won't you go in, Professor?' asks the Baron. 'No, no, it's still not time.' – Finally, from the next room they hear an unmistakable cry of '*Ai, waih, waih* [equivs: 'O weh', 'Oy vay']'; then the doctor throws away his cards and says: 'It's time.'[57]

How pain will allow the original nature to break through all the layers of education, and how an important decision is – rightly – made dependent upon a seemingly unimportant utterance – both are displayed by this good joke in the example of the stage-by-stage transformation in the lamentations of the noble lady in labour.

[L]

We have saved a discussion of another variety of indirect representation in jokes – *metaphor* – until now, on the one hand because in judging it we came across fresh difficulties or alternatively because difficulties that have already arisen on other occasions can be seen particularly clearly. We have already admitted that in many of the examples we investigated we were unable to banish a hesitation as to whether they were to be counted as jokes at all, and we recognized that this uncertainty and the doubts it raised were a great blow to the foundations of our inquiry. However, there is no other material where I feel this uncertainty more forcibly and frequently than with jokes based on metaphor [*Gleichniswitz*]. The feeling that usually tells me well before a joke's hidden, essential nature is revealed – and, it seems, tells a great number of others too – 'this is a joke, this is something you can claim is a joke' – leaves me in the lurch most readily in cases of witty comparisons. Even if I have declared without a second thought that a comparison is a joke, a moment later I believe I have noticed that the enjoyment it gives me is of a different quality from the kind I usually owe to a joke; and the circumstance that witty comparisons are only very rarely capable of rousing that explosive laughter which is the sign of a good joke, makes it impossible for me to evade my doubts as I usually do – by confining myself to the best and most effective examples of its kind.

It is easy to show that there are remarkably fine and effective examples of metaphors that do not impress us at all as being jokes. The lovely comparison in Ottilie's *Journal* between constant tenderness and the English Navy's red thread (see p. 17) is one such; and I cannot resist referring to another with equal pleasure, for I have not yet grown tired of admiring it, nor got over the impression it made on me. It is the metaphor with which Ferdinand Lasalle[58] closed one of his famous speeches for the defence (*Science and the Workers*): 'A man who has dedicated his life to the watchword "Science and the Workers", would, as I have explained, be no more impressed even by a judge's verdict that he encountered on his way through life *than a retort breaking might impress a chemist engrossed in his scientific experiments. Frowning slightly at the resistance of matter, once the disturbance has been removed he goes calmly on with his researches and labours.*'

A rich selection of shrewd and witty metaphors is to be found in Lichtenberg's writings (vol. II, Göttingen ed.); and that is where I shall take the material for our investigation from.

'*It is almost impossible to carry the torch of truth through a crowd without singeing someone's beard.*'

That surely appears to be a witticism, but on closer inspection we note that the witty effect does not come from the metaphor itself, but from a secondary characteristic it has. The 'torch of truth' is actually not a new metaphor, but one that has long been current and reduced to a fixed cliché, as always happens if a metaphor is lucky and gets accepted by linguistic usage. While we scarcely notice the metaphor in 'the torch of truth' any longer, in Lichtenberg's version it is restored to its full original force, for he builds on it further and draws a conclusion from it. But *taking faded phrases in their full meaning* is already familiar to us as a device of joke-technique; it has its place in multiple use of the same material (see p. 26). It might well be the case that the impression made by Lichtenberg's saying derives only from its dependence on this joke-technique.

The same judgement certainly also applies to another metaphor that has the quality of a witticism, made by the same author:

'The man was not *a great light* [*Licht*], it is true, but he was a great *light-holder* [*Leuchter*: 'candlestick'; a near-pun] . . . He was a professor of philosophy.'

To call a scholar a great light, a 'lumen mundi' has long ago lost its force as a metaphor, whether it originally worked as a joke or not. But the metaphor can be refreshed, its full force can be restored by deriving some modification from it and in this way obtaining a second, new metaphor from it. The way in which the second metaphor comes about seems to constitute the requirement for it to be a joke, not the two metaphors themselves. This would be a case of the same joke-technique as in the example of the torch.

The following comparison appears to have the quality of a witticism for a different reason, though one we can judge in similar terms:

'I regard *book-reviews* as being a kind of *children's illness*, to which all new-born books are more or less prone. We have instances where the healthiest die of them, and the sickly ones often pull through. Many don't catch them at all. There have often been attempts to ward them off with the *amulets* of *Preface* and *Dedication*, or even to *shred* [*makulieren*: 'turn to waste paper'] *them by criticism of one's own*; but it doesn't always help.'

The comparison of reviews with children's illnesses is based first of all only on catching them shortly after seeing the light of day. Whether the comparison is a witticism up to that point I do not trust myself to decide. But then it is taken further: it turns out that the later fate of new books can be represented within the framework of the same metaphor or by means of metaphors dependent on it. Taking a comparison further like this is undoubtedly witty, but we already know which technique makes it appear so; it is an instance of *unification*, of creating an unsuspected connection. However, the character of the unification is not altered by the fact that in this case it consists of an extension of the preliminary metaphor.

There are a number of other comparisons where one is tempted to shift the undeniable impression that they are witticisms on to another factor which in itself has again nothing to do with the nature of metaphor in itself. These are the comparisons that contain a striking juxtaposition, often an absurd-sounding combination, or which are replaced by something of the kind as the product of the comparison. Most of the examples from Lichtenberg belong to this group.

'It is a pity that one cannot see into the *entrails of writers' learning*, to find out what they have eaten.' 'Entrails of learning' – that is at first a baffling attributive, really absurd, which is then only explained by the comparison. What if the witty impression made by this comparison were to derive wholly and entirely from the baffling nature of this combination? This would correspond to a joke-technique well known to us: representation by means of absurdity.

Lichtenberg has used the same comparison between ingesting reading-matter and ingesting physical nourishment to create another witticism:

'He had a high opinion of *studying at home*, and so was whole-heartedly in favour of *stall-feeding in learned subjects*.'

The same absurd or at least striking attributives, which, as we begin to notice, are the real vehicles for the joke, can be found in other metaphors from the same author:

'That is the *weather-side of my moral constitution*; I can hold out against things there.'

'Everyone has his *moral backside* [Lichtenberg's English], which he does not display *except in case of need* and which he covers for as long as possible with the *breeches of gentility*.'

'Moral backside' is the striking attributive that has come into being as the product of a comparison. But in addition the comparison is extended with a full-blown play on words ('need') and a second, even more unusual, combination ('the breeches of gentility'), which is perhaps in itself a witticism, for the breeches, because they are the breeches of gentility, as it were, are a witticism themselves. We should not be surprised, then, if the whole impresses us as being a very witty comparison; we begin to notice that in our appreciation we are quite generally inclined to extend a characteristic that belongs only to a part of the whole to the whole itself. Incidentally, the 'breeches of gentility' remind me of a similar baffling line in Heine:

> *Bis mir endlich alle Knöpfe rissen*
> *An der Hose der Geduld.*[59]

[Finally burst all the buttons/ On the breeches of my patience.]

It is obvious that these last two examples have a characteristic that is not to be found in all good, i.e., apt, metaphors. They are to a large extent '*degrading*', one might say; they juxtapose a thing from a high category, an abstraction (here: gentility, patience) with something very concrete, and itself of a low sort (breeches). Whether this peculiarity has to do with jokes is something we shall have to consider later in another connection. At this point let us attempt to analyse another example in which the degrading characteristic is particularly clear. In Nestroy's farce, *Einen Jux will er sich machen*,[60] the shop assistant Weinberl imagines how, when he is a respectable old merchant, he will think back on the days of his youth, saying: '*When we are ʳhatting cosily and the ice is hacked away from in front of the storeroom of memory, and the cellar-door of old times is unlocked again, and the showcase of fantasy is stocked with the wares of long ago.*' These are certainly comparisons of abstractions with very common concrete things, but the joke depends – exclusively or only in part – on the circumstance that it is a shop assistant who is using them, taking them from the field of his everyday business. To bring these abstractions into relationship with these ordinary things, however, is an act of *unification*.

Let us return to Lichtenberg's comparisons.

'*The reasons that move us*[61] *to do something could be arranged like the 32* [directions of the] *winds and their names could be formed in a similar way, e.g., Bread – Bread – Fame or Fame – Fame – Bread.'*

Here too, as so often in Lichtenberg's witticisms, the impression of aptness, wit and perspicacity is so predominant that our judgement on the character of what makes it a witticism is led astray by it. If there is a pinch of wit in the excellent sense of a wise remark like this, it is likely we will be tempted to declare that the entire saying is a splendid witticism. I would rather venture to assert that all that really makes it a witticism arises from our being disconcerted by the curious combination 'Bread – Bread – Fame'. So as a joke it is an instance of representation by means of absurdity.

A curious combination or an absurd epithet on its own may be presented as the product of a comparison.

Lichtenberg: *A woman that sleeps two [zweischläfrig] – a church-pew that sleeps one [einschläfrig].*[62] Hidden behind both is a comparison with a bed; in both, besides bafflement, there is the technical factor of *allusion* at work, in the one instance to the sleep-inducing [also *einschläfrig*] effect of sermons, in the other to the inexhaustible theme of sexual relations.

Though we have discovered so far that whenever a comparison seems to us to be a witticism, this impression is due to the inclusion of one of the joke-techniques familiar to us, finally some other examples seem to attest that a comparison can also be witty in itself.

Lichtenberg characterizes certain odes:

'They are in the field of poetry what Jakob Böhme's immortal works are in prose, *a kind of picnic, to which the writer brings the words and the reader the meaning.*'

'When he *philosophizes*, he casts an *agreeable moonlight* over things, which pleases us overall, but does not show a single thing clearly.'

Or Heine: *'Her face resembled a palimpsest where, beneath the freshly inked monkish script of a Church Father's text, there peeps through the half-obliterated lines of an ancient Greek erotic poet.'*

Or his continued comparisons, with their strongly degrading tendency, in 'Die Bäder von Lucca'.

'Your *Catholic priest* carries on more like a clerk in a *wholesale business*; the Church, the big business, with the pope as its head, gives him a fixed job and a fixed wage for doing it; he works indolently, like anyone who does not work on his own account, has many colleagues, and can easily remain unnoticed in the busy concern – only the credit of the firm is close to his heart, and still more its preservation, for possible bankruptcy would lose him his livelihood. Your *Protestant minister* on the other hand is in all respects his own boss and carries on the business of religion on his own account. He does not go in for wholesale trading, like his Catholic fellow-dealer, but only for *retail*, and as he has to manage this on his own, he cannot be indolent, he has to praise his articles of faith to his customers and run his competitors' wares down; as a proper small tradesman he will stand in his retail stall filled with professional envy for all big business, particularly for the great firm in Rome that employs many thousands of bookkeepers and baggage-hands, and has its agencies in all four corners of the globe.'

In view of this, as of many other examples, we cannot really dispute any longer that a comparison may also be a witticism in itself, without ascribing this impression to its involvement with one of the familiar joke-techniques. But, in that case, what determines the character of the metaphor as a *joke* escapes us entirely, as that certainly does not attach to the metaphor as an expression of the thought, nor to the operation of the comparison. There is nothing we can do but place metaphor under the kinds of 'indirect representation' employed by the joke-technique, and we are forced to leave the problem unsolved, although in metaphor it has come to meet us far more clearly than in the devices used in witticisms which we have dealt with earlier. There must surely be a particular reason too, why we find the decision as to whether something is a joke or not more difficult to make in the case of metaphor than in other forms of expression.

But even this gap in our understanding does not give us any cause to complain that our preliminary investigation has produced no results. Given the close interrelations which we were ready to ascribe to the various characteristics shown by jokes, it would be rash to expect that we could explain one aspect of the problem fully before we had cast a glance at the others. We shall have to attack the problem from a different angle, it seems.

Are we sure that none of the possible joke-techniques has escaped our investigation? Probably not, but if we continue our examination with new material, we shall be able to assure ourselves that we have got to know the most frequent and most important technical devices of the joke-work, at least as far as is needed to come to a judgement on the nature of this psychical process. At present we still do not have such a judgement; on the other hand we have come into possession of an important pointer towards the direction from which we may expect further illumination of the problem. The interesting processes of condensation with substitute-formation which we have recognized to be the core of the joke-technique in verbal jokes pointed us towards the formation of dreams, for the same psychical processes have been discovered in the mechanism at work there. But that is the very same direction to which the techniques of intellectual jokes also point – displacement, faulty thinking, absurdity, indirect representation, representation by the opposite – and all of these without exception recur in the dream-work. Thanks to displacement, dreams have that disconcerting appearance which prevents us from recognizing that they are the continuation of our waking thoughts; the use of absurdity and nonsense in dreams has cost them the dignity of being regarded as a product of our psyche and misled the authorities into assuming that the conditions for dreams to be formed are the disintegration of mental activities and the suspension of criticism, morality and logic. Representation by the opposite is so common in dreams that even popular, quite mistaken, books of dream-interpretation habitually reckon with it; indirect representation, substitution of the dream-thought by an allusion, by a small thing, symbolism analogous to metaphor – these are the very things that distinguish the mode of expression of dreams from that of our waking thought.[63] Such a far-reaching correspondence as the one between the devices of the joke-work and those of the dream-work will hardly be accidental. To demonstrate this correspondence in detail and trace the grounds for it will be one of our later tasks.

Notes

1. The same joke will also engage us later, and we shall have occasion then to make an adjustment to Lipps's rendering, taken up by our own. However, this does not affect the discussion that follows at this point.

2. [Jean Paul, I, section IX, para. 47, quoted by Kuno Fischer, p. 35. The exact quotation runs: 'So sehr siegt überall bloße Stellung, es sei der Krieger oder ihrer Sätze.' ('So much does mere position determine the victory, whether of soldiers or their sentences' (Hale, op. cit., p. 128).)]

3. The same applies to the rendering by Lipps.

4. The syllables common to both words are printed in bold here, in contrast to the type used for the particular components of both words. The second L, which is scarcely pronounced, may of course be ignored. It is obvious that the congruence in the two words of several syllables offers the joke-technique the occasion to create the composite word.

5. ['Ideen: das Buch Legrand': in the second collection of Heine's *Reisebilder* (1827).]

6. Have I the right to do so? At least I have not learned of these witticisms through any indiscretion. They are generally known in this city (Vienna) and to be found on everyone's lips. Eduard Hanslick has made a number of them public in the *Neue freie Presse* and in his autobiography. As for the others, I offer my apologies for any distortions – scarcely avoidable when jokes are handed down by word of mouth – which may have affected them.

7. [Probably Josef Unger (1828–1913), Professor of Jurisprudence and President of the Supreme Court from 1881.]

8. (Weimar edition, XX, p. 212.) [Freud actually placed the quotation containing 'Goethe's lovely analogy' in a footnote on the same page, but rather than lose this important element of his exposition among the endnotes, it has been moved into the body of the text. The translation used is J. R. Hollingdale's (Harmondsworth, 1971), pp. 163–4.]

9. How little this regularly repeated observation concurs with the dictum that a joke is a playful judgement, is something I need only hint at.

10. It is said that the same witty quip was already coined by Heine about Alfred de Musset.

11. One of the complications of the technique of this example is that the modification replacing the omitted insult should be described as an *allusion* to it, as it leads to it only by way of a process of inference. For another factor complicating the technique here, see below.

12. The technique of this witticism is also affected by another factor which I shall keep for later discussion. It concerns the nature of the content in the modification (representation by the opposite, absurdity). There is nothing to prevent the technique of jokes from using several devices simultaneously, though we are only able to get to know them one after another.

13. [Karl Kraus (1874–1936): Viennese polemicist, who edited – and largely wrote – his own influential and exclusive journal *Die Fackel*. The gibe at a journalist is characteristic, for his chief target was the corruption of language as the symptom and cause of the corruption of morality – especially as he found it in the gutter press.]

14. [*Wallensteins Lager* (*Wallenstein's Camp*): the first drama of Schiller's *Wallenstein* trilogy (1800), about power-politics in the Thirty Years War, presents the variety of figures who made up Wallenstein's motley army as the basis of his power. The ingenious extracts here and later are taken from F. J. Lamport's translation in *The Robbers & Wallenstein* (Harmondsworth, 1979), here p. 196.]

15. On the other hand, another factor makes this joke worth rating more highly, but that can be shown only at a later stage.

16. The merit of these jokes derives from the fact that another technical device of a far higher order has come into use at the same time (see below). – Incidentally, I may also draw attention at this point to one way in which jokes are related to riddles. The philosopher Franz Brentano invented a kind of riddle in which a small number of syllables has to be guessed; if joined into a word, or combined in some way, they would yield another meaning, e.g.:

'. . . ließ mich das *Platanenblatt ahnen* [lit: 'the plane-tree leaf made me guess']' or:

'wie du dem *Inder hast verschrieben, in der Hast verschrieben?* [lit: 'as you prescribed for the Indian, (did you) in haste make an error?']'

The syllables to be guessed are to be replaced in the framework of the sentence by the filler 'dal' the appropriate number of times. One of the philosopher's colleagues took clever revenge when he heard of the engagement of the by-no-means young man, asking: Daldaldal daldaldal? [*Brentano brennt-a-no?* lit: 'Brentano – is he afire?']

What is the difference between these daldal-riddles and the jokes above? In the former, the technique is the given condition and the wording has to be guessed, while in the jokes, the wording is overt and the technique is concealed.

[Franz Brentano (1838–1917): Professor of Philosophy in Vienna. Freud attended his lectures as a young student. The echoing phrases of Brentano's riddles make a kind of pun; the sentences containing them need only be syntactically coherent; any actual meaning is fortuitous.]

17. Just as it does not exhaust the technique of a capital joke of Oliver Wendell Holmes's, quoted by Brill: 'Put not your *trust in money*, but put your *money in trust*.' A contradiction is announced here, which then does not come about. The second part of the sentence takes the contradiction back. A good example, incidentally, of the untranslatability of jokes with a technique of this kind.

18. Brill quotes a very similar modification-witticism: *Amantes amentes* [Lovers are fools].

19. [Georg Christoph Lichtenberg (1742–99): Professor of Mathematics at Göttingen, a scientist, eccentric and man of letters who cultivated the small forms of aphorism and essay.]

20. [Friedrich Daniel Schleiermacher (1768–1830): Protestant theologian of the Romantic movement.]

21. [One of those dated topical jokes requiring laborious explanation. Elsa is the heroine of Wagner's *Lohengrin*. Alsace was the disputed territory that was the occasion of war between France and Germany in 1870.]

22. '"When Saphir," as Heymans puts it, "is asked by a wealthy creditor he is visiting: 'Sie kommen wohl um die 300 Gulden? [lit: 'I suppose you've come about the 300 guilders?']', he replies: 'Nein, Sie kommen um die 300 Gulden [lit: 'No, you've lost the 300 [guilders']', exactly what he means is expressed in a form that is both perfectly correct linguistically and not in the least unusual." In fact, that is so: Saphir's reply, *considered in itself*, is perfectly proper. We also understand what he means, that is, that he does not intend to pay his debt. But Saphir uses the same words that were previously used by his creditor. So we cannot help also understanding them in the sense in which the latter had used them. And then Saphir's reply no longer makes sense. The creditor does not "come" at all. He cannot be coming about the 300 guilders, that is, he cannot be coming to bring the 300 guilders. Besides, as creditor, it is not up to him to bring them, but to demand them. The comic nature of Saphir's words comes about as they are recognized in this way to be both sense and nonsense.' (Lipps, p. 97)

According to the version above, reproduced in full for the sake of explanation, the technique of this joke is far simpler than Lipps thinks. Saphir is not coming to bring the 300 guilders, but to fetch them from the rich man. Then the discussion of 'sense and nonsense' in this joke loses its point.

23. *Das große Buch der Witze*, collected and edited by Willy Hermann, Berlin, 1904.

24. For further analysis of this play on words, see below.

25. ['Die Harzreise': the first of Heine's travel-sketches in the first volume of his *Reisebilder* (1826). It included much satire on the University of Göttingen, where he studied. The professors without a name and the beadle occur in chapter I.]

26. [*Eiserne Stirne*: used here in the sense of 'nerve', 'effrontery'; *eiserne Krone*: a minor Austro-Hungarian decoration associated with elevation to the nobility.]

27. [Alfred Dreyfus (1859–1935): French army officer falsely accused by colleagues in 1894 of having passed on military secrets to Germany; court-martialled and imprisoned on Devil's Island. The twelve-year-long *cause célèbre* divided France bitterly between liberals and an anti-Semitic establishment. Freud responded with sadness and bitterness to the verdict in a letter to Fliess (11 September 1899) (Masson, op. cit., p. 371).]

28. Cf. Kuno Fischer on this point (p. 85): he applies the term *'double entendre'*, which I have just used in a different way, for the kind of joke with double meaning in which the two senses are not equally foregrounded, but one lies behind the other. The practice of nomenclature here is a matter of convention; linguistic usage has not come to any hard-and-fast decision.

29. [*Kalauer*: a kind of approximate pun, as Freud explains. The word derives from the French *calembour*, but Freud adds an unauthorized *g*, making a hidden *Kalauer* of his own. In contrast to the *faubourg*, the suburb or *faux bourg*, the *calem-bourg* is the place where jokers go slumming. At least, this play on words might account for his curious *Wohnsitz* metaphor, here rendered by 'dwelling-place'.]

30. [From Lamport, op. cit., pp. 193–4, whose clever variants are a clear illustration of the inappropriateness of mere literal translation of verbal play.]

31. [Frédéric Soulié (1800–1847): French dramatist and novelist.]

32. Heine's reply is a combination of two kinds of joke-technique: diversion with an allusion. He does not say directly: 'He's an ox.'

33. On account of the great variety in its usage, the word 'take' is very suitable for producing a play on words. I shall offer a simple example, in contrast to the displacement joke given above: 'A well-known bank director and speculator on the stock exchange takes a stroll with a friend over the Ringstraße. Outside a coffee-house he suggests to the friend: "Let's go in and *take* something." The friend restrains him: "But, Herr Hofrat, there are people in there."'

34. For the latter, see later sections.

35. Perhaps a few words of further clarification at this point may not come amiss: as a rule displacement occurs between a remark and a reply that carries on the train of thought in a different direction from the one along which it started. The justification for distinguishing displacement from double meaning can best be taken from those examples in which the two are combined, that is, where the wording of a remark admits of a double meaning but which shows the reply the way to making the displacement. (See examples.)

36. [For the essentials of the joke, the actual place does not matter, but for Freud's historical world it certainly does. Pressburg, now Bratislava in Slovakia, was at the heart of old Galicia, with its large population of poor, unassimilated Eastern Jews, who figure in so many of Freud's Jewish jokes.]

37. See below, section III.

38. [See Rosten, op. cit., pp. 364–7.]

39. [Sophocles, *Oedipus at Colonus*. See Sophocles, *The Theban Plays*, tr. E. F. Watling (Harmondsworth, 1947), p. 109.]

40. [*Fliegende Blätter*: comic Munich weekly. For a Jewish variant of this joke, see Rosten, op. cit., p. 268.]

41. [Jules Michelet (1798–1874): French historian, whose *La Femme* (1859) is not regarded as typical of his work.]

42. A similar nonsense-technique can be seen when a joke persists in maintaining a connection which appears to be cancelled by the particular conditions of its content. Among these is Lichtenberg's *knife without a blade with a missing handle*. Similarly the joke told by J. Falke (loc. cit.): 'Is that the place where the Duke of Wellington spoke these words?' – *Yes, that's the place, but he never spoke the words*.

43. 'Kück' [a Yiddish-coloured word] from 'gücken', that is, a gaze, a distant gaze.

44. [Variant of Propertius, *Elegies*, X, 6.]

45. [Freud appears to be having a joke with his insider-audience at the expense of his outsider-audience. His irony here is of a different order from the simple stable irony he analyses as 'representation by the opposite' on p. 63, but of the deep-revolving sort that plays with different levels of knowledge.]

46. I shall make use of the peculiar negative relation, already referred to, of jokes to riddles – that the one hides what the other displays – in order to give a better description of 'unification' than the examples above allow. Many of the riddles with which the philosopher G. Th. Fechner whiled away the period of his blindness are distinguished by a high degree of unification, which makes them especially attractive. Take, for example, the fine riddle no. 203 *Rätselbüchlein von Dr Mises*, 4th augmented ed. n.d.):

Die beiden ersten finden ihre Ruhestätte
Im Paar der andern, und das Ganze macht ihr Bette.

[My first two (*Toten*: 'the dead') find their resting-place in the pair of the others (*Gräber*: 'graves'), and my whole (*Totengräber*: 'grave-digger') makes their bed.]

We are given no information about the two pairs of syllables to be guessed except their relation to one another, and about the whole we are given only its relation to the first pair. Or the following two examples of description by means of relation to the same or slightly modified third element.

No. 170
Die erste Silb' hat Zähn' und Haare,
Die zweite Zähne in den Haaren.
Wer auf den Zähnen nicht hat Haare,
Vom Ganzen kaufe keine Ware.

[My first syllable has teeth and hair (*Ross*: 'horse'), my second teeth in hair (*Kamm*: 'comb'). Anyone who has no teeth on his hair (i.e., who can't look out for himself) should beware of buying any goods from my whole (*Rosskamm*: 'horse-dealer'.]

No. 168
Die erste Silbe frißt,
Die andre Silbe ißt,
Die dritte wird gefressen,
Das Ganze wird gegessen.

[My first syllable devours (*Sau*: 'pig'), the other syllable eats (*er*: 'he'), the third is devoured (*Kraut*: 'cabbage'), my whole (*Sauerkraut*) is eaten.]

The most perfect unification is to be found in a riddle of Schleiermacher's, which is nothing if not witty:

Von der letzten umschlungen
Schwebt das vollendete Ganze
Zu den zwei ersten empor.

[Encircled by my last (*Strick*: 'rope'), my completed whole (*Galgenstrick*: 'rogue', 'gallows-bird') swings aloft to my two first (*Galgen*: 'gallows').]

The vast majority of syllable-riddles lack unification, i.e., the feature by which the one syllable is to be guessed is quite independent of the one indicating the second or third syllable, and also of the point of reference for guessing the whole by itself.

[Gustav Theodor Fechner (1801–87): romantic philosopher and psychologist, who renewed interest in the relations of body and soul. His pseudonymous *Rätselbüchlein* was first published in 1850. In the final chapter of *The Interpretation of Dreams* Freud adopted Fechner's phrase 'a different scene of action' for the location of dreams in the psyche.]

47. [For a variant on this joke, though used to illustrate brevity, see Jean Paul (1804!) (Hale, op. cit., p. 162).]

48. [Disaster brought upon himself by *Der hinterlistige Heinrich*, who teased the geese and was carried aloft by them and dropped in the soup. Minor work by Wilhelm Busch (1832–1908), whose tremendously popular comic picture-stories combined slapstick, sadism and *schadenfreude* with *petit-bourgeois* proprieties: chaos is followed by order restored. Freud borrows this example from Lipps (*Komik und Humor*, p. 177), but it is an indication of how widely Busch was known that neither thought it necessary to give an attribution.]

49. After a model in the *Greek Anthology*. [Gotthold Ephraim Lessing (1729–81, 'Auf die Galathee', *Sinngedichte*.]

50. [*Simplizissimus*: comic Munich journal with a very gifted team of writers and cartoonists.]

51. [The term *intellektueller Witz* was used by Kuno Fischer as an alternative to his coinage *Gedankenwitz*, the term adopted by Freud. Fischer coined the word by borrowing the form of the literary term *Gedankenlyrik* – which has no exact equivalent in English – used to classify those lyrics whose subject-matter is ideas rather than emotions. Freud uses the word to make his distinction between *Gedankenwitz*, the intellectual joke, and what he calls the *Wortwitz*, the verbal joke, which he had discussed earlier. However, the elegant similarity of formulation in fact fudges a categorical distinction between the two: in Fischer's *Gedankenwitz*, as in the *Gedankenlyrik*, ideas are the subject-matter; in Freud's *Wortwitz*, words are the material and the medium.]

52. [In his literary study *Der Wahn und die Träume in W. Jensens 'Gradiva'* (*Delusion and Dream in Jensen's 'Gradiva'*) (1907), Freud draws attention to extended passages of speech which are ambiguous in just this sense, chosen intentionally by the character Zoë so that her reality might match

her lover Hanold's delusion. Freud's comment: 'It is a triumph of wit [*Witz* – which one might be tempted to render as 'ingenuity', but not in the light of his present argument] to be able to represent delusion and truth in the same expressive form' (*Studien Ausgabe*, X, pp. 76–7). Here, as so often in the present work, there is a sense that Freud is on the brink of a more general aesthetic theory.]

53. [*Artritis/arthritis*: equivalents for Freud's *Dichteritis/Diphtheritis*. *Dichter*: 'poet'.]

54. [Probably Karl Kraus is meant; see note 13.]

55. [August, Graf von Platen-Hallermünde (1796–1835): poet of highly wrought verse, who spent much of his life in Italy. His anti-Semitism, homosexuality and the formality of his lyrics together provoked Heine's nasty attacks on him. Those quoted here occur in chapters IX and XI of 'Die Bäder von Lucca'.]

56. [Freud has the Yiddishism 'Aesoi', which might be soberly rendered by the equivalents of 'Ach so!' or 'So that's how it is.' But I am persuaded by Rosten's happy analysis of *ai-ai-ai* in its many modulations – 'this exquisite exclamation' (op. cit., p. 7) – to adopt it here. Like the following joke, this too is an 'unmasking', though explicitly so.]

57. [Rosten (op. cit., pp. 134–5) tells the same story of the apocryphal Countess Misette de Rothschild – but less subtly gives her final cry as 'Ge-valt!' What is 'unmistakable' about Freud's 'Ai, waih, waih' is the Yiddish 'Oy vay [is mir]' audible behind it. His Baroness has modulated in language and register from aristocratic French through literate German to a not yet wholly inarticulate cry – not only to the universal nature Freud ascribes to a woman in labour, but also to her social origins. This is the 'joke' he later describes as an unmasking.]

58. [Ferdinand Lasalle (1825–64): founder of the socialist *Allgemeiner deutscher Arbeiterverein*. His death in a duel entered one of Freud's dreams; see *The Interpretation of Dreams*, VI.V.]

59. ['Jehuda ben Halevy' in Heinrich Heine, *The Complete Poems*: *A Modern English Version*, tr. Hal Draper (Boston, 1982), p. 674.]

60. [Johann Nepomuk Nestroy (1801–62): popular Viennese writer of comedies. *Einen Jux will er sich machen* (1842) has been adapted by Thornton Wilder as *The Merchant of Jonkers* (1938) and by Tom Stoppard as *On the Razzle* (1981).]

61. Today we would say 'motives'.

62. [The German terms refer to double and single beds, but Lichtenberg also exploits the double meaning of *einschläfrig*.]

63. Cf. my *Interpretation of Dreams*, section VI, 'Die Traumwerk' ['The Dream-work'].

III The Tendencies of the Joke

[A]

At the end of the previous section, as I was writing down Heine's comparison of the Catholic priest with an employee and the Protestant minister with an independent retailer, I was aware of an inhibition prompting me not to use this metaphor. I told myself that among my readers there would probably be some who venerated not only religion, but also its governance and its officers; these readers would only become indignant at the comparison and get into a state of high affect – which would rob them of any interest they might have in distinguishing whether the metaphor appeared to be witty in itself or witty only as a consequence of anything added. With other metaphors – for example, the neighbouring one of the agreeable moonlight cast on things by a certain philosophy – there would be no need to worry about an influence of this kind on some of our readers, which would get in the way of our investigation. The most devout of men would still be in a frame of mind to form a judgement on our problem.

It is easy to make out the character of those jokes associated with differences in audience-reaction to them. Sometimes the joke is an end in itself and serves no particular purpose; at others, it does put itself in the service of such a purpose; it becomes *tendentious*. Only the joke that has a tendency or intention runs the risk of coming up against persons who do not want to listen to it.

Theodor Vischer labelled the non-tendentious joke an 'abstract' joke; I prefer to call it 'innocuous'.

Since we have already separated jokes into verbal jokes and

intellectual jokes, according to the material worked on by their technique, we are obliged to examine the relation of this classification to the new one I have just introduced. There is no relationship of reciprocal influence between verbal jokes and intellectual jokes on the one hand, and abstract jokes and tendentious jokes on the other; they are two classifications of the jokes we produce which are quite independent of each other. Perhaps someone might have received the impression that innocuous jokes are predominantly verbal, while the more complicated technique of intellectual jokes is mainly put to use by strong intentions and tendencies. However, there are innocuous jokes that work with verbal play and punning, and equally there are innocuous ones that make use of all the resources of the intellectual joke. It is equally easy to show that a tendentious joke may be simply verbal in technique. Thus, for example, jokes 'playing' on proper names[1] often have an insulting and hurtful tendency, and obviously belong to the verbal jokes. On the other hand, the most innocuous of all jokes are again verbal, for example, the *Schüttelreime* [extended rhyming spoonerisms] that have become popular recently. Their technique is made up of the multiple use of the same material with a quite peculiar modification:

Und weil er Geld in Menge hatte,
lag stets er in der Hängematte.

[lit: 'And because he had money in quantity, he always lay in his hammock.'[2]]

No one will dispute, I hope, that the amusement we have in this kind of otherwise humble rhyming is the same enjoyment that makes us recognize a joke.

Good examples of intellectual jokes and witticisms that are abstract or innocuous are to be found in abundance among Lichtenberg's comparisons, some of which we have already met. I shall add a few more:

'They had sent an octavo volume to Göttingen, and got back a quarto in body and soul.'

'To build this structure properly, the most important thing is to

*lay a good foundation, and I do not know of any firmer than if on
every course of bricks pro one immediately lays a course contra.'*

'*One* [thinker] *begets the thought, another lifts it from the baptis-
mal font, the third produces children with it, the fourth visits it on
its deathbed, and the fifth buries it.*' (Metaphor with unification.)

'*He not only didn't believe in ghosts, he wasn't even afraid of
them.*' The joke here exists simply and solely in the absurd mode of
representation, putting what is usually reckoned to be the lesser in
the comparative and taking what is regarded as the more important
as the positive. If we dispense with the witty way of clothing it
[*Einkleidung*[3]], it would say: it is much easier to dismiss our fear of
ghosts rationally than guard yourself against it when the occasion
arises. This is no longer a joke at all – though it is a true psychological
insight still too little appreciated, the same insight, in fact, as Lessing
expressed in his well-known words:

'Not all are free, who mock their chains.' (*Nathan der Weise*,
IV.iv.2757–8.)

This is an opportunity for me to clear up a misunderstanding that
might be a possibility in any case. For an 'innocuous' or 'abstract'
joke should certainly not mean the equivalent of an 'empty' joke
with no content [*gehaltlos*], but simply the opposite of the 'tendentious' jokes I shall discuss later. As the example above demonstrates,
an innocuous, i.e., un-tendentious, witticism can also be very rich in
content [*gehaltvoll*], and say something worthwhile. However,
the content [*Gehalt*[4]] of a joke is separate from the joke, and is the
content of the thought, which is expressed as a joke by a particular
contrivance. Indeed, just as clockmakers are accustomed to fit a
particularly fine mechanism with a precious case, it may also be so
with jokes that the finest feats of joke-making are used to clothe
thoughts that are richest in content.

Now in the case of jokes based on ideas, if we keep our eye on
the distinction between the content of the thought [*Gehalt des
Gedankens*] and its clothing as a joke, we shall arrive at an insight
that can shed light on much of our uncertainty in judging jokes. For
it turns out – and this is the surprising thing – that we ascribe our
enjoyment of a joke to the combined impression made by the content

and the success of the joke [*Witzleistung*] together, and we allow ourselves to be pretty well deceived by the one factor over the extent of the other. Only a reduction of the joke will clear up this deception of our judgement for us.

Moreover, the same thing also applies to verbal jokes. When we hear: 'Experience consists of experiencing what we wish we had not experienced' – we are baffled; we think we are being told some new truth, and it takes a while before we recognize behind this disguise the truism: 'One learns from experience' (Kuno Fischer). The splendid achievement of this joke [*Witzleistung*] in defining 'experience' almost exclusively by using the word 'experience' deceives us into overestimating the content of the statement. The same thing happens with Lichtenberg's unification joke about 'January' (p. 57), which tells us no more than we already know: that New Year's wishes are as rarely fulfilled as other wishes – and in many other similar instances.

We meet the contrary in other jokes where we have obviously been captivated by the aptness and truth of the thought, so that we call the statement a brilliant joke, while only the thought is brilliant and the feat of joking [*Witzleistung*] often feeble. In Lichtenberg's witticisms in particular, their central thought frequently has much more value than the way they are clothed as a witticism, though we extend our appreciation of the former quite unjustifiably to it. For example, his remark about 'the torch of truth' (p. 71) as a comparison is scarcely a witticism, but it hits the mark so neatly that we are tempted to draw attention to the statement as being particularly witty.

Lichtenberg's witticisms are outstanding above all on account of their thought-content and sureness in hitting the mark. Goethe rightly said of this author that the jokes and jests flashing into his mind pin-point the places where problems are hiding, more exactly, that they touch on the solution to problems. When, for example, he notes down what came to him as a witty idea:

'He always read *Agamemnon* instead of *angenommen* [lit: 'assumed'] – he had read so much Homer' (technically, this is an example of stupidity + punning). What he has done is nothing less than uncover the secret of misreading.[5] That witticism (p. 51) whose technique appeared so very unsatisfactory to us is similar:

'*He was astonished that cats had two holes cut in their fur in the very place where they had eyes.*' The stupidity on show here is only apparent; in reality, behind this simple-minded remark there lies hidden the great problem of teleology in animal anatomy; it was by no means so obvious that the fissure of the eyelids should open just where the cornea is exposed until evolution shed light on this coincidence.

Let us keep in mind that what we receive from a witty remark is a total impression, in which we are not able to separate the share contributed by the thought-content [*Gedankeninhalt*] from the share made by the success of the joke [*Witzleistung*]; perhaps later we shall find an even more significant parallel to this.

[B]

For our purpose of throwing theoretical light on the nature of jokes, innocuous jokes are bound to be of greater value to us than tendentious ones, jokes lacking content [*Gehalt*] of greater value than profound ones. Innocuous play on words without any content, I suggest, will present us with the problem of jokes in its purest form, because in these instances we escape the danger of being confused by the tendency a joke may have, or of being deceived in our judgement by its good sense. Using material of this kind, it is possible to take a new step forward in our knowledge.

I shall choose the most innocuous example of a verbal joke I can find:

A visitor is announced to a girl still at her toilette, who complains: 'Oh what a pity, just when one is *at one's most anziehend* [pun: both 'attractive' and 'getting dressed'], one can't make an appearance.'[6]

But as I begin to doubt whether I am right in claiming that this is an un-tendentious joke, I shall replace it with another, blessedly simple-minded, which is perhaps not open to such objections.

In a house where I am invited as a guest, at the end of the meal the pudding called a *roulade* is served, which requires some skill in the cook to prepare. So one of the guests inquires 'Home-made?', and our host replies: 'Certainly, it's a *Home-roulade* (Home-Rule[7]).'

This time we shall not examine the joke's technique, but propose to turn our attention to another factor, indeed, the most important one. Listening to this improvised joke gave those present much amusement – I recall it clearly – and made us laugh. In this case, as in countless others, the listeners' feeling of pleasure cannot derive from the joke's tendency or from its thought-content [*Gedankeninhalt*]; all that is left is for us to relate this feeling of pleasure to its technique. So the technical resources we have already described – condensation, displacement, indirect representation, etc. – have the power to arouse a feeling of pleasure in the listener, then, even though as yet we cannot see how they have come by this power. In this easy way we have arrived at our second proposition towards an explanation of jokes; the first (p. 12) was that the jokiness of a joke depended on its form of expression. Let us call to mind that the second proposition does not really tell us anything new. It only picks out what was already contained in an observation we made earlier. We recall – do we not? – that when we succeeded in reducing a joke, that is, in replacing its [form of] expression by another one while carefully preserving its sense, this eliminated not only its character as a joke, but also the effect of laughter, that is, our enjoyment of the joke.

We cannot go any further at this point without first getting to grips with our philosophical authorities.

The philosophers, who include the joke under the category of the comic and treat the comic itself within aesthetics, characterize the way our imagination works aesthetically [*das ästhetische Vorstellen*] by the condition that then we demand nothing of things, nor wish to do anything with them; we do not need them for the satisfaction of our great vital needs, but are content with contemplating them and enjoying the imagined idea. 'This enjoyment, this mode of imagining, is the purely aesthetic mode, which rests only in itself, has its end only in itself and fulfils none of the other ends of life' (Kuno Fischer, p. 68).

We shall scarcely be taking a position that contradicts these words of Fischer's – perhaps only translating his thoughts into our way of expressing them – when we stress that the activity of joking cannot be said to have no aim or purpose, for it has set itself the unmistakable aim of arousing pleasure in the listener. I doubt whether we are capable of undertaking anything that does not take some intention into account. If we are not actually using our psychical apparatus to realize one of our indispensable satisfactions, we let it work towards pleasure, we try to obtain pleasure from its own activity. I would surmise that this is really *the* prerequisite for the aesthetic working of the imagination in general [*alles ästhetische Vorstellen*], but I understand too little of aesthetics to be inclined to pursue this proposition; but of joking I can say on the basis of the two insights just gained that it is an activity whose aim it is to obtain pleasure from psychical processes – intellectual or otherwise. There are certainly other activities that have the same goal. Perhaps what distinguishes them is the field of psychical activity they seek to draw pleasure from, perhaps the method they employ in doing so. At present this is something we cannot decide; but we do maintain firmly that the joke-technique and the tendency towards economy which partly governs it (pp. 34–5) have now been brought into connection for the production of pleasure.

But before we set about solving the puzzle of how the technical resources of the joke-work are able to produce pleasure in the listener, let us remind ourselves that for the sake of simplification and greater transparency we have pushed tendentious jokes entirely to one side. Still, we must attempt to throw light on what the intentions and tendencies of [this kind of] joke are, and how it serves these tendencies.

One observation above all warns us not to leave tendentious jokes to one side when we are investigating the source of the pleasure we take in jokes. The pleasurable effect of an innocuous joke is mostly a moderate one; a distinctly agreeable feeling, a slight smile, is usually all it is able to provoke in the listener, and part of this effect can probably be put down to thought-content, as we have seen in appropriate examples (pp. 90–91). An un-tendentious joke scarcely ever achieves those sudden outbursts of laughter that make tendentious jokes so irresistible. As the technique can be the same in both, we may find the suspicion stirring that a tendentious joke has sources of pleasure at its disposal – by virtue of its tendency – to which innocuous jokes have no access.

It is now easy to give an overview of the tendencies present in jokes. Where a joke is not an end in itself, i.e., innocuous, it puts itself at the service of two tendencies only, which can themselves be merged into a single viewpoint; it is either a *hostile* joke (used for aggression, satire, defence) or it is an *obscene* joke (used to strip someone naked [*Entblößung*]). Again, we should note from the start that the technical variety[8] [*Art*] of the joke – whether it is a verbal or an intellectual joke – bears no relation to these two tendencies.

But it will take us longer to lay out the way in which jokes serve these tendencies. In this investigation I would like to begin not with hostile jokes but with obscene jokes. It is true, the latter have been deemed worthy of study far less often, as if a revulsion from their subject-matter had carried over to the object. However, let us not be thrown off course by this, for straight away we are about to come upon a borderline kind of joke which promises to throw light on more than one dark point.

We know what is understood by 'bawdry': deliberately emphasizing sexual facts and relations by talking about them. However, this definition is no more conclusive than any other. A lecture on the anatomy of the sexual organs or on the physiology of reproduction, despite this definition, need not have a single point of contact in common with bawdry. It is also characteristic of bawdy talk that it is directed at a particular person by whom the speaker is sexually aroused, and is meant to make them aware of this arousal by listening to the bawdry and so becoming sexually aroused themselves. Instead of being aroused, the person might also be made to feel shame or embarrassment, which only implies a reaction against their arousal and, in this roundabout way, an admission of it. Bawdy talk, then, is in origin directed at women and is to be regarded as the equivalent of an attempt at seduction. So if a man in male company enjoys telling or listening to bawdy stories, the original situation – which cannot be realized on account of social impediments – is also imagined as well. Anyone who laughs at the bawdy talk they have heard, is laughing like a spectator at an act of sexual aggression.

The sexual subject-matter that forms the content of bawdry includes more than what is specific to either sex; over and above this, it includes what the two sexes have in common to which the feeling of shame extends, that is, excremental subject-matter in all its range. But this is the range that sexual subject-matter has in childhood; in the imagination at this stage there exists a latrine, as it were, where what is sexual and what is excremental are distinguished badly or not at all.[9] Everywhere in the field of thinking investigated by the psychology of neuroses the sexual still includes the excremental, and is understood in the old, infantile, sense.

Bawdry is like an act of unclothing the person of different sex at whom it is directed. By voicing the obscene words it forces the person attacked to imagine the particular part of the body or the act involved and shows them that the aggressor himself is imagining it. There is no doubt that the pleasure in gazing on what is sexual revealed in its nakedness is the original motive of bawdy talk.

It can only help to clarify matters if at this point we go back to fundamentals. The inclination to gaze on what is specific to each sex in its nakedness is one of the original components of our libido. Perhaps it is already a substitute itself, deriving from the pleasure, posited as being primary, of touching what is sexual. As so often, gazing has replaced touching here too.[10] The libido for looking and touching is of two kinds in everyone, active and passive, masculine and feminine, and develops in the one or the other direction according to which sexual character is predominant. In young children it is easy to observe the inclination to show themselves naked. Where the germ of this inclination does not meet the usual fate of eclipse and suppression, it develops in adult men into the perversion known as exhibitionism. In women, the passive inclination to exhibitionism is almost invariably eclipsed by the magnificent reactive feat of sexual modesty – but not without saving a little escape hatch for it in their clothes. I need only hint at how versatile and variable according to convention and circumstance is the measure of exhibitionism that women are permitted to retain.

In men a high degree of this urge persists as a component of the libido and serves to introduce the sex act. If this urge asserts itself on the first approach to the woman, it has to make use of speech for two reasons. First, to lay claim to the woman, and second, because by summoning up the idea the words spoken may kindle the corresponding state of arousal in the woman herself and waken her inclination to passive exhibitionism. These words of solicitation do not go as far as bawdry, but can pass over into it. For in a situation where the woman soon becomes willing, the obscene speech is short-lived, it promptly gives way to a sexual action. It is different if the woman's willingness cannot be counted on, and a defensive reaction on her part makes its appearance instead. Then the sexually arousing speech becomes – in the form of bawdry – an end in itself; as the sexual aggression is checked in its advance towards the act, it lingers on the evocation of arousal and derives pleasure from signs of it in the woman. In doing so, the aggression probably also changes character, in the same way as every movement in the libido does when it meets an obstacle; it becomes plain hostile, cruel, that is, it calls on the sadistic components of the sexual drive for help against the obstacle.

The woman's intransigence, then, is the most immediate prerequisite for bawdry to develop, though one which merely seems to imply postponement, offering the prospect that further efforts might not be in vain. The ideal case of this kind of resistance on the woman's part occurs if another man, a third party, is present at the same time, for then any immediate acquiescence from the woman is as good as out of the question. This third party soon becomes very important for the development of the bawdry; but above all we should not disregard the presence of the woman. Among country people or in lower-class taverns one can observe that it is only when the barmaid or the landlady comes on the scene that the bawdry gets going; the opposite occurs only when we reach a higher social level, and the presence of a female person puts an end to the bawdry; the men save this kind of conversation – which originally presupposed the presence of a woman made ashamed – until they are 'among themselves'. And so gradually, instead of the woman, it is the spectator or in this case the listener who becomes the target audience for the bawdry, and this transformation already makes the bawdry approach the character of a joke.

From this point on, there are two factors that will claim our attention: the part played by the third person, the listener, and the conditions governing the content of the bawdy joke itself.

In general, a tendentious joke requires three persons: apart from the one who is telling the joke, it needs a second person who is taken as the object of the hostile or sexual aggression, and a third in whom the joke's intention of producing pleasure is fulfilled. We shall have to look for the deeper grounds for these relations later, but for the moment let us keep to the fact they signal: the person who tells the joke is not the one who also laughs at it and so enjoys the pleasure it produces, but the inactive listener. In the case of bawdry, the three persons have the same relations. The course of its development can be described thus: as the first person finds his satisfaction inhibited by the woman, his libidinal impulse develops a hostile tendency towards this second person and calls on the third, originally the intruder, to be his ally. The first person's bawdy talk strips the woman naked before the third, who is now, as listener, bribed – by the effortless satisfaction of his own libido.

It is curious how very popular bawdy exchanges of this kind are among the common people and how they never fail to rouse a mood of cheerful humour. But it is also worth noticing that in this complicated process, which has so many of the characteristics of the tendentious joke, none of the formal requirements that are the sign of a joke are expected of bawdry. To talk dirty without disguising it gives pleasure to the first person and makes the second laugh.

Only when we rise into more cultivated society do we find the addition of the formal requirements for jokes. The bawdry becomes witty, and is tolerated only if it is witty. The technical device it uses most is allusion, i.e., replacement by something small, something remotely related that the listener can reconstruct in his imagination into a full and plain obscenity. The greater the disproportion between what is given directly in the joke and what it has necessarily aroused in the listener, the subtler the joke, and the higher it may dare enter into good society. Apart from allusion, coarse or subtle, the bawdy joke has all the other devices of verbal and intellectual jokes at its disposal, as can easily be shown in examples.

Here at last we can understand what a joke can do for its tendency. It makes the satisfaction of a drive possible (be it lustful or hostile) in face of an obstacle in its way; it circumvents this obstacle and in doing so draws pleasure from a source that the obstacle had made inaccessible. The obstacle in the way is actually nothing other than woman's increased inability, in conformity with a higher cultural and social level, to tolerate sexual matters undisguised. The woman thought of as being present in the original situation is simply kept on as if she were there, or, even in her absence, her influence continues to have the effect of making the men abashed. One may observe how men of a higher social level are prompted by the presence of girls of a lower class to let their bawdy jokes revert to simple bawdy talk.

The power that makes it difficult or impossible for women, and to a lesser extent men too, to enjoy undisguised obscenity we call 'repression', and we recognize in it the same psychical process which in cases of serious [psychological] illness keeps entire complexes of impulses as well as their issue far from consciousness, and which has turned out to be one of the main causal factors in what are called the psycho-neuroses. We grant that higher culture and education have a great influence on the development of repression, and we assume that under these conditions a change in psychical organization comes about, which could also be contributed by an inherited disposition, with the result that what was once felt to be agreeable now appears unacceptable and is rejected with all the force of the psyche. Through our culture's work of repression, primary possibilities of enjoyment, now spurned by the censorship within us, are lost. But all renunciation is very difficult for the human psyche, and so we find that tendentious jokes provide a means of reversing [the process of] renunciation and of regaining what was lost. When we laugh at an indecent joke that is subtle, we are laughing at the same thing that causes the bumpkin to laugh in a coarse obscenity; in both cases the pleasure is drawn from the same source; but we would not be capable of laughing at the coarse obscenity, we would be ashamed, or it would appear disgusting to us; we can only laugh when the joke has come to our help.

What we surmised at the outset, then, seems to be confirmed: that the tendentious joke has other sources of pleasure at its disposal than the innocuous kind, where all the pleasure is somehow linked to technique. We can also emphasize afresh that in tendentious jokes we are not capable of distinguishing by our feeling which share of our pleasure has its source in technique, and which in tendency. *So we do not in the strict sense know what we are laughing at.* In the case of all obscene jokes, we are subject to gross illusions of judgement as to how 'good' the joke is, in so far as this depends on formal requirements; the technique of these jokes is often pretty feeble, the laughter they provoke tremendous.

[C]

Let us now examine whether the part played by jokes is the same when they serve a hostile tendency.

From the start we come upon the same conditions here. Our hostile impulses towards our fellows – ever since our childhood as individuals as well as since the childhood of human culture – have been subject to the same restrictions, the same progressive repressions, as our sexual urges. We have not advanced so far that we are able to love our enemies, nor, being smitten on the right cheek, turn the left also;[11] and today, even, all the moral precepts restraining us from putting our hate into action still carry the clearest indications that they were originally meant to apply to the small community of our fellow-tribesmen. As well as legitimately feeling that we belong to one people, we also permit ourselves to disregard most of these restraints in our attitude towards an alien people. All the same, within our own circle we have made some progress in mastering our hostile impulses; as Lichtenberg puts it so sharply:

'Where we now say "Excuse me", we once used to give them a cuff over the ear.' Violent hostility, forbidden by law, has given way to verbal invective, while better knowledge of how human impulses are interconnected, together with the 'tout comprendre c'est tout pardonner' which follows logically from it, robs us more and more of the ability to get angry with the fellow-creature[12] who has got in our way. As children still endowed with powerful dispositions towards enmity, we later learn in the course of our more highly developed personal culture that it is unworthy to call people names; and even where a fight is actually permitted, the number of things that may not be employed as a means of carrying it on have increased markedly. Ever since we have had to give up expressing hostility by our actions – deterred from doing so by the unimpassioned third person, for it is in their interest that the safety of their persons should be preserved – we have developed a new technique of insult, just as we did in the case of sexual aggression, which aims to draw this third person into becoming an ally against our enemy. By making our enemy small, mean, contemptible, comical, we take a roundabout route to getting for ourselves the enjoyment of vanquishing him, which the third person – who has gone to no effort – endorses with his laughter.

We are now prepared for the part played in hostile aggression by the joke. The joke will allow us to turn to good account those ridiculous features in our enemy that the presence of opposing obstacles would not let us utter aloud or consciously; again, that is, it will *get around restrictions and open up sources of pleasure that have become inaccessible*. It will, further, bribe the listener with his own gain in pleasure into taking our side without probing very far, just as on other occasions we ourselves, bribed by an innocuous joke, usually overestimate the content of a statement if it is wittily expressed. Our language has a saying, 'to have the laugh on one's side', which hits the mark exactly.

Let us look, for example, at the witticisms made by Herr N. which were scattered over the previous pages. They are all of them insults. It is as if Herr N. wanted to shout out loud: 'But the Minister of Agriculture is an ass himself!' [pp. 20–21] 'Don't talk to me about

***; he's bursting with vanity!' [p. 19] 'I've never read anything more boring than this historian's essays on Napoleon in Austria!' [p. 17]. But his high degree of personal cultivation makes it impossible for him to give vent to these judgements of his in this form. That is why they have recourse to jokes, for jokes will ensure them a reception with the listener which, despite the truth they might well contain, they would never have found in an unjoking form. One of these jokes – the 'roter Fadian' [p. 17] – is particularly instructive, perhaps the most convincing of them all. What is there about it that compels us to laugh and diverts our interest so completely away from asking whether it is doing the poor writer an injustice or not? Certainly the joking form, the joke, that is; but what are we laughing at when we do? Without doubt at the person himself who is presented to us as the 'roter Fadian', and at his red hair in particular. The cultivated person has got out of the habit of laughing at physical disabilities, nor in his eyes does having red hair count as one of the physical disadvantages worth laughing at either. But it certainly still does to schoolboys and the common people, and even at the cultural level of certain Municipal Councillors and Members of Parliament. And now this joke of Herr N.'s has in the cleverest way made it possible for us, delicate-minded adults that we are, to laugh like schoolboys at the historian's red hair. This was certainly not Herr N.'s intention; but it is very doubtful whether anyone who gives his jokes free rein is bound to be aware of their precise intention.

While in these cases the obstacle to the aggression that the joke helped to get round was internal – an aesthetic objection to the insult – in other cases it may be purely external. As in the case where His Majesty is struck by the stranger's striking resemblance to his own person and asks him: 'Was your mother once in service at the palace?' and the stranger's quick-witted reply is: 'No, but my father was' [p. 58]. He would surely like to knock the insolent questioner down for daring to cast aspersions on the memory of his beloved mother with such an insinuation; but this insolent questioner is His Majesty, and one may not knock him down or even insult him if one does not wish to pay for this revenge with one's whole existence. The thing to do, then, would be to swallow the insult in silence; but

99

fortunately the joke shows the way to repaying the insult unscathed – by picking up the allusion in the technical device of unification and turning it against the assailant. Our impression that this is a joke is so strongly determined here by its tendency, that in view of the joking riposte we are inclined to forget that the assailant's question, in its use of allusion, is a joke itself.

The prevention of an insult or an abusive reply by external circumstances happens so often that the tendentious joke is a particular favourite for use in enabling criticism or aggression towards persons in high places who claim authority [to be voiced]. The joke then represents a rebellion against such authority, a liberation from the oppression it imposes. This is the factor, of course, that also makes caricature so attractive to us – we laugh at it even when it is badly done, merely because we consider rebellion against authority to be a creditable thing.

If we bear in mind that the tendentious joke is so well suited to attacking the great, the dignified and the mighty – powers protected from direct disparagement by internal inhibitions or external circumstances – then we are forced into a particular view of certain groups of jokes which seemingly have to do with inferior and powerless figures. I mean the marriage-broker stories, some of which we met when we were examining the various techniques employed in the intellectual joke. In some of them, e.g., in the examples 'And she's deaf as well' [p. 55] and 'Who would lend these people anything!' [p. 55], the marriage-broker was laughed at for being an indiscreet and thoughtless figure who became comical because he let out the truth automatically, as it were. But does what we have learned about the nature of the tendentious joke on the one hand and the great amusement we have from these stories on the other chime with the wretchedness of the figures the joke seems to be laughing at? Are they worthy adversaries for the joke? Is it not rather the case that the joke is only pushing the brokers into the foreground in order to hit a more important target, or, as the saying is, 'striking the sack, and intending the ass'? This view really cannot be dismissed.

This interpretation of the marriage-broker stories can be taken further. It is true that I do not need to go into them closely; I can be content with regarding these stories as *Schwänke* [comic folk-tales], and deny that they have the character of a joke. So what is taken to be a joke, then, also depends on subjective factors of this kind; this is something we have now noticed and shall have to examine later on. It means that only what I say is a proper joke is a joke. What is a joke to me can be just a comic story to someone else. But if a joke admits of this doubt, it can only be because it has one side for show, a façade – in our instances a comical façade – which will satisfy the eyes of one viewer, while another may try to look behind it. The suspicion may begin to stir that this façade is meant to dazzle the probing eye, that stories of this kind have something to hide.

In any case, if our marriage-broker stories are jokes, they are all the better as jokes because their façade has put them in a position to hide not only what they have to say, but also that they have something – forbidden – to say. But if we take the interpretation further and reveal what is hidden, unmasking these stories with their comical façade as tendentious jokes, it would run as follows: anyone who lets the truth slip like this in an unguarded moment is actually glad to be free of the pretence. That is a true psychological insight of deep penetration. Without some assent of this kind, no one would allow themselves to be overcome by the automatism that brings the truth to light in these stories.[13] But this now transforms the ridiculous figure of the *Schadchen* into a sympathetic and pitiable one. How happy the man must be that at last he can throw off the burden of pretence, if he promptly takes the first opportunity to cry aloud the final scrap of truth! As soon as he sees that the cause is lost, that the bride does not charm the young man, he will gladly reveal that she has yet another hidden flaw that the suitor has not noticed, or he will take advantage of the occasion when he has to come up with an argument settling a detail to express his contempt for the people he is working for: I ask you, who would lend those people anything! The entire ridicule now falls on the parents, only touched on in the story, for approving of such a swindle just to get their daughters a husband, on the pitiful situation of girls who let themselves be married under such arrangements, and on the shamefulness of marriages contracted after such introductions. The broker is the right man to express such criticism, for he more than anyone knows of these abuses, but he may not broadcast them aloud, as he is a poor man who can make a living only by exploiting them. But a similar conflict also marks the popular mind that created these and similar stories; for it knows that the sanctity of marriages already contracted will fare ill if attention is drawn to the procedures that go on in contracting them.

Let us recall what we observed in examining the technique of jokes: that absurdity in a joke frequently substitutes for mockery and criticism in the thought behind the joke – and in this respect the joke-work is doing the same as the dream-work; here we find this state of affairs freshly confirmed. That the mockery and criticism is not directed at the person of the broker, who makes his appearance in the previous examples just as the whipping-boy, can be demonstrated by a number of other jokes in which the broker, quite to the contrary, is described as the figure who comes out on top, with an argument to deal with every difficulty. These are the stories with a logical façade, instead of a comical one, sophistical intellectual jokes. In one of these (pp. 53–4), the broker has the art of arguing away the flaw of the bride's limp. It is at least 'ready-made'; by contrast, another wife whose limbs were straight would be in constant danger of falling down and breaking a leg, and then there would be the illness, the pain, the doctor's bills, which the husband would save if his wife had a limp already. Or in another story he knows how to refute any number of the suitor's objections to the bride, with a good argument for each one, answering him then at the last, unwhitewashable, one: 'So? She's not to have one single fault?' [p. 52], as if some remnant were not necessarily left over from the earlier causes for demur. It is not difficult to point out the weak point in the argumentation in both examples; we already did so when we examined their technique. But now something else interests us. If the broker's words are given such a strong appearance of logic, which reveals itself on careful scrutiny to be [just that] – appearance – then the truth behind it is that the joke declares the broker is in the right; the thought is not bold enough to say he is in the right seriously, and replaces this serious truth with the appearance presented by the joke. But here as so frequently the jest betrays the serious truth. We will not go astray if we assume that all these stories with a logical façade really mean what they say with their intentionally faulty reasoning. It is only its use of sophistry for the hidden representation of the truth that makes it a joke in character, one, that is, mainly dependent on its tendency. For in both stories what is meant to be suggested is that the suitor is really making himself ridiculous when he goes looking so carefully for the bride's separate good points, which all turn out to be handicaps, forgetting as he does so that he has to be prepared to take for his wife a human being with unavoidable frailties, while on the other hand the only quality that would make marriage with the more or less imperfect personality of the wife tolerable would be fondness on both sides and readiness for loving adaptation – which is not once mentioned in the entire transaction.

The mockery of the suitor in these examples – where the broker now most appropriately plays the part of the figure who comes out on top – is expressed far more clearly in other anecdotes. The more transparent these stories are, the less joke-technique they contain; they are, as it were, only borderline cases of jokes, rather sharing with their technique only the formation of a façade. But as they have the same tendency and also hide it behind a façade, it is appropriate that they should have the full effect of a joke. In addition, their poverty in technical resources explains why so many jokes of this kind cannot do without the comical element of argot – which has a similar effect to a joke – without losing a great deal.

The following is a story of this kind; for all its power as a tendentious joke, it no longer shows any trace of joke-technique: 'The broker asks: "What do you want of your bride?" – Answer: "She must be beautiful, she must be rich, and educated." – "Fine," says the broker, "but I make that three wives."' Here the rebuke is delivered to the husband directly, no longer in the disguise of a joke.

In the examples so far the veiled aggression was still directed against people, in the marriage-broker stories against all the parties taking part in the marriage transaction: bride, bridegroom and their parents. But the joke's objects of attack could just as well be institutions, persons in so far as they are representative of the institutions, moral or religious precepts, philosophies of life enjoying such great respect that any criticism of them can only make an appearance masked as a joke, that is, as a joke hidden by its façade. However few the topics this tendentious joke has for a target, its forms and disguises are extremely various. I think we are right to give this group of tendentious jokes a distinctive name. Which name is the appropriate one will emerge after we have interpreted some examples.

I recall the two stories – the one of the impoverished gourmet who was caught out eating 'salmon with mayonnaise' [pp. 41–2], and the other of the alcoholic tutor [p. 44] – which we got to know as sophistical displacement jokes. I shall take their interpretation further. We have since heard that if a story's façade has the appearance of logic attached to it, the thought would probably like to say seriously: 'the man is right' – but on account of some opposition countering it, it is not bold enough to say so except by making the one point where it is easy to show that he is wrong. The 'pointe' chosen is the precise point of compromise between where he is right and where he is wrong – which is certainly not a decision, but corresponds, I suggest, to the conflict in ourselves. The two stories are simply epicurean. They are saying: 'Yes, the man is right; there is nothing greater than enjoyment, and it doesn't really matter how you get it.' That sounds terribly immoral, and it probably is not much better than the 'carpe diem [seize the day]'[14] of the poet, who appeals to the insecurity of life and the barrenness of virtuous self-denial; fundamentally, that is what it is. If the idea that the man in the 'salmon with mayonnaise' joke is supposed to be right puts us off so much, this does not come about because it is illustrating a truth with an indulgence of the lowest sort which, it seems to us, we can well do without. In reality, every one of us has had hours and times when he has given this philosophy of life its due and upbraided morality for only being able to make demands without any compensations. Ever since we no longer believe the directive [to think on] the Beyond, where all self-denial shall be rewarded with gratification –

there are, by the way, very few of the godly if we make self-denial the distinguishing mark of faith – ever since then, 'carpe diem' has become a serious reminder. I would gladly postpone my gratification, but do I know if I'll still be there tomorrow?

'Di doman' non c'è certezza [There is no certainty about tomorrow].'[15]

I would gladly do without all the avenues to gratification that society disapproves of, but am I certain that society will reward my self-denial – even though with some postponement – by opening to me one of the permitted avenues? It is possible to say out loud what these jokes whisper: that the wishes and desires of human beings have a right to make themselves heard as much as demanding and ruthless morality, and in our times it has been said in forceful and stirring sentences[16] that this morality is only the selfish ordinance of the rich and powerful few who are able to satisfy their wishes without postponement at any time. As long as the art of healing has not gone further in making our life more certain, and as long as social arrangements do not do more to make it more agreeable, the voice in us that rebels against the demands of morality will not be stifled. In the end every honest person will make this admission, at least to themselves. This conflict can only be decided by a roundabout route via a fresh insight. We must link our lives to that of others in such a way, we must be able to identify with others so closely, that we are able to overcome the curtailment of our own lifetime; and we may not fulfil the demands of our own needs illegitimately, but must leave them unfulfilled, because only the continued existence of so many unfulfilled demands is able to develop the power to change the social order. But not all personal needs can be postponed and transferred to others in this way, and a universal and ultimate solution to the conflict does not exist.

Now we know what we should call jokes like the last [two] we have interpreted: they are *cynical* jokes, and what they conceal are *cynicisms*.

Among all the institutions the cynical joke habitually attacks, there is none more important, more powerfully protected by moral precepts, nor more inviting of attack than the institution of marriage, which is, accordingly, also the target for the majority of cynical jokes. No claim is more personal than that for sexual freedom, and nowhere has culture attempted to exercise greater suppression than in the field of sexuality. For our purposes one single example will suffice, from the 'Entry in the Joke Book of Prince Carnival' mentioned on p. 67:

'*A wife is like an umbrella. After all, before long one takes a cab.*'

We have already discussed the complicated technique in this example: a baffling, apparently impossible, comparison, but one which, as we now see, is not in itself a joke; in addition, an allusion (cab = public vehicle), and, as its most powerful technical device, an omission which increases its unintelligibility. The comparison could be analysed in the following way: one marries to be safe from the onslaughts of sensuality, and then all the same it turns out that marriage does not allow the satisfaction of rather stronger needs, just as one takes an umbrella for protection against the rain and then still gets wet in the rain. In both cases one has to look around for stronger protection, in the one a public vehicle, in the other women available for money. The joke is now almost entirely replaced by cynicism. That marriage is not an institution that satisfies the husband's sexuality is something one is not bold enough to say out loud and in public, unless perhaps one is driven to it by the love of truth and reforming zeal of a Christian von Ehrenfels.[17] For the strength of this joke lies in the fact that it has, after all, by all manner of roundabout routes, said it.

A situation particularly favourable to the tendentious joke is set up when the intended criticism of protest is directed against one's self, or, put more circumspectly, against a person in whom that self has a share, a collective person, that is, one's own people, for example. This determinant of self-criticism may explain to us how it is that a number of the most telling jokes – of which we have given plenty of examples – have grown from the soil of Jewish popular life. They are stories invented by Jews and aimed at Jewish characteristics. The jokes made about Jews by outsiders [*Fremden*] are mostly brutal comic anecdotes, in which [the effort of making] a proper joke is saved by the fact that to the outsider the Jew counts as a comical figure. The Jewish jokes originating with Jews admit this too, but they know their real faults and how they are related to their good points; and the share the raconteur's own person has in what is being criticized creates the subjective conditions for the joke-work that are otherwise difficult to set up. By the way, I do not know whether it often happens in other instances that a people should make fun of its own nature to such an extent.

As an example of this I can draw attention to the story mentioned on p. 69 of the Jew on the train who promptly abandoned all decent manners the moment he recognized that the new arrival in the carriage was of the same religion. We met this joke as an instance of illustration by a detail, of representation by means of something very small; it is meant to illustrate the democratic style of thinking among Jews, which does not acknowledge any difference between master and man, but unfortunately also upsets discipline and co-operation. Another, particularly interesting, group of jokes portrays the relations of poor and rich Jews to one another; their heroes are the *Schnorrer* and the charitable householder or the Baron. The *Schnorrer*, who is admitted as a guest to the same house every Sunday, appears one day accompanied by an unfamiliar young man who looks set to sit down and join everyone at table. 'Who's he?' asks the master of the house, and receives the reply: 'He's my son-in-law as of last week; I've promised him his board for the first year.' The tendency in these stories is always the same. It will come to the fore most clearly in the following one: the *Schnorrer* begs the Baron for money to make a sea journey to Ostend; the doctor has recommended sea-bathing for his complaints. In the Baron's opinion, Ostend is a particularly expensive place to stay; somewhere cheaper would also do. But the *Schnorrer* rejects this suggestion with the words: 'Herr Baron, for my health, nothing is too expensive.' This is a splendid displacement joke, which we could take as the model of its genre. The Baron clearly wants to save his money, but the *Schnorrer* answers as if the Baron's money were his own, which he may then of course regard as less important than his health. We are invited to laugh here at the effrontery of the claim, but it is exceptional for these jokes not to be provided with a façade to mislead our understanding. The truth behind this one is that the *Schnorrer* who in his thoughts treats the rich man's money as his own, has, according to the sacred ordinances of the Jews, in reality almost a right to make this mix-up. The protest that created this joke is of course directed against the Law that presses heavily upon even the pious.

Another story tells of how on the steps of a rich man's house a *Schnorrer* encounters a fellow in his trade who advises him not to continue his way. 'Don't go on up today, the Baron's in a bad mood, he's not giving anyone more than one florin.' – 'I will go up all the same,' says the first *Schnorrer*. 'Why should I give him the one florin. Is he giving *me* anything?'

This joke makes use of the technique of absurdity by having the *Schnorrer* assert that the Baron is giving him nothing at the very moment he is getting ready to beg for the gift. But the absurdity is only apparent; it is almost true that the rich man is giving him nothing, for he is obliged by the Law to make the beggar a gift of alms, and, strictly speaking, should be grateful to him for giving him the opportunity to do good. The common, middle-class view of charity is in conflict here with the religious one. It is in open revolt against the religious view in the story of the Baron who is moved so deeply by the *Schnorrer*'s tale of suffering that he rings for his servants: 'Throw him out – he's breaking my heart!' This open declaration of its tendency again produces a borderline joke. The only difference between the complaint (for it is no longer a joke): 'It is really no advantage to be a rich man among Jews. Other people's misery doesn't give you the chance to enjoy your own good fortune' and these last stories, is that the stories illustrate it in a single situation.

Other stories that again are technically borderline jokes testify to a deeply pessimistic cynicism – such as the following: A man who is hard of hearing consults the doctor, who makes the correct diagnosis: the patient probably drinks too much brandy and that's why he is deaf. He advises the deaf man against drinking, and the deaf man promises to take the advice to heart. After a while the doctor meets him in the street and asks him in a loud voice how he is feeling.

'Thank you,' comes the reply, 'you don't have to shout, doctor, I've given up drinking and I can hear again very well.' A while later they encounter each other once more. The doctor asks in his ordinary voice how his patient is feeling, but notices that he is not being understood. 'What's that?' – 'It seems to me that you're back to drinking brandy,' the doctor shouts in his ear, 'and that's why you can't hear anything again!' 'You may be right,' replies the man who is hard of hearing. 'I'm back to drinking brandy, but I'll tell you why. As long as I wasn't drinking, I could hear; but nothing I heard was as good as the brandy.' Technically, this joke is simply an illustration; argot and skill in storytelling are needed to help in raising a laugh, but behind the anecdote there lurks the unhappy question: 'Wasn't the man right in his choice?'

What these pessimistic stories are alluding to is the manifold and hopeless misery of the Jews, and it is on account of this wider connection that I have to include them among the tendentious jokes.

Other similarly cynical jokes, not only Jewish anecdotes, attack religious dogmas and even belief in God. The story of the Rabbi's [miraculous] 'gaze' [p. 54], where the technique consisted of the flaw in thinking that equated fantasy and reality (it would also be tenable to interpret it as displacement), is a cynical or critical joke of this kind directed at the miracle-worker and certainly against belief in miracles too. As a dying man, Heine is supposed to have made a joke that in his situation was positively blasphemous. When the priest in his kindness reminded him of God's mercy and gave him hope that in God he would find forgiveness for his sins, he is said to have replied: 'Bien sûr qu'il me pardonnera; *c'est son métier.*' That is a degrading comparison, technically more or less with the value of an allusion, for a *métier*, a job or a calling, is something a tradesman has, maybe, or a physician, that is, he has only one *métier*. But the power of the joke lies in its tendency. What it intends to say is simply and solely: of course he will forgive me – after all, that's what he is there for; I haven't taken him on for any other purpose (as one retains a physician or a lawyer). And so in the dying man, lying there powerless, there stirs the consciousness that he has created God and endowed him with power so that he can make use of him when required. Shortly before its annihilation the supposed creature God still declares itself to be the creator.

[D]

To the genres of tendentious jokes we have dealt with so far,

> jokes that strip naked, or obscene jokes,
>
> aggressive (hostile) jokes,
>
> cynical (critical, blasphemous) jokes,

I should like to add a new one as the fourth and least common, whose characteristics can be illustrated by a good example.

Two Jews meet in a railway carriage at a station in Galicia. 'Where are you travelling?' asks the one. 'To Cracow,' comes the answer. 'Look what a liar you are!' the other protests. 'When you say you're going to Cracow, you want me to believe that you're going to Lemberg. But I know that you're really going to Cracow. So why are you lying?'

This delicious story, with its impression of extravagant logic-chopping, clearly works by means of the technique of absurdity. The second Jew is to take being upbraided for his lies because he says he is travelling to Cracow – which is in fact his destination! But here, this powerful technical device – absurdity – is coupled with another technique, representation by the opposite, for according to the unspoken assertion of the first Jew, the other is lying when he is telling the truth, and telling the truth with a lie. But the more serious content of this joke is the question of what determines truth. Again, the joke is pointing to a problem and exploiting the uncertainty of one of our most common concepts. Is it truth when we describe things as they are, without bothering about how our listener will understand what we have said? Or is this only a jesuitical truth, and does not genuine truthfulness rather consist in taking the listener into account and conveying to him a true likeness of our own knowledge? I regard jokes of this kind as being sufficiently distinct from the others to be allotted a special position. What they are attacking is not a person or an institution, but the very certainty of our knowledge itself, one of our speculative goods. The name of *'sceptical'* jokes, then, would be the appropriate one for them.

[E]

In the course of discussing the tendencies and intentions of the joke we have perhaps been able to cast light on many aspects, and we have certainly found ample incentive for further investigations. But the results we have reached in this section combine with those in the previous one to produce a difficult problem. If it is true that the pleasure given by a joke is attached on the one hand to its technique and on the other to its tendency and intention, what is the common aspect under which these two sources of pleasure in the joke – so different from each other – can be united?

Notes

1. [Freud seems to have been stung by such games with his own name, which means 'joy'. See *The Interpretation of Dreams*, V.B.]
2. [The literal rendering, of course, has no relevance to the playful interchange of consonants.]
3. [A telling metaphor, which indicates the degree to which Freud is prepared to separate content and form – despite his insistence on how the effectiveness of a joke depends on its form (which he always refers to as its 'expression'), and despite his elaborate taxonomy of forms following from this. His 'reductions', of course, assume this separability from the start, and his suggestion that the (still indispensable) form of the joke ultimately functions only as fore-pleasure builds on it. Freud is on the edge here of a larger literary theory, one that runs counter to the classical aesthetics he found in Kuno Fischer. The metaphor itself is an ancient religious trope for the relation of body to soul.]
4. [Freud uses this word rarely, elsewhere preferring *Inhalt*, to which he reverts in the last paragraph of this section. *Gehalt* is a word in which literary and chemical usages conflict. In chemistry, it indicates quantitative content; in aesthetics – as distinguished by Goethe in his *Noten und Abhandlungen*

zum West-östlichen Divan (*East-west Divan*) (1819) – it indicates the meaning intrinsic to the form. Freud's use appears to be closer to the former sense, and he uses the word interchangeably with his preferred *Inhalt*, i.e., 'content as contained' – like the clock in the case, or the thought in the joke. I have rendered both words by 'content', but indicated locally where *Gehalt* is used.]

5. Cf. my *Psychopathologie des Alltagslebens* [*Psychopathology of Everyday Life*], Berlin: S. Karger, 1904, 4th ed. 1912 [X].

6. R. Kleinpaul, *Die Rätsel der Sprache*, 1890.

7. [Home Rule for Ireland was a recurring question in the last decades of the nineteenth century. Freud is probably referring here to the debates before and after Gladstone's Second Home Rule Bill of 1893, which, like its predecessor, was defeated in the House of Lords.]

8. [I have used 'variety' here and elsewhere for the German *Art*. A flatter way of rendering it would be by the all-purpose 'kind', but the specialized nature of Freud's discourse requires something more distinctive. One would expect him here to use the specific literary term *Gattung* [genre], but in fact, that is a word he rarely uses, preferring *Art*, the term used in the natural sciences for 'species' or 'variety'. Cumulative use of 'species' as a category term would tend to over-scientize the text, so I have settled largely for the word that is at home in the natural sciences, but not exclusively so.]

9. See my *Drei Abhandlungen über die Sexualtheorie* [*Three Essays on the Theory of Sexuality*], 1905, appearing at the same time as this study, 2nd ed. 1910.

10. Moll's contrectation drive (*Untersuchungen über die Libido sexualis*, 1898).

11. [Variant of Matthew 5.39.]

12. [Echo of Matthew 5.22.]

13. It is the same mechanism that governs 'slips of the tongue' and other self-betraying phenomena.

14. [Horace, *Odes*, I.xi.8.]

15. Lorenzo de' Medici. [From *Il Trionfo di Bacco e di Arianna*.]

16. [Possibly Nietzsche's?]

17. See his essays in the *Politisch-anthropologische Revue* II, 1903.

B Synthetic Part

IV The Mechanism of Pleasure and the Psychological Origins of the Joke

[A]

Our knowledge of where the peculiar pleasure afforded us by jokes has its sources is something we can now take as our starting-point, regarding it as established. We know that we may succumb to the illusion of confusing our enjoyment of a statement's thought-content with our actual pleasure from it as a joke, but that the latter has itself essentially two sources: in its technique and in its intention or tendency. What we would now like to find out is *how* this pleasure arises from these sources, the mechanism of this pleasurable effect.

It seems that the explanation we are looking for will be found much more easily in tendentious jokes than in the innocuous sort. So we shall begin with the former.

Our pleasure in a tendentious joke arises from the satisfaction of an intention or tendency which – the satisfaction – would not otherwise have taken place. That such satisfaction is a source of pleasure needs no further explanation. But the way in which a joke will bring about this satisfaction is linked to particular conditions from which further information may perhaps be gained. Two cases are to be distinguished here. The simpler case is when satisfying the intention is barred by some external obstacle which the joke is able to get round. This is what we found, for example, in the answer His Royal Highness received when he asked whether the mother of the man he was addressing had ever lived in the palace [p. 58], or in the connoisseur's when the two rich rogues exhibited their portraits [p. 64]: 'And where is the Saviour?' The intention in the one instance aims at paying back a slur in the same coin, in the other at offering an insult instead of the expert opinion required; it is faced with purely external factors, the powerful positions of the persons the insults are aimed at. All the same, it may strike us that these and similar jokes of a tendentious nature, however much they may satisfy us, are not able to provoke a great deal of laughter.

It is different if the bar to realizing the intention directly is not any external factor but an internal obstacle, if the intention is opposed by an inner impulse. On our assumption, this condition would be realized, for example, in the aggressive witticisms of Herr N., in whose person a strong inclination to invective is held in check by a highly developed aesthetic cultivation. In this particular case, internal resistance is overcome and inhibition lifted with the aid of a joke. This enables the intention to be satisfied, as it was in the case of an external obstacle, and suppression avoided, together with the 'psychical damming-up'[1] involved; to this extent, the mechanism giving rise to pleasure would be the same in both cases.

At this point, though, we feel inclined to go more deeply into the differences in psychological situation between the cases of internal and external obstacle, as we have an inkling that lifting the inner obstacle might possibly give rise to an incomparably greater contribution to the pleasure. But I suggest we remain moderate at this point and for the moment content ourselves with the one firm observation which for us is still the essential thing. The only difference between cases of external and internal obstacle is that in the latter an inhibition which already existed is lifted, while in the former the creation of a new one is avoided. So we shall not be speculating overmuch if we declare that in creating, as in maintaining, a psychical inhibition some 'psychical expenditure' is required. Now, if it follows that in both cases where a tendentious joke is employed, pleasure is produced, then it is reasonable to assume *that this gain in pleasure corresponds to the saving in psychical expenditure*.

With this we seem to be coming again upon the principle of *economizing*, which we first met in the technique of verbal jokes. But whereas to start with we believed we found economizing in the use of as few and as similar words as possible, here we begin to suspect that economizing in psychical expenditure altogether must have a far more comprehensive meaning, and we must consider it a possibility that a closer definition of this still very unclear concept of 'psychical expenditure' may bring us closer to the essential nature of the joke.

A certain lack of clarity, which we have not been able to overcome in dealing with the mechanism of pleasure in tendentious jokes, is something we will accept as a fair punishment for having attempted to explain the more complicated thing in advance of the simpler, tendentious jokes before innocuous ones. We note that *'saving in effort spent on inhibition or suppression'* seemed to be the secret of the pleasurable effect of tendentious jokes, and turn to the mechanism of pleasure in innocuous jokes.

From suitable examples of innocuous jokes, where there was no risk that either content or intention would upset our judgement, we were obliged to conclude that the technical devices of jokes were themselves sources of pleasure, and we shall now examine whether this pleasure could perhaps be traced back to economizing on psychical expenditure. In one group of these jokes (word-play) the technique consisted of drawing the attention of our psyche to the sound of a word instead of to its sense, making our (acoustic) representation of the word [*Wortvorstellung*] itself take the place of its meaning as conferred on it by its relations to the representations we make of the thing [*Dingvorstellungen*]. We may really suspect that this brings great relief to the work of the psyche, and that when we are using words for serious purposes, we have to make a certain effort to refrain from this convenient procedure. We can observe that pathological states of thought-activity, in which the possibility of concentrating psychical expenditure on one point is probably limited, do in fact bring this kind of representation of a word's sound to the fore more than its meaning, and that when they are speaking, such pathological cases proceed according to the 'external' instead of the 'internal' associations of the word-representation, as the formula has it. In the case of children too, who are of course still used to treating words as things, we note their inclination to look for the same sense behind the same or similar sound, which becomes the source of many of the mistakes that grown-ups laugh at. If it then affords us unmistakable enjoyment in a joke when the use of the same or a similar word takes us from one sphere of ideas to another, remote, one (as the 'Home-roulade' joke [pp. 91–2] takes us from the kitchen to politics), it is surely correct to trace this enjoyment back to an economizing on psychical expenditure. Our pleasure in a joke afforded by a 'short-circuit' of this kind also seems to be the greater the more alien the two spheres of ideas that are brought into connection by the same word are to each other. The further apart they are from each other, the greater the consequent saving effected by the joke's technique in the route taken by our thoughts. Let us note, by the way, that the joke is making use of a linking device here that is rejected by serious thinking and scrupulously avoided.[2]

There is a second group of technical devices in jokes – unification, identity of sound, multiple use, modification of familiar sayings, allusions to quotations – where we can pick out their common characteristic being the rediscovery in each case of something familiar where we might have expected something new instead. This rediscovery of the familiar is pleasurable, and again it will not be difficult for us to to recognize this pleasure as the pleasure of economizing, and relate it to economizing on psychical expenditure.

That the rediscovery of what is familiar, 're-cognition', is pleasurable seems to be generally admitted. Groos[3] says (p. 153) 'Recognition is everywhere – where it is not over-mechanized (putting on one's clothes, for instance ...) – connected with feelings of pleasure. The mere quality of familiarity is already accompanied by that gentle sense of ease which fills Faust when he re-enters his study after an uncanny encounter...'[4] 'If the act of re-cognition rouses pleasure in this way, then we may expect that mankind will start thinking of exercising this capacity for its own sake, that is, of experimenting with it in play. In fact, Aristotle saw the basis for the enjoyment of art in the delight we take in recognition, and there is no denying that this principle should not be overlooked, even if it does not have such far-reaching significance as Aristotle assumed.'

Groos goes on to discuss those games characterized by intensifying our delight in recognition by putting obstacles in its way, that is, by bringing about a 'psychical damming-up', which is removed with the act of recognition. However, his attempt at explanation abandons the assumption that recognition is pleasurable in itself when he uses these games as the basis for training our enjoyment of recognition back to our *delight* in *power*, in overcoming a difficulty. I regard this factor as secondary, and see no cause to depart from the simpler conception that recognition, by relieving our psychical expenditure, is in itself pleasurable, and that the games based on this pleasure are just making use of this damming mechanism to increase the amount of pleasure.

Likewise, it is generally acknowledged that rhyme, alliteration, refrain and other poetic forms that repeat similar verbal sounds are also exploiting the same source of pleasure, the rediscovery of what is familiar. A 'feeling of power' does not play any perceptible part in these techniques, which show such a great correspondence to 'multiple use'.

Given the close relations between recognizing and remembering, it is no longer a daring hypothesis to propose that there is also such a thing as a pleasure in remembering, that is, that the act of remembering is intrinsically accompanied by a pleasurable feeling with a similar origin. Groos does not seem disinclined to make such an assumption, but again he derives pleasure in remembering from a 'feeling of power', which is where he looks for the chief ground of the enjoyment to be had in almost all games – in my opinion, wrongly.

The use of another technical resource in jokes, not so far discussed, also depends on the 'rediscovery of what is familiar'. I mean the factor of *topicality*, which presents a rich source of pleasure in very many jokes and will explain some peculiarities in the life-history of jokes. There are jokes that are perfectly free of this requirement, and in a treatise on jokes we are obliged to make use of examples of this kind almost exclusively. But this should not make us forget that there are other jokes which we may perhaps have laughed at even more heartily than at those of the perennial sort, but which we now have difficulty in using because they would call for such long commentaries, and even with that help would not have the effect they once did. These last jokes contain allusions to persons and events which were 'topical' at the time, roused general interest and kept it alert and alive. After this interest had died down, after the affair in question had been settled, these jokes too lost a part of their pleasurable effect, indeed, quite a considerable part. For example, the joke made by my kind host when he called the pudding being served a 'Home-roulade' does not seem to me nearly as good now as it did then, when Home Rule was a permanent headline above the political columns in our newspapers. If I try to assess the merits of this joke *now* by describing how that one word, by saving us a great detour in our thinking, leads us out of the sphere of ideas associated with the kitchen into the remote one of politics, *then* I would have had to alter this account to 'how this word from the sphere of ideas of the kitchen is taking us to the sphere of politics, which is so remote from it but which is sure of our lively interest because it is actually occupying our minds all the time'. Another joke: 'This girl reminds me of Dreyfus: the army doesn't believe in her innocence' has lost its force today, even though all its technical resources must have remained unchanged. Our bafflement at the comparison and the *double entendre* of the word 'innocence' cannot make up for the fact that the allusion, which at the time touched on a matter charged with recent excitement, reminds us today of an interest that is over and done. A joke that is still topical, such as the following, for example: Crown Princess Louise had inquired of the Crematorium in Gotha about the cost of a cremation. The management replied: 'Normally 5,000 marks, but you would only be charged 3,000, as you have already been "durchgebrannt" [lit: 'been burnt'; slang: 'eloped'] once' – a joke like this appears irresistible today; after a time it will have sunk in our estimation very considerably, and a while later still, when one will not be able to tell it without adding in a commentary on who Princess Louise was, and how her 'being burnt [having eloped]' is meant, it will, despite the neat play on words, remain without effect.

In this way a large number of jokes at present doing the rounds attain a certain lifespan, in fact a life-history, consisting of a flowering and a decline, and ending in complete oblivion. The need of human beings to obtain pleasure from the processes of their thinking is constantly creating new jokes, following the new interests of the day. The vitality of topical jokes is not authentically their own; it is borrowed by way of allusion from those other interests, and the course these run determines the fate of the joke as well. The factor of topicality – a transient source of pleasure, it is true, but one making a particularly fruitful addition to the pleasure peculiar to the joke itself – cannot simply be equated with the rediscovery of the familiar. Rather, it is a matter of a particular qualification of what is familiar: it has to be fresh, recent, untouched by forgetting. In the formation of dreams, too, we meet a particular preference for what is recent, and cannot resist supposing that the association with what is recent is rewarded, that is, made easier, by a distinctive bonus of pleasure.

Unification, which after all is only repetition in the field of thought-connections instead of subject-matter, found particular recognition from Fechner as a source of pleasure in jokes. He writes (*Vorschule der Ästhetik*, I, XVII): 'As I see it, in the field we are looking at here, the main part is played by the principle of the unification of multiplicity, but it also needs to be supported by minor additional requirements in order to push the enjoyment afforded by these cases, with its distinctive character, over the threshold.'[5]

In all these instances of repeating the same connection or the same verbal material, and of rediscovering what is familiar and recent, there is nothing to prevent us arguing that the pleasure taken in them comes from saving psychical expenditure, as long as this view proves fruitful in explaining details and reaching new generalizations. We know that we still have to make it clear how this saving comes about, and what the expression 'psychical expenditure' means.

The third group of joke-techniques – mostly in intellectual jokes – which includes faulty logic, displacements, absurdity, representation by the opposite, etc., may on first appearance carry its own particular imprint and betray no relation to the techniques of rediscovering the familiar or substituting verbal associations for associations with objects. Nevertheless, these jokes above all are where it is very easy to apply the theory of economizing or relief [*Erleichterung*] to advantage.

It is easier and more convenient to stray from a line of thought once started than hold on to it, easier to jumble up diverse things than arrange them as antitheses, especially convenient to accept modes of inference rejected by logic, and finally to ignore the fact that in putting words and thoughts together they should also make sense – of course there is no doubt about this, and this is just what the joke-techniques under discussion do. But we will be disconcerted by the proposition that activity of this kind by the joke-work should open up a source of pleasure, for when we encounter such inferior intellectual performance outside jokes, we have only unpleasurable feelings of rejection towards them.

In serious life, 'pleasure in nonsense', as we may call it for short, is concealed to the point of vanishing. To demonstrate it we have to follow up two cases, one in which it is still visible and the other in which it becomes visible once more: the behaviour of the learning child and of the adult in a toxically altered state of mind. In the period when the child is learning to handle the vocabulary of his mother tongue, he takes obvious pleasure in 'experimenting playfully' (Groos) with this material, joining the words together to get the pleasurable effect of the rhythm or rhyme, without being tied to the requirement that they should make sense. This pleasure is gradually denied him, until the only word-combinations left that he is allowed are those that make sense. In later years, attempts to get outside the hard-learned restrictions in the use of words can still be seen, as he distorts them with special suffixes, alters their forms in certain systematic ways (syllabic repetition, *Zittersprache* ['zitter' – slang': a secret language of children]) or even invents a language of his own for use among playfellows – efforts that go on to surface again in certain categories of the mentally ill.

As I see it, whatever motive the child was pursuing when he began with such games, as he develops further he indulges in them in the consciousness that they are nonsensical, and discovers enjoyment in the charm of what his reason forbids. He now makes use of play to escape the pressure of critical reason. But much more powerful are the restrictions that are bound to take effect in the course of being educated to think logically and to separate what is true in reality from what is false; that is why the rebellion against the compulsions of logic and reality goes so deep and lasts so long; even the manifestations of imaginative activity come under this viewpoint. The power of criticism has usually grown so great in the later part of childhood and in the period of learning which extends beyond puberty that pleasure in 'nonsense unbound' ['*befreiten Unsinn*[6]] is only rarely bold enough to express itself directly. We do not dare to talk nonsense; but the inclination characteristic of young boys to get up to absurd and pointless activities seems to me to be the direct issue of pleasure in nonsense. In pathological cases it is easy to see this inclination intensified to such an extent that it dominates the schoolboy's speech and replies; in some grammar-school boys [*Gymnasiasten*] suffering from neurosis, I was able to convince myself that the unconscious pleasure they took in the nonsense they produced had no less a share in their slips and stumbles [*Fehlleistungen*[7]] than their real ignorance.

Later, the university student does not give up demonstrating against the compulsion of logic and reality, for he feels its authority with less and less patience or restraint anyway. A good part of student ragging belongs to this reaction. Human beings are simply 'tireless pleasure-seekers' – I don't remember where I found this happy expression – and to give up any pleasure once enjoyed is very hard for them. With the merry nonsense of a drunken oration [*Bierschwefel*], the student will attempt to salvage some pleasure for himself from a freedom of thought which he progressively loses in the course of his academic training. Indeed, much later still, as a mature man, when he he has met up with others at a scientific conference and had the feeling that he is in the position of a learner again, the bar-room newspaper [*Kneipzeitung*], which distorts his newly won insights into nonsense, has to compensate him for his newly acquired intellectual inhibition.

'Drunken oration', 'bar-room newspaper', the very names testify that the critical attitude which has repressed the pleasure in nonsense has already become so strong that it cannot be thrust aside even for a while without toxic assistance. Altering our state of mind is the most valuable thing that alcohol has done for humankind, and that is why this 'poison' [*Gift*[8]] is not equally indispensable for everyone. A cheerful mood, whether it has originated from within or been toxically produced, reduces the inhibitory forces – criticism among them – and so makes the sources of pleasure, on which the suppression has been weighing, accessible again. It is exceedingly instructive to see how what we expect from a joke sinks as our mood lifts. The mood simply substitutes for the joke, just as the joke has to try to substitute for the mood in which possibilities of enjoyment, otherwise inhibited, – among them pleasure in nonsense – may assert themselves.

Mit wenig Witz und viel Behagen.[9]

[With little wit and much enjoyment.]

Under the influence of alcohol the adult becomes a child again, finding pleasure in having the course of his thoughts freely at his disposal without having to keep to the compulsion of logic.

We hope that we have now set out how the joke's absurdity-techniques correspond to a source of pleasure. We need only repeat that this pleasure comes from an economizing in psychical expenditure and a relief from the compulsion of criticism.

Looking back once again at the three groups of joke-techniques we have distinguished, we observe that the first and third of these groups, the substitution of object-associations with verbal associations and the use of absurdity, can be brought together as ways of restoring old freedoms and of disburdening us from the compulsion of our intellectual education. They are means of psychical relief, which can be contrasted in a certain way with the economizing that makes up the technique of the second group: specifically, relief for what is already there, and economizing on a psychical expenditure only just being called for. All joke-techniques go back to these two principles, then, and consequently so does all the pleasure arising from these techniques. Moreover, the two kinds of technique and of obtaining pleasure coincide – at least on the whole – with the division of jokes into verbal and intellectual.

[B]

The preceding discussion has led us unexpectedly to an insight into the evolution or psychological origins of the joke, which we will now approach more closely. We have got to know the joke's preliminary stages; their development as far as the tendentious joke is probably able to reveal fresh relationships between its various characteristics. Prior to any joke or witticism there is something we may call play or 'fun'. Play – let us keep to this name – makes its appearance in children while they are learning to use words and put thoughts together. This play is probably complying with one of the drives that compel children to exercise their capacities (Groos). As they do so they come upon pleasurable effects arising from the repetition of what is similar, the rediscovery of what is familiar, similar sounds, etc., which can be explained as unexpected savings in psychical expenditure. It is not surprising that these pleasurable effects encourage children in the habit of playing, and cause them to carry on with it regardless of the meaning of the words or the coherence of their sentences. So *play* with words and thoughts, motivated by certain pleasurable effects, would be the first preliminary stage of the joke.

This play is brought to an end by the strengthening of a factor that deserves to be called an attitude of criticism, or rationality. Play is now rejected as being meaningless or plainly absurd. On account of this critical attitude it becomes impossible. It is also out of the question now, except by accident, to obtain any pleasure from those sources of rediscovery of what is familiar, etc. – unless the young person growing up is overcome by a pleasurable mood which, like the child's cheerfulness, lifts the inhibiting effect of his critical judgement. In this case alone his old way of getting pleasure from play becomes possible once again. But he does not want to wait and do without his old familiar pleasure, so he looks for ways and means to make himself independent of the pleasurable mood. The further development towards the joke is determined by these two aims: to evade the criticism and to find a substitute for the mood.

With these aims the second preliminary stage of the joke is brought into action: *pleasantry* or *banter* [*Scherz*]. The purpose now is to achieve the pleasure obtained in play, but in doing so also to silence the critical objections that would not allow the pleasurable feeling to emerge. There is only one way leading to this end: the meaningless combination of words or absurd string of thoughts does have to have some meaning after all. The entire art of the joke-work is mustered to discover the words and constellations of thought in which this condition is fulfilled. All the technical resources of the joke or witticism are already put to use here, in the pleasantry; indeed, linguistic usage does not make any consistent distinction between pleasantry and joking. What separates a pleasantry from a joke is that the meaning of the statement that has evaded criticism does not need to be new or valuable or even merely sensible; it just has to be said the way it is said, however feeble, pointless or futile it is to say it that way. In the pleasantry, the satisfaction of having made possible what criticism has forbidden takes the foreground.

It is a mere pleasantry, for example, when Schleiermacher defines jealousy as a passion that seeks with zeal what makes suffering ['Eifersucht ist eine Leidenschaft, die mit Eifer sucht, was Leiden schafft,' p. 27]. It is a pleasantry when Professor Käster, who taught physics in Göttingen in the 18th Century – and made jokes – asked a student called *Kriegk* at registration for his age; told that he was thirty years old, the professor commented: 'Oh, then I have the honour of seeing the Thirty Years' Krieg [War].'[10] Asked what professions his four sons had taken up, the great Rokitansky gave the bantering reply: 'Zwei heilen und zwei heulen [Two heal and two howl]' (two physicians and two singers). The information was correct and therefore incontestible; but it did not add anything to what might have been contained in the bracketed phrase. It is obvious that his reply took the other form only on account of the pleasure deriving from the unification and from the similar sound of the two words.

I think that at last we are able to see clearly. It has always bothered us in considering joke-techniques that these do not only belong to the joke alone, and yet the joke's essential nature has seemed to depend on them, for when we removed them by reduction, their jokiness and the distinctive pleasure they gave as jokes were lost. We now note that what we described as joke-*techniques* – and in a certain sense we must continue to give them this name – are rather the *sources* from which the joke obtains the pleasure; and we do not feel disconcerted that other procedures should draw from the same sources to the same end. But the technique proper to jokes or witticisms and belonging to them alone consists in their method of making their use of these pleasure-producing devices proof against the objections from criticism that would annul the pleasure. There is little of a general nature that we can say of this procedure; the joke-work reveals itself, as we have already said, in its choice of such verbal material and such intellectual situations as will allow the old play with words and ideas to pass the test of rational criticism; and to this end all the oddities of vocabulary and all the constellations and combinations of ideas have to be most skilfully exploited. Perhaps we may later reach the point where we are in a position to characterize the joke-work by one specific feature; for the moment it remains unexplained *how* the choice so fertile for generating jokes is made. However, the purpose and function of the joke – to protect the pleasure-producing combinations of words and ideas – has already turned out to be the essential characteristic of the pleasantry. From the start the pleasantry's function has been to lift internal inhibitions and make sources of pleasure which these had made inaccessible flow freely once more; and we shall find that throughout its entire development it remains true to this nature.

We are now also in a position to assign the right place to that factor of 'sense in nonsense' (see Introduction, p. 6) to which our authorities ascribed such great importance in characterizing the joke and explaining its pleasurable effect. The two fixed points determining [the nature of the] joke, the tendency it pursues to perpetuate pleasurable play, and the trouble it takes to protect itself from the criticism of reason, are grounds enough to explain why a particular joke may appear nonsensical from one point of view, but must make good – or at least admissible – sense from another. How it does this is still the joke-work's affair; where a joke has not been successful, it is just rejected as 'nonsense'. But in any case, we do not need to trace the pleasurable effect of a joke back to the conflict of feelings produced by its simultaneous sense and nonsense, whether directly or by way of 'bafflement and light dawning'. There is just as little necessity for us to go further into the question of how pleasure can arise from the alternation between thinking-a-joke-is-nonsense and recognizing-it-has-sense. The psychological origins of the joke have taught us that our pleasure in a joke comes from play with words or from unleashing nonsense, and that the sense of a joke is only intended to protect this pleasure from being annulled by rational criticism.

In that case, the problem of the joke's essential nature would already be explained with the explanation of the pleasantry. Let us turn to the further development of the pleasantry to its highest point in the tendentious *joke* or *witticism*. The pleasantry still puts the intention of amusing us first and is satisfied if what it says does not appear nonsensical or completely empty of content [*gehaltlos*]. If what it says does have content [*Gehalt*] and value, the pleasantry turns into a joke. A thought that would have been worthy of our interest, even if expressed in the plainest form, is now clad in a form which is bound to arouse our pleasure in itself.[11] We must certainly think that such an alliance has not come about unintentionally, and we shall try to guess what the intention underlying the formation of the joke may be. An observation we made earlier, seemingly by the way, will put us on the track. We have remarked above that a good joke makes a general impression of pleasing [*Wohlgefallen*], so to speak, without our being capable of distinguishing directly what part of the pleasure [*Lust*] comes from the form of the joke and what from its admirable thought-content [*Gedankeninhalt*] (p. 91). We are constantly deluding ourselves on this division, now overestimating the quality of the witticism on account of our admiration for the thought it contains, now, contrariwise, the value of the thought on account of the amusement we have from how it is clad in a joke. We do not know what is amusing us or what we are laughing at. This uncertainty of judgement, which we may take as fact, may have been the actual motive for the formation of the joke. The thought seeks the guise of a joke because this will commend it to our attention, making it appear more significant and valuable to us, but above all because this costume bribes our critical reason and confuses it. We are inclined to credit the thought with what has pleased us in the joke's form, and we are also no longer inclined to find anything that has amused us false or wrong, for that would block or bury a source of pleasure for ourselves. Also, if a joke has made us laugh, we are put into a frame of mind most unfavourable for criticism, for something has made us succumb to that mood which had once been satisfied by play and which the joke has endeavoured with all its resources to replace. Although we have already established that jokes of this kind are to be described as innocuous, not yet tendentious, we must not let it escape our notice that strictly speaking only the pleasantry is un-tendentious, that is, serves only the aim of producing pleasure. The joke or witticism – even if the thought it contains is not tendentious, that is, serves merely theoretical intellectual interests – is actually never without tendency; it pursues the second aim of helping the thought along by strengthening it [*Vergrößerung*] and securing it against rational criticism. Here again the joke reveals its original nature in its opposition to an inhibiting and restrictive power – in this case critical judgement.

This, the first use of the joke to go beyond the production of pleasure, points the way to further uses. The joke is now recognized as a powerful psychological factor, whose weight can be decisive if it is thrown into the one scale or the other. The major tendencies and drives of our inner life make use of it for their own ends. The originally un-tendentious joke, which began as play, *secondarily* comes into relation with tendencies which nothing formed in our psyche can in the long run escape. We already know what feats jokes can perform in the service of an intention to unclothe someone, or of a hostile, cynical or sceptical tendency. In the obscene joke, which evolved out of dirty talk, it turns the third person, originally the intruder in the sexual situation, into an accomplice in whose presence the woman is made to feel shame, by bribing him with a share of the pleasure gained. A joke with an aggressive tendency transforms the initially indifferent audience by the same means into accomplices in hate or scorn, and creates an army of foes for its enemy, where once there was only one. In the first case it overcomes the inhibitions of shame and decency with the bonus of pleasure it offers; but in the second it again overturns the critical judgement that would otherwise have scrutinized the dispute. In the third and fourth instances, in the service of a cynical or a sceptical tendency, the joke will severely shake the listener's respect for institutions and truths he has believed in, on the one hand by reinforcing the argument, but on the other by cultivating a new kind of attack. Where an argument tries to draw the listener's criticism on to its side, a joke attempts to thrust it aside. There is no doubt that the joke has chosen the way with the greater psychological effectiveness.

In this review of the achievements of tendentious jokes, what is easier to see – the effect of the joke on the listener – has made its way to the fore. But it is more important for us to understand the functions the joke performs in the inner life of the person who makes it, or – the only way to put it correctly – the person it occurs to. We have already made the proposal once – and we have occasion to repeat it here – that we should study the psychical processes in jokes as they are shared between two persons. For the moment let us suppose that the psychical process aroused in the listener will in most cases be formed after the model of the one taking place in the joke's creator. The external obstacle to be overcome in the listener corresponds to an inner inhibition in the joker. At the least, the expectation of an external obstacle is present in the latter as an inhibiting idea. In particular cases, the internal obstacle overcome by the tendentious joke is obvious; with regard to Herr N.'s witticisms, for example, we may assume that they make it possible not just for his listeners to enjoy aggression in the insults, but above all for him to produce them. Among the kinds of internal inhibition or suppression there is one that deserves our especial interest because it is the most far-reaching; it goes by the name of 'repression' and is recognized by its function of barring the impulses that have succumbed to it – as well as their offspring – from becoming conscious.

We shall learn that tendentious jokes are able to release [*entbinden*] pleasure even from those sources that are subject to repression. If the overcoming of external obstacles can be traced back to inner inhibitions and repressions in the way we have indicated above, we may say that out of all the developmental stages of the joke, the most important characteristic of the joke-work – that it sets pleasure free by removing inhibitions – is most clearly shown in the tendentious joke. It reinforces the tendencies it serves by bringing them assistance from impulses kept suppressed, or it puts itself generally at the disposal of suppressed tendencies.

We may readily admit that these are the functions of the tendentious joke, but we must still bear in mind that we do not understand how it succeeds in performing these functions. Its power lies in the gain in pleasure it draws from the sources of word-play and liberated nonsense, and, to judge by the impressions we have had from un-tendentious pleasantries, we cannot possibly think the amount of this pleasure to be so great that we could credit it with the force to remove deep-rooted inhibitions and repressions. Actually, this is not a simple effect of force but a more complicated situation of releasing [*Auslösung*]. Instead of giving an account of the long roundabout way I took to reach an insight into this situation, I shall attempt to present it along a short, synthetic route.

In his *Vorschule der Ästhetik* (vol. I, V), G. T. Fechner set up the 'principle of aesthetic support [*Hilfe*] or intensification', which he explains in the following words: '*Arising from the convergence of non-contradictory determinants of pleasure which have little effect by themselves, there emerges a greater, often much greater, pleasure than the pleasure-value of the individual determinants by themselves, greater than could be explained as the sum of the single effects; indeed, a convergence of this kind can produce a positive outcome of pleasure and overstep the threshold of pleasure even where the separate factors are too weak to do so; though in comparison with others they must show a perceptible advantage in pleasingness* [*Wohlgefälligkeit*].'[12] I do not think the topic of jokes gives us much opportunity to confirm the correctness of this principle, though it can be demonstrated in many other forms of artistic production. We have learned something else from jokes which at least approaches this principle: that when several factors producing pleasure are working together, we are not in a position to ascribe to each the real share in the outcome that is properly theirs (see p. 91). But it is possible to vary the situation postulated in the principle of support, and aim at putting a number of questions worth answering to these new determinants. What generally happens when determinants of pleasure come together in the same constellation with determinants of un-pleasure? What does the outcome, positive or negative, depend on? Among these possibilities, the case of the tendentious joke is a special one. There is an impulse or effort present which has wanted to release [*entbinden*] pleasure from a certain source, and which would, unhindered, indeed do so; besides this, there is another impulse working against this emergence of pleasure, that is, inhibiting or suppressing it. The suppressing current must be to some degree stronger than the suppressed, as the outcome shows, but the one suppressed is still not removed on that account.

Now suppose a second impulse also came on to the scene which would release pleasure from the same process, though from other sources – operating, that is, with the same intent as the suppressed. What can the outcome be in such a case? An example will show us how the land lies better than this schematic account. We have an impulse to insult a certain person; but our sense of propriety, our aesthetic cultivation, is such a barrier to it that the insult cannot take place; if it *were* able to break through, for example on account of a change in affect or mood, this eruption would be experienced in retrospect with unpleasurable feelings. So the insult does not take place. But we might be offered the possibility of turning the material of words and thoughts used for the insult into a good joke or witticism, that is, of releasing pleasure from other sources that are not obstructed by the same suppression. But this emergence of pleasure still could not take place unless the insult were permitted; but once it is permitted, the new release of pleasure is still bound up with it. Our experience with the tendentious joke shows that the suppressed tendency can obtain enough strength from the support given by the pleasure of the joke to overcome the – otherwise stronger – inhibition. The insult takes place, because it is possible to make a joke with it. But the pleasure aimed for is not only the pleasure generated by the joke; it is incomparably greater – so much greater than the pleasure from the joke that we have to assume that the previously suppressed tendency has succeeded in getting through, possibly without any loss. Under these circumstances, it is the tendentious joke that makes us laugh the most heartily.

Perhaps we shall arrive at a clearer idea of the process of support given by jokes against suppression when we examine the determinants of laughter. But even now we can see that the case of tendentious jokes is a special case of the principle of support. One possible means of producing pleasure enters to join a situation in which another one is thwarted and so unable to yield any pleasure by itself; the result is a far greater production of pleasure than that of the possibility that has entered. This last has acted as an *enticement bonus*, as it were; supported by the offer of a small amount of pleasure, a very great amount, otherwise difficult to attain, has been gained. I have good reason to surmise that this principle corresponds to an arrangement that holds good for many fields remote from one another in our inner life, and I think it will be useful to call the pleasure that serves to trigger the major release of pleasure *fore-pleasure* and call the principle itself the *fore-pleasure principle*.

We can now formulate how the tendentious joke functions: using the fore-pleasure of the pleasure afforded by the joke, it puts itself at the service of tendencies and intentions to produce new pleasure by lifting suppressions and repressions. If we now review its development, we may say that from its beginning to its consummation, the joke has remained true to its nature. It begins as play – in order to get pleasure from using words and thoughts freely. As soon as the strengthening of reason dismisses playing with words as senseless and playing with thoughts as nonsense, it is transformed into pleasantry – in order to hold on to these sources of pleasure and be able to obtain new pleasure from the liberation of nonsense. As a joke proper, still un-tendentious, the joke then gives its support to thoughts, strengthening them against attack from critical judgement;

in doing so, it is helped by the principle of confusion of sources of pleasure. And finally it allies itself with strong tendencies struggling against suppression in order to remove their internal inhibitions according to the principle of fore-pleasure. Reason – critical judgement – suppression – these are the powers it fights one after the other; it holds on to the original sources of pleasure in words, and from the stage of pleasantry onwards opens up new sources of pleasure for itself by lifting inhibitions. The pleasure it generates, whether it is the pleasure of play or of lifting inhibition, we can in all cases derive from savings in psychical expenditure – with the proviso that this view does not contradict the nature of pleasure and proves fruitful in other fields.[13]

Notes

1. [The phrase is Lipps's, first used in his *Grundtatsachen des Seelenlebens* (1883), which Freud found such a valuable text, and again in *Komik und Humor*. It indicates a blocking of the discharge of ideas [*Vorstellungsabfluß*].]

2. If I may be allowed to anticipate the account in the text, I am able to cast some light at this point on the requirement that linguistic usage seems to treat as the criterion for calling a joke 'good' or 'bad'. If an ambiguous or slightly modified word has got me by a short route from one sphere of ideas to another, without also setting up a meaningful connection between the two spheres of ideas, then I have made a "bad' joke. In this bad joke, the one word, the 'point', is the single link between the two disparate ideas. The example used above, the 'Home-roulade', is an instance. But a 'good' joke comes about when the children's expectation holds good and with the similarity of words another, essential, similarity of meaning is really indicated at the same time, as in the example: 'Traduttore – Traditore.' The two disparate ideas linked here by an external association have a meaningful connection as well, declaring their affinity. The external association only takes the place of the internal connection; it serves to point it out, or make it clear. The 'translator' does not only have a similar name to the traitor; he *is* a kind of traitor too, his name is, as it were, justly borne.

The distinction developed here is identical to the division of 'pleasantry' from 'joke'. But it would be wrong to exclude examples like 'Home-roulade' from a discussion of the nature of jokes. Once we begin to consider the pleasure peculiar to jokes, we find that 'bad' jokes are by no means bad as jokes, that is, unsuited to producing pleasure.

3. *Die Spiele des Menschen*, 1899.

4. [The reference is to Faust's return to his study (Goethe, *Faust*, I.3) after his first meeting with Mephistopheles – in the guise of a dog.]

5. Section XVII is headed: 'On Ingenious and Joking comparisons, Word-play and other Instances having the Character of Amusement, Fun and Ridiculousness'.

6. [The quotation marks are Freud's, suggesting some literary reference, perhaps on the model of Tasso's *Gerusalemma Liberata*, rendered in German as *Das befreite Jerusalem*.]

7. [The famous Freudian slip.]

8. [Is Freud making a little pun in English here?]

9. [Mephistopheles in Goethe's *Faust*, I.8.]

10. Kleinpaul, *Die Rätsel der Sprache*, 1890.

11. As an example clearly showing the distinction between a pleasantry and a proper joke, let us take the excellent witticism with which a member of the 'Bourgeois Ministry' in Austria answered a query about the cabinet's solidarity: 'How are we to *stand up for* [*einstehen*] one another when we can't *stand* [*ausstehen*] one another?' Technique: use of the same material with slight (antithetical) modification; the thought, accurate and apt: 'There is no solidarity without personal *rapport*.' The antithesis in the modification (*einstehen–aus*stehen) corresponds to the divisions stated by the thought and is used to represent it.

[The 'Bourgeois Ministry' was the Reformist cabinet appointed in 1868 by Franz Josef, led by the liberally inclined Prince Auersperg, but with a number of ministers of bourgeois origin. Warmly welcomed by Freud's father (see *The Interpretation of Dreams*, V.B). By 1871 it had broken up.]

12. See p. 51 of the 2nd ed., Leipzig, 1897. The italics are Fechner's.

13. Nonsense jokes, to which I have not done full justice in this account, deserve a brief, belated, consideration.

Given the importance our theory ascribes to the factor of 'sense in nonsense', one might be tempted to expect that every joke must be a nonsense joke. But this is not necessary, because only play with ideas inevitably leads to nonsense, while the other source of pleasure in jokes, play with words, only occasionally makes this impression and does not invariably summon up the attitude of criticism connected with nonsense. The dual root of pleasure in jokes – from playing with words and playing with ideas, corresponding to the most important division into verbal jokes and intellectual jokes – creates appreciable difficulties in making a neat formulation of general statements about the joke. Word-play generates evident pleasure on account of the factors listed above: recognition, etc., and consequently it is prone to suppression only in small measure. Playing with ideas cannot be motivated by this pleasure; it is subject to very forceful suppression, and the pleasure it is able to deliver is only the pleasure that comes from lifting an inhibition; accordingly, one could say that pleasure in jokes displays a kernel of the original pleasure of play and a shell of the pleasure of lifting inhibition. – Naturally, we are not aware that our pleasure in a nonsense joke derives from our success in liberating nonsense in spite of suppression, whereas we notice as a matter of course that playing with words has given us pleasure. – The nonsense that remains in the joke based on ideas secondarily acquires the function of sharpening our attention by baffling us; it acts as a means of strengthening the effect of the joke, but only when it is obtrusive, so that our bafflement outstrips our understanding by a noticeable instant of time. It can be seen from the examples on pp. 47ff. that nonsense in a joke can also be used to represent a judgement contained in the thought. But this too is not the primary significance of nonsense in jokes.

We can attach to the nonsense jokes a number of joke-like productions which lack a suitable name, but which might have a claim on the label 'silliness in the guise of a joke'. They are legion; I will select only two as samples. As he is being served fish at dinner, a man reaches with both hands into the mayonnaise and rubs it into his hair. His neighbour looks at him in astonishment, so he seems to notice his mistake and apologizes: 'Excuse me, I thought it was spinach.'

Or: 'Life is a suspension-bridge,' says the one. 'How is that?' asks the other. – 'How do I know?' comes the answer.

These extravagant examples function by arousing the expectation of a joke, so that we try hard to find the hidden sense behind the nonsense. But we find none. They really are nonsense. The pretence makes it possible for a moment to liberate our pleasure in nonsense. These jokes are not entirely without tendency; they are 'teasers', giving the teller a certain pleasure by misleading the listener and annoying him. The latter then stifles his annoyance by intending to tell them himself.

v The Motives for Jokes – The Joke as Social Process

To talk of the motives for jokes might seem unnecessary, for the aim of obtaining pleasure has to be recognized as a sufficient motive for the joke-work. However, it is not impossible on the one hand that other motives also take part in producing them; while on the other, in the light of certain familiar experiences, we are bound to raise the general issue of subjective determinants for jokes.

Two factors above all challenge us to do so. For although the joke-work provides an excellent route to gain pleasure from psychical processes, we can still see that not everyone is capable of making use of this means in the same way. The joke-work is not at everyone's command, and in general there are only a few who have it in great measure, and we mark them out by saying that they are possessed of 'wit'. 'Wit' in this context appears as a special talent, rather of the order of the old 'mental faculties', and when it makes an entry it turns out to be pretty independent of the others: intelligence, imagination, memory, etc. So in witty persons certain aptitudes or psychical determinants permitting or favouring the joke-work are to be assumed.

I am afraid that we will not get very far in exploring this topic. We are only once in a while successful in progressing from understanding a particular joke or witticism to a knowledge of the subjective psychical determinants of the person who invented it. Quite by chance it happens that the very example where we began our examination of joke-technique also gives us a glimpse into the subjective determination of a joke. I mean Heine's joke, which also caught the attention of Heymans and Lipps:

'. . . I was sitting next to Salomon Rothschild and he treated me just like his equal, quite famillionairely ("Die Bäder von Lucca").'

Heine put these words into the mouth of a comic figure, Hirsch-Hyacinth, lottery-agent, quack-surgeon and valuer from Hamburg, valet to the noble Baron Cristoforo Gumpelino (formerly Gumpel). The poet obviously takes great pleasure in this his creature, for he makes Hirsch-Hyacinth a great boaster and gives him the most amusing and outspoken things to say, almost lending him the practical wisdom of a Sancho Panza. It is a great pity that Heine, who does not seem to have been inclined towards dramatic composition, dropped this delightful character so soon. There are not a few passages where it seems as if the poet himself were speaking through Hirsch-Hyacinth's mouth from behind a flimsy mask, and we soon become certain that in this figure the poet is only parodying himself. Hirsch recounts his reasons for casting off his earlier name and for now calling himself Hyacinth. 'And I also have the advantage,' he continues, 'that there is already an H. on my seal, so I don't have to have a new one engraved.' But Heine himself was able to make the same economy when he exchanged his first name of 'Harry' for 'Heinrich' at his baptism. Now anyone familiar with the poet's biography must recall that in Hamburg, which the figure of Hirsch-Hyacinth also indicates, Heine had an uncle of the same name, who played a very great role in his life as the rich man of the family. And this uncle was also called – Salomon, just like old Rothschild, who welcomed poor Hirsch so famillionairely. What seemed to be a mere pleasantry in Hirsch-Hyacinth's mouth soon reveals a bitterly serious background if we ascribe it to the nephew Harry-Heinrich. But *he* was a member of the family, after all; indeed, we know it was his ardent wish to marry this uncle's daughter, but his cousin turned him down, and his uncle always treated him rather 'famillionairely' as a poor relation. His rich cousins in Hamburg never really appreciated him; I recall an old aunt of mine, who had married into the Heine family, telling of how, as a good-looking young woman, she found herself one day sitting at the family table next to a fellow-guest who seemed to her rather unprepossessing and was treated with some disdain by the others; she did not feel she should be any more amiable towards him. Many years later she realized that this negligent and neglected cousin had been the poet Heinrich Heine. There is a great deal of evidence as to how much Heine suffered from this rejection by his rich relations, both as a young man and later. It was from the soil of this subjective emotion that the 'famillionairely' witticism then grew.

One could guess at similar subjective determinants in many other witticisms from the great satirist, but I do not know of any other example where they can be demonstrated as convincingly as here; so it is tricky if one wants to make any more precise statement about the nature of these personal determinants; and, of course, one has no wish a priori to claim determinants as complicated as these for the origin of every joke. The insights we are looking for are not accessible any more easily from jokes produced by other famous men; one rather gets the impression that the subjective determinants of the joke-work are often not far away from those of neurotic illness – when one learns of Lichtenberg, for example, that he was a great hypochondriac, afflicted with all kinds of eccentricities. The great majority of jokes, particularly the new ones constantly being produced to meet the occasions of the day, circulate anonymously; one could inquire curiously about the kind of person to whom one might trace back the production of these jokes. If one has occasion as a physician to get to know one of those people who may not be outstanding in other respects but are known in their circle to be jokers and the authors of a number of passable witticisms, one may be surprised to discover that this humorist is a divided personality prone to nervous illnesses. But the inadequacy of the documentation will certainly keep us from proposing that a psycho-neurotic constitution of this kind should be an invariable or necessary subjective determinant for the formation of jokes.

Jewish jokes once again offer a more transparent case, for, as I mentioned, they have been altogether invented by Jews themselves, whereas anecdotes about them coming from other sources scarcely ever rise above the level of the farcical tale or of brutal derision (pp. 108–9). The involvement of the persons concerned seems to stand out as the determinant here, as it did in Heine's 'famillionairely' witticism; and its significance seems to be that direct criticism or aggression is more difficult for the person to make directly, and only made possible by roundabout routes.

Other subjective factors determining or favouring the joke-work are less shrouded in darkness. The motive behind the production of innocuous jokes is quite often the ambitious urge to show off how clever one is, to display oneself, a drive to be equated with exhibition-ism in the field of sexuality. The presence of several inhibited drives, whose suppression has remained to some degree unstable, will provide the most favourable disposition for producing tendentious jokes. In particular, single components of a person's sexual consti-tution may make their appearance as motives in the formation of jokes. A great number of obscene jokes allow us to infer a hidden propensity towards exhibitionism in their authors; tendentious jokes of the aggressive kind are most successfully made by those in whom the presence of a powerful sadistic component, more or less inhibited in life, can be shown in their sexuality.

The second fact challenging us to investigate the subjective deter-minants for jokes is the universal and familiar experience that no one is content with making a joke for themselves alone. The urge [*Drang*] to communicate the joke is indissolubly linked to the joke-work; indeed, this urge is so strong that it will quite often ignore weighty second thoughts as long as it is realized. With the comic too, communicating it to another person confirms the enjoyment, but it is not imperative; if one happens upon what is comical, one can enjoy it alone. On the other hand one is compelled to pass on a joke; the psychical process of joke-formation does not seem to be over when the joke occurs to its author; something is left that tries to complete this unknown process of joke-formation by passing the joke on.

At first we cannot guess at the reasons for this impulse [*Trieb*] to tell the joke to someone else. But there is another oddity we note in the joke which once again distinguishes it from the comic. When something comic confronts me, I am able to laugh heartily at it by myself – though I am also delighted if I can make someone else laugh by telling him about it. But I am unable to laugh by myself at a joke that has occurred to me, despite the unmistakable enjoyment that it gives me. It is possible that my need to pass it on to someone else is somehow connected to the laughter effected by the joke which is denied to me but manifest in the other person.

So why do I not laugh at my own joke? And what is the part played in the process by the other person?

Let us turn first to the latter question. Generally, where the comic is concerned, two persons come under consideration: apart from my own self, the person in whom I find something comical; if *things* appear comical to me, this comes about through a kind of personification which is a fairly frequent mode of representation in our inner life. These two persons, my own self and the person-as-object [*Objekt-Person*], are sufficient for the comic process; a third person can join it, but is not essential. Joking in the form of play with one's own words and thoughts at first does without a person-as-object, but as early as the preliminary stage of pleasantry – if it has been successful in making play and nonsense proof against the objections of reason – it already demands another person to whom it can communicate what it has produced. However, in the case of a joke, this second person does not correspond to the person-as-object in the comic process, but to the third person, the 'someone-else'. It seems that in a pleasantry, the decision whether the joke-work has been successful in fulfilling its task is transferred to the other person, as if the first person, the 'I', were not certain of its judgement. The innocuous joke, too, the joke that reinforces the thought, needs the 'someone-else' in order to test whether it has fulfilled its aim. If the joke puts itself at the service of hostile tendencies or intentions to strip someone, it can be described as a psychical process requiring three persons, the same ones as in the comic process, but the part played by the third person is different in this case; the psychical process of the joke is consummated between the first person, the 'I', and the third, the person from outside, not, as it is in the comic process, between the self and the person-as-object.

In the third person required by the joke too, the joke comes up against subjective determinants which may make the aim of arousing pleasure unattainable. As Shakespeare reminds us:

A jest's prosperity lies in the ear
Of him that hears it, never in the tongue
Of him that makes it . . . (*Love's Labours Lost*, V.ii.869–71)

Someone under the sway of a mood linked to serious thoughts is not the right person to reassure the pleasantry that it has been successful in rescuing the pleasure yielded by words. He must be in a cheerful frame of mind himself, or at least an indeterminate one, to play the part of the third person in the case of a pleasantry. The same obstacle goes on to affect innocuous and tendentious jokes; but in the latter a fresh obstacle makes its appearance, the contrary of the tendency that the joke is aiming to serve. It is impossible to prompt someone to laugh at an excellent obscene joke if the stripping is meant for a respected figure related to the third person; in a gathering of priests and ministers no one would dare come out with Heine's comparison of Catholic and Protestant clergy with retailers and employees of a wholesale concern; and before an audience of my enemy's devoted friends, the wittiest diatribes I could utter would not make their point as witticisms but as diatribes, and would produce indignation, not pleasure, among their hearers. Some degree of inclination, or a certain indifference, the absence of any factor that might provoke strong feelings opposing the joke's tendency, is the indispensable requirement if the third person is to play a part in consummating the process of the joke.

Where such obstacles to the effectiveness of the joke are absent, the phenomenon we now propose to investigate makes its appearance: the pleasure produced by the joke turns out to be more evident in the third person than in its author. We must be content with saying 'more evident' though we would really like to ask whether the pleasure of the listener is not 'more intense' than that of the one who made it, for clearly we have no means of measuring or comparing. But we do see that the listener declares his pleasure by bursting into laughter, after the first person has mostly come out with the joke wearing a straight face. If I pass on a joke I myself have heard, in telling it I must behave just like the person who made it, so as not to spoil its effect. The question now is whether the dependence of laughter on these conditions enables us to draw any conclusions about the psychical process that takes place when jokes are formed.

Now we cannot possibly propose to consider everything that has been said and published about the nature of laughter here. We may be frightened off such an aim by the proposition put by Dugas, a student of Ribot's, at the head of his book *La Psychologie du Rire* (1902). 'Il n'est pas de fait plus banal et plus étudié que le rire; il n'en est pas qui ait en le don d'exiler d'avantage la curiosité du vulgaire et celles des philosophes; il n'en ait pas sur lequel on ait recueilli plus d'observations et bâti plus de théories, avec cela il n'en est pas qui demeure plus inexpliqué, on serait tenté de dire avec les sceptiques qu'il faut être content de rire et de ne pas chercher à savoir pourquoi on rit, d'autant que peut-être le réflexion tue le rire, et qu'il serait alors contradictoire qu'elle en découvrit les causes [There is no subject more ordinary and more often studied than laughter. There is not one that has been more able to rouse the curiosity both of the common people and of the philosophers; there is not one which has been more observed or on which more theories have been built, but for all that there is not one that remains more unexplained. One might be tempted to say with the sceptics that we should be content to laugh and not seek to know why we laugh, for it may be that reflection kills laughter, and so it would be a contradiction to think that it could discover its causes]' (p. 1).

On the other hand, we shall not fail to make use for our own ends of a view on the mechanism of laughter which fits in excellently with our own thinking. I mean Herbert Spencer's attempt at an explanation in his essay 'The Physiology of Laughter'.[1]

According to Spencer, laughter is a manifestation of the discharge [*Abfuhr*] of psychical excitation and evidence that the psyche's use of this excitation has suddenly come up against an obstacle. He describes the psychological situation that issues in laughter in the following words: 'Laughter naturally results only when consciousness is unawares transferred from great things to small – only when there is what we may call a *descending* incongruity.'[2]

French authorities (Dugas) describe laughter along similar lines as a 'détente', a manifestation of relaxation of tension, and A. Bain's formula: 'Laughter is a relief from restraint' seems to me to depart far less from Spencer's theory than many authorities would have us believe.

We do, it is true, feel the need to modify Spencer's theory, partly putting its ideas more precisely, partly altering them. We would say that laughter arises when an amount of psychical energy previously used in charging certain psychical pathways has become unusable, so that it can be freely released. We are quite clear that we shall place ourselves in 'bad odour' with such a theory, but we shall venture to quote an excellent sentence from Lipps's work *Komik und Humor*, which casts light on more than just the comic and humour: 'Ultimately, separate psychological problems always lead us quite deep into psychology, so that fundamentally no psychological problem can be treated in isolation' (p. 71). The concepts of 'psychical energy' and 'discharge', and treating psychical energy as a quantity have become habitual in my thinking ever since I began to marshal the facts of psychopathology philosophically. In my *Interpretation of Dreams* (1900), I was already attempting, as Lipps was, to argue that it is the essentially unconscious psychical processes and not the contents of consciousness that are 'the actual effective factors in the psyche'.[3] It is only when I talk of 'charging psychical pathways' that I seem to depart from the metaphors current in Lipps. It was my experiences of how psychical energy is so readily displaceable along certain paths of association, and of how indestructible is the persistence of the traces made by psychical processes, that in fact suggested to me that I should try out this kind of transposition into imagery [*Verbildlichung*] for the unknown. To avoid misunderstanding, I must add that I am not attempting to proclaim that cells and fibres, or the neurone systems that are taking their place nowadays, are these psychical pathways, although it would have to be possible to represent such pathways – even if it cannot yet be indicated how – by organic elements of the nervous system.

In laughter, then, according to our hypothesis, the determinants are given for an amount of psychical energy, used until then for charging, to be freely released. And since laughter – not all laughter, it is true, but certainly laughter at jokes – is a sign of pleasure, we shall be inclined to relate this pleasure to the lifting of the energy-charge present up until then. When we see that the person listening to a joke is laughing, whereas its creator is unable to laugh, this is as good as telling us that in the listener some expenditure in energy-charge is being lifted and released, while in the formation of the joke obstacles have arisen either to the lifting or to the possibility of release. The psychical process in the listener, in the joke's third person, can scarcely be more aptly characterized than by emphasizing that he purchases the pleasure of the joke with a very small expenditure of his own. He is made a present of it, as it were. The words of the joke he is listening to necessarily evoke in him the imagined idea [*Vorstellung*] or combination of thoughts which in him too was confronted by such great internal obstacles to forming it. He would have had to make an effort of his own to bring it about as the first person, and to do so he would have had to expend at least as much psychical energy as matched the strength of its inhibition, suppression or repression. He has saved himself this psychical expense; following our earlier discussions (pp. 116–17), we would say his pleasure corresponds to these savings. Following our insight into the mechanism of laughter, we should rather say that because the forbidden imagined idea has been produced by auditory perception, the charge of energy used for inhibition has suddenly become superfluous and so is ready to be released by laughter. In essentials the two descriptions amount to the same thing, for the expenditure saved corresponds exactly to the inhibition that has become superfluous. But the last description illustrates the process more aptly, for it allows us to say that the person listening to the joke is laughing with the amount of psychical energy that has become free through the lifting of the inhibitory energy-charge; he is laughing away this amount, as it were.

If the person in whom the joke is formed cannot laugh, we have just said this indicates a departure from the process going on in the third person, which affects either the lifting of the inhibitory energy-charge or the possibility of its release. But the first of these two cases does not apply, as we are bound to see at once. The inhibitory charge of energy must have been lifted in the first person, too, otherwise no joke would have come about – after all, it was formed in order to overcome such resistance. Also, it would be impossible for the first person to feel the pleasure of the joke – after all, we had to trace this back to the lifting of the inhibition. So we are left with only the other alternative, where the first person is unable to laugh, although he may feel pleasure, because there is an interference in the possibility of release. Such interference in enabling release to take place may arise if the liberated inhibitory energy is immediately shifted to some other use within the psyche. It is good that our attention has been drawn to this possibility; we shall give it our further consideration directly. However, in the first person of the joke, another condition, leading to the same result, may be realized. It may be that no quantity of energy capable of manifestation has been set free at all, despite the lifting of the inhibitory energy-charge that has occurred. For of course the joke-work that has to correspond to a definite amount of new psychical expenditure goes on in the first person of the joke. That is, the first person himself generates the force that lifts the inhibition; this certainly results in a gain in pleasure for him – in the case of a tendentious joke indeed a considerable gain – for the fore-pleasure obtained by means of the joke-work itself takes over any further lifting of inhibitions; but the expenditure on the joke-work is subtracted in every case from the gain made by lifting the inhibition, the same expenditure which the person listening to the joke does not make. To support this argument, one may also observe that the joke loses its effect of laughter even in the third person as soon as he is expected to spend some effort on intellectual work. The allusions made in a joke have to be obvious, its omissions easy to fill; once a conscious intellectual interest is awakened, the effect of the joke as a rule is made impossible. An important distinction between jokes and riddles is to be found here. It may be that the psychical constellation in the course of the joke-work is in general not favourable to the free discharge of what has been gained. We are probably not in a position at this point to reach any deeper insight. We have been able to explain the one part of our problem – why the third person laughs – better than the other part – why the first person does not.

At any rate, if we hold on to these views as to the conditions for laughter and for the psychical process going on in the third person, we are in a position to give a satisfactory explanation of a great number of peculiar features in the joke which have been known but not understood. If an amount of energy-charge capable of release is to be freed in the third person, there are several requirements which have to be fulfilled, or which are desirable to encourage the process. 1. It must be ensured that the third person really makes this expenditure in energy-charge. 2. Once liberated, this energy-charge must be prevented from finding another psychical use, instead of proffering itself for motor release. 3. It can only be advantageous if the charge to be freed in the third person has been strengthened, intensified, beforehand. All these aims are served by particular devices of the joke-work which we may sum up as secondary or auxiliary techniques.

The first of these requirements lays down one of the qualities in the third person needed to make him a suitable listener to the joke. He must definitely be compatible psychically with the first person to the extent of sharing the same internal inhibitions that the joke-work overcame in the first. Someone given to dirty talk will not be able to derive any pleasure from jokes that do their stripping wittily; Herr N.'s aggressive witticisms will not be understood by uncultivated folk who are used to giving free rein to their pleasure in swearing. For every joke demands its own audience, and laughing at the same jokes is evidence of far-reaching psychical compatibility. We have, by the way, arrived at a point here which allows us to guess more precisely the process going on in the third person. He must be able as a matter of habit to set up in himself the same inhibition that the joke overcame in the first person, so that as soon as he hears the joke the readiness for this inhibition is compulsively or automatically aroused. At the same time, this readiness for inhibition, which we cannot but think of in terms of a real expenditure [of energy] analogous to mobilization in the army, is recognized as being unnecessary or as coming too late, and so released *in statu nascendi* by laughter.[4]

The second requirement for creating a free discharge – preventing the liberated energy from being put to a different use – appears to be the more important by far. It provides the theoretical explanation for the unreliability of a joke's success when ideas [*Vorstellungen*] with a strong and arousing effect are called up in the listener by the thoughts expressed in it, for then whether his attention remains with the joking-process or withdraws from it depends on the compatibility or disparity between the tendency of the joke and the train of thought controlling the listener. But even greater theoretical interest lies in a number of the joke's auxiliary devices which evidently serve the aim of drawing the listener's attention away from the joking-process altogether, leaving the latter to run its course automatically. I purposely say 'automatically' and not 'unconsciously', because the latter description would be misleading. In this case it is only a matter of keeping the increased charge of attention away from the psychical process while the joke is being heard. The usefulness of these auxiliary devices leads us to surmise that it is this very charge of attention that has a major share in the monitoring and fresh use of the liberated charge of energy.

It does not seem easy in any case to avoid the endopsychical use of energy-charges that have become superfluous, for of course in our thought-processes we are constantly acting to displace such charges from one path to another without losing any of their energy through release. To do this the joke makes use of the following means. First, it aims to be expressed as briefly as possible, so as to offer fewer targets for the attention. Second, it observes the requirement that it should be easily understood (see above); for as soon as it demanded intellectual work requiring a selection among various pathways of thought, the joke could not help endangering its effect not only by the unavoidable effort entailed in thinking, but also by arousing the attention. But as well as this, it uses the ploy of distracting the attention by offering something that will capture it in the way the joke is expressed, in such a way that meantime the inhibitory charge may be liberated and its release accomplished undisturbed. The omissions in the wording of a joke already fulfil this aim; they provoke us to fill in the gaps and in this way enable the joking-process to escape the attention. Here the technique of riddles, which attract the attention, is used as it were in the service of the joke. Even more effective are the façade-forms which we found especially in some groups of tendentious jokes (see p. 103). The syllogistic façade splendidly fulfils the aim of capturing our attention by setting it a task. Even while we are beginning to consider what might be wrong with the reply, we are already laughing; our attention has been caught on the hop; the release of the liberated inhibitory charge is accomplished. The same applies to jokes with a comic façade, where the comedy comes to the assistance of the joke-technique. A comic façade enhances the effect of a joke in more ways than one; it not only makes the automatism of the joking-process possible by arresting our attention, but it also makes the release brought about by the joke easier, by preceding it with a release brought about by the comic. In this respect the comedy works just like the bribe of fore-pleasure, and this may explain how some jokes are able to do without the fore-pleasure produced by the other devices entirely, and use only the comic for fore-pleasure. Of the actual joke-techniques themselves, it is displacement and the representation of the absurd in particular that – besides being suitable for other functions – provide the desirable distraction of the attention.[5]

We already have an inkling of something we shall see more clearly: that in the requirement that the attention should be distracted we have discovered a feature of the psychical process in the listener to the joke that is by no means inessential. And, in connection with this, there are some other things we can understand too. First, how it comes about that we scarcely ever know what it is we are laughing at in a joke, even though we can settle it by analytic investigation: this laughter is just the result of an automatic process which is only made possible by keeping our conscious attention at bay. Second, we come to understand that odd feature jokes have of being able to manifest their full effect on the listener only when they are new to him, and come to him as a surprise. This characteristic, which determines their ephemeral nature and spurs us to produce more and more new jokes, obviously derives from the fact that it is in the nature of a surprise or sudden attack that it cannot succeed a second time. When a joke is repeated, our attention is drawn to the first time we heard it by our dawning memory of it. This opens the way to understanding the urge to tell a joke we have just heard to others who do not yet know it. One is probably recovering some of the potential enjoyment – missing because the joke is no longer novel – from the impression it makes on the newcomer. And a similar motive may have driven the creator of the joke to pass it on to someone else in the first place.

Third, I shall note as advantageous to the joking-process, though no longer as requirements for it, those auxiliary technical devices of the joke-work that are intended to increase the amount [of energy] achieving discharge and so to heighten the effect of the joke. It is true, they mostly heighten the attention paid to the joke as well, but they neutralize its influence again by simultaneously capturing it and inhibiting its mobility. Anything that arouses interest and bafflement acts in these two directions – that is, the absurd, and contraries above all, and the 'contrast of ideas' which some authorities have wanted to make the essential characteristic of the joke, but which I regard as nothing but a means of reinforcing its effect. Anything baffling summons up in the listener that state of energy-distribution which Lipps called 'psychical damming-up', and no doubt he is also right to assume that the 'release' [*Entladung*] turns out to be all the more powerful, the greater the prior damming. It is true, Lipps's account is not concerned expressly with jokes, but with the comic in general; but it seems to us very likely that the discharge [*Abfuhr*] brought about in jokes, which releases [*entladet*] an inhibitory charge of energy, is increased in the same way by the damming-up.

It now begins to dawn on us that the joke-technique is in general determined by two kinds of tendency, those making the creation of the joke in the first person possible, and others intended to guarantee the joke the greatest possible pleasurable effect on the third person. The Janus-like double-facedness of the joke, which secures its original gain of pleasure against the attacks of critical rationality, and the mechanism of fore-pleasure belong to the first tendency; the further complication of technique by the requirements spelt out in this section arises from taking the joke's third person into account. So the joke is essentially a double-dealing rogue who serves two masters at once. Everything in the joke aimed at gaining pleasure is calculated with an eye to the third person, as if insuperable internal obstacles in the first person stood in its way. This is what gives the strong impression of the indispensability of this third person to consummating the joking-process. But whereas we are able to gain a fairly good insight into the nature of this process in the third person, we sense that the corresponding process in the first person is still shrouded from us in darkness. Of the two questions: 'Why can't we laugh at our own jokes?' and: 'Why are we driven to tell our own jokes to someone else?' an answer to the first has so far eluded us. We can only surmise that there is an intimate connection between the two facts, and that the *very reason* we are compelled to pass on our joke to someone else is *because* we are unable to laugh at it ourselves. From our insights into the conditions for gaining pleasure and for release in the third person, we may infer that in the first the conditions for discharge are lacking and those for gaining pleasure are perhaps only incompletely fulfilled. If so, it is not implausible that we supplement our own pleasure by achieving the laughter that is not possible for ourselves by the roundabout way of the impression on the person who has been made to laugh. We laugh as it were 'par ricochet', as Dugas puts it. Laughter belongs to the highly infectious expressions of psychical states; if I make someone else laugh by telling them my joke, I am actually making use of him to arouse my own laughter, and one can in fact observe how someone who has just told a joke with a straight face then goes on to join in the other's laughter – with a moderate laugh. So it would seem that telling my joke to someone else serves several purposes: first, to give me objective reassurance that the joke-work has been successful; second, to supplement my own pleasure when the effect of the joke on this other person rebounds on to me; and third – when I repeat a joke not my own – to remedy my loss of pleasure when the joke has ceased to be a novelty.

At the end of this discussion of the psychical processes in jokes as they are enacted between two persons, we may cast a glance back at the factor of economizing, which we have had in mind as an important issue in the psychological conception of jokes ever since we first began to explain their technique. The most immediate but also the most naïve conception of this economizing – that it is simply concerned with avoiding any psychical expenditure at all, which is achieved by using the narrowest range of words possible and by setting up connections between ideas – is something we have left far behind us. Even then we said to ourselves: pithy, laconic – not enough for a joke. The brevity of a joke is a special one – the 'joking' brevity itself. The original gain in pleasure produced by playing with words and ideas did derive from mere economies in expenditure, it is true, but as play developed into making jokes, the tendency towards economy also had to shift its aims, for the savings made by using the same words or by avoiding a fresh combination of ideas would count for nothing against the enormous expenditure involved in the activity of thinking. We may do well to allow ourselves to compare the economy of the psyche with a business concern. As long as the business turnover is very small, the main thing of course is that on the whole not much is spent and that the running costs are kept extremely low. The frugality applies to the absolute height of the expenditure. Later, when the business has expanded, the importance of running costs lessens; it no longer matters how high the amount of expenditure becomes as long as the turnover and returns can be sufficiently increased. Restraint in expenditure for running the business would be petty, indeed positively unprofitable. However, it would be wrong to assume that given the absolute amount of the expenditure there would be no more room for the tendency towards economy. The boss's thrifty-mindedness will now turn to parsimony in single items, and feel satisfied if the same activity can now be managed at a lower cost when its previous costs were higher, however small the economy may appear in comparison with the total expenditure. In a quite analogous way, economy in details remains a source of pleasure in the complicated business of our psyche, too, as everyday occurrences can show us. Anyone who used to light his room with a gas lamp and has now gone over to electric light will have a distinct feeling of pleasure for quite a while as he turns on the electricity, that is, for the moment when the memory of the complicated arrangements required to light the gas revives in him. Similarly, the savings in inhibitory expenditure made by the joke – very slight in comparison with the total psychical expenditure – remain a source of pleasure for us because they economize on a particular expense which we are used to making and which we were already prepared to make on this occasion too. That the expenditure is expected, prepared for, comes unmistakably to the fore as a factor.

A localized saving, such as the one we have just considered, will not fail to afford us momentary pleasure, but it does not bring about a lasting relief as long as what has been saved here can be employed elsewhere. It is only if this further disposal can be avoided that the particular saving is transformed back into a general relief of psychical expenditure. In this way, with our greater insight into the psychical processes of jokes, we see that the factor of relief takes the place of economy. The former evidently gives the greater feeling of pleasure. The process in the joke's first person produces pleasure by lifting inhibition, reducing local expenditure; it does not seem to come to rest until, by the introduction of the mediating third person, it has obtained general relief by means of a discharge [of energy].

Notes

1. Herbert Spencer, 'The Physiology of Laughter' (first published in *Mac-Millan's Magazine*, March, 1860), *Essays*, vol. II, 1901.
2. Various points in this definition would require close examination in an investigation of comic pleasure; this has already been undertaken by other authorities, and in any case it does not lie on our path. – Spencer does not seem to me to have been fortunate in his explanation of why the discharge finds the very pathway whose excitation results in the somatic picture of laughter. I should like to make just one contribution to the topic of the physiological explanation for laughter, that is, to the derivation or interpretation of its characteristic muscular actions – something which has been thoroughly dealt with both before and since Darwin, but has still not been

finally settled. To my knowledge, the grimace of drawing back the corners of the mouth in a smile makes its first appearance in the satisfied and surfeited infant as he slips from the breast and falls asleep. There it is an authentic expressive movement, for it tallies with the decision to take in no further nourishment, as it were representing an 'enough', or rather 'more than enough'. This original meaning of pleasurable repletion may have imparted to the smile – which after all is still the fundamental manifestation of laughter – its later relation to pleasurable processes of discharge.

3. Compare the section in the book by Lipps just mentioned, chapter VIII: 'On psychical energy', etc. (see *The Interpretation of Dreams*, chapter VIII [F]). – 'Hence the general proposition holds good: the factors of psychical life are not the contents of consciousness, but unconscious psychical processes which are essentially unconscious. The task of psychology, then, if it does not merely want to describe the contents of consciousness, must be to infer the nature of these unconscious processes from the constitution of the conscious contents and their temporal connections. Psychology must be a theory of these processes. But a psychology of this kind will very soon discover that these processes have many and varied qualities which are not represented in the corresponding contents of consciousness' (Lipps, pp. 123–4).

4. The *status-nascendi* argument has been put by Heymans (*Zeitschrift für Psychol.* XI) in a rather different connection.

5. Using an example of a displacement joke, I should like to discuss another interesting feature of the joke-technique. On one occasion the great actress Gallmeyer is said to have replied to the unwelcome question 'How old?' 'with innocent voice and eyes modestly cast down' with the answer 'In Brünn.' That is the very model of a displacement; asked about her age, she replies with her birthplace, that is, she anticipates the next question and implies 'This particular question I would like to see passed over.' And yet we have a feeling that the jokiness of the joke is not being expressed unalloyed. The question-skipping is all too clear, the displacement all too obvious. Our attention grasps immediately that it is a case of an intended displacement. In other displacement jokes the displacement is disguised, our attention arrested by the effort to locate it. In one of the displacement jokes (p. 46) – 'And what am I supposed to be doing in Pressburg at half-past 6?' as an answer to a recommendation of a saddle-horse – the displacement is similarly intrusive, but to make up for that it has in its absurdity a confusing effect on our attention, whereas in the actress's interrogation we are able to accommodate her displacing reply at once. – What we call '*bantering questions*' diverge from the joke in a different direction, though otherwise

they may make use of the best techniques. The following is an example of a bantering question using the technique of displacement: What is a cannibal who has eaten his father and mother? – Answer: An *orphan*. – And when he has eaten all his other relations as well? – *Sole heir*. – And where will such a monster find sympathy? – *In the dictionary under 'S'*. Bantering questions are not fully-fledged jokes because it is not possible to guess the joking answers they are asking for, unlike the allusions and omissions, etc., in a joke.

C Theoretical Part

VI The Relation of the Joke to Dreams and to the Unconscious

At the end of the section concerned with discovering the technique of jokes (p. 77), we stated that the processes of condensation (with or without substitute-formation), displacement, representation by absurdity or by the opposite, indirect representation, etc., which we found taking part in the creation of jokes, all show a far-reaching agreement with the processes of the 'dream-work'. And we held in reserve both making a closer study of these similarities and investigating what might be the common ground that seemed to be suggested by such similarities. It would be much easier for us to develop this comparison if we could assume that one of the elements compared – the 'dream-work' – were widely known. But we shall probably do better not to make this assumption; for I have had the impression that my *Interpretation of Dreams*, published in 1900, may have produced more 'bafflement' than 'light dawning' among my professional colleagues; and I know that my wider readership has been content to reduce the substance of the book to one catchword ('wish-fulfilment'), which is convenient to remember and easy to misuse.

However, in continuing my pursuit of the problems treated there – which my medical practice as a psychotherapist gives me ample opportunity to do – I have not come up against anything that would have required me to alter or improve my line of thought, so I can wait quietly until my readers' understanding has caught up with me, or until intelligent criticism has proved to me the fundamental errors in my view. In order to make the comparison with jokes, I shall recapitulate the essentials on the subject of dreams and the dream-work here in brief and concentrated form.

We know a dream from our memory of it, which seems mostly fragmentary and sets in after we have woken up. Then it is a tissue of sense-impressions – mainly visual, though there are also other kinds – which have feigned a living experience, and in which thought-processes ('knowledge' in dreams) and expressions of affect may be mingled. I call what we remember of a dream in this way the '*manifest dream-content*'. Often it is completely absurd and confused, at other times only the one or the other; but even if it is quite coherent, as it is in some anxiety dreams, it confronts us as something alien in our inner life, nor can we account for its source. An explanation for these characteristics has until now been sought in the dream itself, regarding them as symptoms of a disorderly, dissociated and so to speak 'sleepy' activity of the nervous elements.

As against that, I have shown that this – so strange – 'manifest content' can invariably be made intelligible as the mutilated and altered transcript of certain psychical formations with their own rationale [*korrekt*], which have earned the name '*latent dream-thoughts*'. We obtain our knowledge of them by breaking the manifest dream-content down into its constituent parts without regard for any apparent sense it may have, and then by pursuing the threads of association leading out from each of the isolated elements. These interweave with one another and ultimately bring us to a tissue of thoughts which not only have a perfectly good rationale, but can also be fitted easily into the familiar context of our inner life. In the course of this 'analysis', the dream-content will have cast off all those oddities we found so strange; but if our analysis is to be successful, we must, while it is going on, steadfastly reject the critical objections that will constantly be raised against our reproduction of the separate intermediary associations.

As the result of our comparison between the manifest dream-content as it is remembered and the latent dream-thoughts as we have uncovered them, we arrive at the concept of the 'dream-work'. Dream-work is the name we shall give to the sum total of those transformatory processes that have transposed the latent dream-thoughts into the manifest dream. And it is to the dream-work that the sense of strangeness previously aroused in us by the dream now clings.

But the function of the dream-work can be described in the following way: an often very complicated tissue of thoughts that has been set up during the day and left unresolved – a residue of the day – holds on to the amount of energy it demanded – our interest – during the night as well, and threatens to disturb our sleep. This residue of the day is transformed by the dream-work into a dream, so that sleep is left unharmed. To give the dream-work something to come to grips with, the day's residue must be capable of forming a wish, not a very difficult condition to fulfil. The wish arising from the dream-thoughts forms the preliminary stage and later the kernel of the dream. Our experience of analyses – not the theory of dreams – tells us that in children *any* wish left from waking life is enough to summon up a dream, which turns out continuous and inventive, though usually brief, and can easily be recognized as a 'wish-fulfilment'. In adults, the general condition holding good for a wish to create dreams seems to be that the wish should be alien to our conscious thought, that is, that it should be a repressed wish, or at any rate have reinforcements unknown to consciousness. Without the assumption of the unconscious as I have explained it above, I could not have developed the theory of dreams further, nor interpreted the empirical material of the dream-analyses. The influence of this unconscious wish on the material fit for consciousness [*bewußtseinskorrekt*] of the dream-thoughts now produces the dream. In the process, this material is as it were drawn down into the unconscious or, more exactly, is exposed to treatment habitual on the level of unconscious thought-processes and characteristic of this level. So far our knowledge of the characteristics of unconscious thinking and of the difference between it and 'pre-conscious' thought – thought capable of becoming conscious – comes only from the results of this same 'dream-work'.

A novel theory, not simple, and going against the habits of our thinking, can hardly gain in clarity from a concentrated account. So all I can aim to do with this discussion is to refer [the reader] to the fuller treatment of the unconscious in my *Interpretation of Dreams*, and to Lipps's writings, which seem to me to be highly significant. I know that anyone under the spell of a good old philosophical schooling, or remotely dependent on what is called a philosophical system, will resist the hypothesis of the 'psychical unconscious' as Lipps and I understand it, and would most like to prove from their definition of the psychical that it is impossible. But definitions are matters of convention, and can be changed. It has often been my experience that persons who argue that the unconscious is absurd or impossible had not drawn their impressions at the wells that flowed to force me, at least, to acknowledge it. These opponents of the unconscious had never shared in witnessing [*mitangesehen*] the effect of post-hypnotic suggestion, and the instances I reported to them from my analyses of neurotics without using hypnosis filled them with the greatest astonishment. They had never realized the idea that the unconscious is something that we really do not know, while we are forced by the most compelling inferences to fill it in; instead they understand it as something that is capable of becoming conscious, something that one had not been thinking of just then, that was not placed in the 'focus of attention'. They had also never tried to convince themselves of the existence of such unconscious thoughts in their own inner life by analysing a dream of their own, and when I attempted to do so with them, they could only take in the ideas that occurred to them with amazement and confusion. It has also been my impression that essentially affective resistances stand in the way of accepting the 'unconscious'; I base it on the fact that no one wants to get to know their unconscious, so the most convenient thing is to deny the possibility completely.

The dream-work, then, to which I return after this excursus, submits the thought-material presented in the optative mood to a very curious working-over. Initially, it takes the first step from the optative to the present [indicative], it replaces an 'Oh, if only I could . . .' with an 'It is . . .' This 'It is' is destined for hallucinatory representation – what I have called the 'regression' in the dream-work, the path taken from thoughts to perceptual images, or, if we want to put it in terms of the topography – as yet unknown and not to be understood anatomically – of the psychical apparatus, it takes the path from the region of thought-formations to that of sense-perceptions. Along this path, which runs in the opposite direction to the line of development of psychical complication, the dream-thoughts acquire visualizable form [*Anschaulichkeit*]; ultimately a graphic [*plastisch*] situation emerges as the kernel of the manifest 'dream-image'. In order to be representable in sensory form, the dream-thoughts have had to undergo strong interventions to recast their expression. But while the thoughts are being transformed back into sense-perceptions, further transformations appear in them; some of these can be understood as necessary, others are surprising. One understands it as a necessary side-effect of regression that almost all the logical relations between the thoughts which have given them articulation are lost in the manifest dream. The dream-work accepts as it were only the raw material of the ideas [*Vorstellungen*] for representation, but not the relations that the thoughts have to one another as well, or at least it retains the freedom to ignore them. On the other hand, there is another part of the dream-work which we cannot derive from regression, from the transformation of thoughts back into sensory images – the very part that is important for our analogy with the formation of jokes. During the dream-work, the material of the dream-thoughts undergoes a quite extraordinary concentration or *condensation*. Its starting-points are items with features in common [*Gemeinsamkeiten*] which are present within the dream-thoughts either by accident or in keeping with the content; since these items themselves are not as a rule sufficient for large-scale condensation, new, artificial and fleeting common ground is created in the dream-work; and to this end it is even fond of using words in whose sound various meanings coincide. The common features newly created by condensation enter the manifest dream-content as representatives of the dream-thoughts in such a way that one element in the dream corresponds to a point of connection, a junction for the dream-thoughts, and in this regard it must be called generally 'overdetermined'. The fact of condensation is the part of the dream-work that is most easily recognizable; it is enough to compare the reported wording of a dream with the transcription of the dream-thoughts obtained by analysis to get a good impression of the scale and range of condensation.

It is less comfortable to be persuaded of the second major transformation which the dream-work effects in the dream-thoughts, the process I have called dream-*displacement*. It shows itself in this way: taking centre-stage in the manifest dream and appearing with great sensory intensity is what lay on the periphery of the dream-thoughts and was quite unimportant; and likewise vice versa. This makes the dream appear displaced in comparison with the dream-thoughts, and it is this very displacement that makes it come to meet our waking inner life as something alien and incomprehensible. For such displacement to come about, it had to be possible for the energy-charge to pass unhindered from important ideas [*Vorstellungen*] to unimportant – and this, in normal thinking capable of consciousness, can produce only the impression of 'flawed thinking'.

Transformation of dream-thoughts so that they become representable, condensation and displacement are the three major functions we may ascribe to the dream-work. A fourth, perhaps dealt with too briefly in *Die Traumdeutung* [*The Interpretation of Dreams*], does not for our purposes come under consideration here. To work out the ideas on 'the topography of the psychical apparatus' and 'regression' fully and consistently – and only that would give these working hypotheses any value – one would have to attempt to determine at which stages of regression the various transformations of the dream-thoughts took place. This attempt has not yet been seriously undertaken; but at least we can say of displacement with certainty that it has to happen in the thought-material while that material is still at the stage of the unconscious processes. Condensation we shall probably have to imagine as a process extending over the entire course [of dream-formation] until it reaches the perceptual region. But in general we shall have to be content to assume that all the forces taking part in the formation of dreams take effect simultaneously. Given the restraint one must understandably preserve in dealing with such problems, and with respect to the doubts in principle – which are not for discussion here – about putting the question in such terms, I would put my trust broadly in the proposition that the process of the dream-work preparatory to the dream is to be located in the region of the unconscious. It seems that in the formation of dreams, roughly speaking, there are three stages in all to be distinguished: first, the transposition of the preconscious residue of the day into the unconscious, a process in which the conditions governing the state of sleep must also have had a part; then the actual dream-work in the unconscious; and third, the regression of the worked-over dream-material to perception. And it is as such that the dream becomes conscious.

The forces that take part in the formation of dreams can be recognized as: the wish to sleep; the charge of energy still left to the day's residue after it has been lowered by the state of sleep; the psychical energy of the unconscious wish that forms the dream; and the resistant power of the 'censorship', dominant in waking life and not entirely lifted during sleep. It is above all the task of dream-formation to overcome the inhibitions created by the censorship, and it is this very task that is accomplished by the displacements of psychical energy within the material of the dream-thoughts.

Now we recall what it was that prompted us in our investigation of jokes to think of dreams. We found that the character and effect of jokes were bound up with certain forms of expression, technical resources among which the various kinds of condensation, displacement and indirect representation are the most striking. But processes leading to the same results of condensation, displacement and indirect representation have become familiar to us as characteristics of the dream-work. Does not this agreement suggest to us that joke-work and dream-work must be identical, at least in one essential point? The dream-work, as I see it, lies with its most important characteristics unveiled before us; but in the psychical processes of the joke, the very part we are able to compare with the dream-work, the process of joke-formation in the first person, is still shrouded from us. Should we not yield to the temptation of constructing [*konstruieren*] this process by analogy to the formation of a dream? Some of the features of dreams are so foreign to jokes that we cannot carry even the corresponding part of the dream-work over to the formation of jokes. The regression of the train of thought to perception certainly does not apply to jokes; but the two stages in the formation of dreams, the descent of a preconscious thought to the unconscious and unconscious revision, would, supposing we adopted them for the formation of jokes, supply the self-same result as we are able to see in jokes. Let us decide, then, to propose the hypothesis that this is the course taken by joke-formation in the first person. *A preconscious thought is given over for a moment to unconscious revision, and the result promptly grasped by conscious perception.*

But before we test this proposition in detail, let us consider an objection which can become a threat to our premiss. We are starting from the fact that the techniques of the joke point towards the same processes that are familiar to us as characteristics of the dream-work. Now against this it is easy to say that we would not have described the techniques of the joke as condensation, displacement, etc., and would not have arrived at such far-reaching congruities between jokes and dreams in their means of representation, if our previous knowledge of the dream-work had not prejudged our conception of the joke-technique, so that fundamentally we are only finding in the joke the confirmation of the expectations with which we approached it from the dream. Such an origin for their congruity would not be a sure guarantee for its survival outside our prejudice. And, indeed, no other author has in fact applied the aspects of condensation, displacement and indirect representation to forms of expression in the joke. That would be a possible objection, but it does not make it a justified one. It could just as well be that the sharper focus to our view given by our knowledge of the dream-work might be indispensable to recognizing the congruity as it exists in reality. In any case, the decision will depend only on whether a critical scrutiny can prove from particular examples that such a view of joke-technique is a forced one, and that other conceptions, more probable and more profound, have been suppressed in its favour, or whether it will have to admit that the expectations based on the dream really can be confirmed in the joke. It is my opinion that we have nothing to fear from such criticism, and that our method of reduction (see

p. 17) reliably showed us the forms of expression in which the techniques of the joke were to be sought. Giving these techniques names that already anticipated the result – the congruity between joke-technique and dream-work – is something I did entirely as of right and really nothing more than an easily justifiable simplification.

Another objection might not damage our cause so much, but it might not be possible to refute it on such strong grounds either. It could be argued that the joke-techniques – which tally with our purposes so well – do indeed deserve to be acknowledged, but that they are still not all the possible techniques there are, nor all the ones that are used in practice. Influenced by the model of the dream-work, it might be objected, we have picked out only the joke-techniques that fit it, while others, which we have overlooked, would not have demonstrated that such congruity was generally present. Now I am really not so bold as to maintain that I have succeeded in throwing light on the technique of all the jokes in circulation, so I shall leave it an open possibility that my enumeration of joke-techniques will reveal many gaps. However, I have not intentionally excluded from discussion any kind of technique that became transparent to me, and I can affirm that the most frequent, the most important, the most characteristic technical devices to be found in jokes have not escaped my attention.

Jokes possess another characteristic that fits satisfyingly into our conception of the joke-work, deriving as it does from the dream. It is true, we say one 'makes' a joke, but we sense that when we do so, we are behaving differently from when we make a judgement or make an objection. A joke has quite outstandingly the character of a 'bright idea', occurring to us involuntarily. It is not so much that one does not know a moment beforehand what joke one is going to make, which one then only needs to clothe in words. One senses rather something undefinable, which I would best compare with an *absence*, a sudden letting-go of intellectual tension, and then all at once the joke is there, for the most part simultaneously clad in words. Some of the devices found in jokes are also used outside them in expressing thoughts: metaphor and allusion, for example. I may intend to make an allusion. In the process, I first have the direct expression of my thought in mind (in my inner ear), but in uttering it I inhibit myself with scruples appropriate to the situation, I almost make up my mind to replace the direct expression by some form of indirect expression and then produce an allusion; but an allusion that has arisen in this way, under my continual control, is never a joke, however useful it may be otherwise; a joking allusion, on the other hand, will appear without my being able to pursue these preparatory stages in my thinking. I do not want to attach over-much importance to this behaviour; it is scarcely definitive, but it surely accords well with our assumption that in forming a joke one lets go of a train of thought for a moment, and then it suddenly surfaces from the unconscious as a joke.

Jokes also display a curious behaviour in respect of associations. Frequently they are not at the disposal of our memory when we want them, but turn up at some other time as if inadvertently, at places in our train of thought where we do not understand how they come to butt in. Again, these are only minor features, but all the same they do indicate that they came from the unconscious.

Let us now draw together those characteristics of the joke that can be referred to its formation in the unconscious. There is above all its peculiar brevity – not an essential mark, it is true, but an unusually distinctive one. When we first met it we were inclined to see it as an expression of economizing tendencies, but we had obvious objections to this view ourselves. It appears to us now to be rather a sign of the unconscious revision that the joke has undergone. For we cannot connect the corresponding process in dreams, condensation, to any other other factor except to its localization in the unconscious, and we must assume that the conditions for condensation lacking in the preconscious are present as given in the unconscious thought-processes.[1] It is to be expected that in the process of condensation, some of the elements affected by it will be lost, while others, taking over the energy that had charged the lost elements, will be made more powerful, or even over-powerful, by the condensation. That is, the brevity of the joke would be like that of the dream, a necessary by-product of condensations occurring in both, in both instances a phenomenon resulting from the condensation-process. It is to this origin that the brevity of the joke also owes its peculiar character, which we are unable to describe any further, though we sense how striking it is.

Earlier (p. 121) we understood the one product of condensation – multiple use of the same material, word-play, punning similarity of sound – in terms of localized economizing, and we argued that the pleasure given by the (innocuous) joke derived from an economizing of this kind; later we found that the original intention of the joke lay in making words yield the kind of pleasure that it had enjoyed unconfined at the stage of play, but which had been blocked by rational criticism in the course of intellectual development. We have now decided to proceed on the hypothesis that condensations of the kind that serve the joke-technique arise automatically, without any particular intention, during the thinking-process in the unconscious. Are these not two different, apparently incompatible, views of the same fact? I do not think so; it is true, they are two different views, and they do require reconciling, but they do not contradict each other. The one is merely foreign to the other, and once we have established a relationship between them, we shall probably have come a step further in our knowledge. That such condensations are sources for obtaining pleasure is quite consistent with the hypothesis that they easily find the conditions for their emergence in the unconscious; contrariwise, we see the motivation for the plunge into the unconscious in the circumstance that the pleasure-bringing condensation required by the joke emerges there easily. Two other factors too, which at first sight seem completely foreign to each other, meeting as if by unwelcome chance, can be seen on deeper scrutiny to be intimately linked, indeed, identical in nature. I mean the two propositions that on the one hand, during its development on the level of play – in the childhood of reason, that is – the joke is able to produce these pleasure-bringing condensations; and that, on the other hand, it performs the same feat on a higher level by plunging the thought into the unconscious. For the infantile is the source of the unconscious; unconscious processes are nothing more than those produced simply and solely in early childhood. The thought, plunging into the unconscious in order to form the joke, is only revisiting the ancient home of its erstwhile play with words. For a moment thinking is transposed back to the childish stage, in order to repossess the childish source of pleasure. Even if we did not already know it from research into the psychology of neuroses, we could not but surmise from jokes that the strange unconscious revision is nothing other than the infantile type of thinking. In children it is just not very easy to catch this infantile thinking on the wing, with its peculiarities which have been preserved in the adult's unconscious, because it is usually being corrected *in statu nascendi*, so to speak. Still, in a number of cases, it does happen, and when it does we always laugh at the 'childish silliness'. Whenever something unconscious of this kind is revealed, it generally affects us as being 'comic'.[2]

The characteristics of these unconscious thinking-processes are easier to grasp in the expressions of those suffering from certain psychical disorders. It is very probable, as old Griesinger suspected, that we would be in a position to understand the deliria of the mentally ill and see them as messages if we did not apply the demands of conscious thinking to them, but instead treated them with our art of interpretation, rather like dreams.[3] And for dreams too, we did indeed once confirm the 'return of our inner life to the embryonic point of view'.[4]

In dealing with the processes of condensation, we discussed the significance of the analogy between jokes and dreams so thoroughly that we may be more brief in what follows. We know that displacements in the dream-work indicate the influence of the censorship on conscious thinking; accordingly, we shall be inclined to assume when we meet displacement among the techniques of the joke that some inhibiting power also plays a part in its formation. We already know, too, that this is quite generally the case; in normal moods, the joke's efforts at obtaining the old pleasure in nonsense or word-play are inhibited by the objections of critical reason; this has to be overcome in each individual instance. But the way in which the joke-work deals with this task reveals a far-reaching difference between jokes and dreams. In the dream-work the problem is solved as a rule by displacements, by the selection of images [*Vorstellungen*] that are remote enough from the contested ones for the censorship to let them through, but which are still their offspring and have taken over the full transference of their [energy-]charge. That is why displacements are never absent from any dream and are far more thoroughgoing; not only diversions from a train of thought but also all the varieties of indirect representation are to be counted among the displacements, particularly the substitution of a significant but offensive element by one that is neutral, appearing innocuous to the censorship, and related to the first as the most distant allusion, as well as substitution by symbolism, metaphor, or something small. It is indisputable that parts of this indirect representation already come about in the dream's preconscious thoughts – symbolic or metaphorical representation for example – because otherwise the thought would not have got as far as the level of preconscious expression at all. Indirect representations of this sort and allusions whose reference to what is actually meant is easy to discover are indeed accepted and much-used expressive means in our conscious thinking too. But the dream-work exaggerates the use of these means of indirect representation beyond all bounds. Under pressure from the censorship any kind of connection is good enough for substitution by allusion, displacement from one element to any other is permitted. What is particularly striking and characteristic of the dream-work is that for internal associations (similarity, causal connection, etc.) it substitutes what are called external ones (simultaneity, contiguity in space, identity of sound).

All these displacement devices also occur as joke-techniques, but when they do, they usually keep to the limits drawn for their use in conscious thinking, and they may be missing entirely, even though jokes too invariably have the task of dealing with inhibitions. We can understand that displacements should fall back in this way if we recall that the joke generally has another technique at its command to fend off the inhibition – indeed, that we have not found anything more characteristic of jokes than this very technique. For the joke does not create compromises, as the dream does, it does not evade the inhibition, rather it insists on keeping up its play with words or nonsense, but limits itself to a choice of instances in which this play or nonsense can also appear acceptable (in pleasantries) or meaningful (in jokes), thanks to the ambiguity of words and the variety of relations between thoughts. Nothing distinguishes the joke more clearly from all other psychical formations than this its two-sidedness and two-facedness, and from this aspect at least, in their emphasis on 'sense in nonsense', our authorities have come closest to an understanding of the nature of the joke.

Given the total ascendancy of this technique, peculiar to jokes, in overcoming their inhibitions, we might regard it as superfluous that they should make use of the technique of displacement in individual cases at all. However, on the one hand, certain varieties of this technique still remain valuable to the joke as aims and sources of pleasure – such as true displacement (diversion of thoughts), which indeed shares in the nature of nonsense; and on the other hand, we should not forget that the highest stage of joking, the tendentious joke, frequently has two kinds of inhibition to overcome, those opposing the joke itself and those opposing its tendency (pp. 98–9), and that allusions and displacements are well suited to enabling it to perform this task.

The ample and unbridled use of indirect representation, displacements and especially allusions in the dream-work has a consequence which I mention not on account of its own significance, but because it was the subjective occasion for me to become interested in the problem of jokes. If one gives an account of a dream-analysis to someone who is not conversant with such things, in which, of course, the curious and – to waking thought – repugnant pathways of the allusions and displacements employed by the dream-work is described, the reader is subject to an uncomfortable impression, declares that these interpretations are 'jokey' [*witzig*], but obviously regards them not as successful jokes but as being forced, and as somehow breaking the rules of the joke. This impression is now easy to explain: it is because the dream-work operates with the same devices as the joke, but in their use oversteps the limits that the joke respects. We shall soon learn that as a consequence of the role played by the third person, the joke is bound by a certain condition which does not affect the dream.

Among the techniques common to jokes and dreams, representation by the opposite and the use of absurdity claim a certain interest. The first belongs to resources of the joke that have a very powerful effect, as we could see, among other things, from the examples of 'going-one-better' jokes (pp. 61–2). Representation by the opposite, by the way, cannot escape conscious attention, unlike most of the other joke-techniques; anyone trying to set the mechanism of the joke-work going in himself as deliberately as possible – the habitual joker – is usually quick to discover that one can most easily respond to a remark with a joke if one asserts its opposite and leaves it to the inspiration of the moment [*Einfall*] to ward off the anticipated objection by changing one's meaning. Perhaps representation by the opposite owes this privileged place to the circumstance that it forms the kernel of another pleasure-bringing mode of expression in thought, which we do not need to bother the unconscious to understand. I mean *irony*, which approaches the witticism very closely, and is counted among the subspecies of comedy. In essence it consists in stating the opposite of what one intends to say to the other, but sparing him the contradiction by giving him to understand – by tone of voice, by accompanying gestures – by fine stylistic indications, when it is a matter of writing, – that in fact one means the opposite of what one is saying. Irony can only be used where the other person is prepared to hear the opposite, so that he cannot but be inclined to contradict. Because it is dependent on this condition, irony very easily runs the risk of not being understood. It gives the person using it the advantage of evading the difficulties of direct expression with ease – in invective, for example; in the listener it produces a comic pleasure, probably by provoking him to an expenditure of energy on contradiction – which is promptly recognized to be superfluous. A comparison of this kind with a genre of the comic closely related to it may strengthen us in our assumption that what is special about the joke is its relation to the unconscious – which may also perhaps distinguish it from the comic.[5]

Representation by the opposite plays a far greater part in the dream-work than in the joke. The dream is not only fond of representing two contraries by one and the same compound image; it also transforms an object from the dream-thoughts into its opposite so often that this creates a great difficulty in the work of interpretation: '. . . at first one cannot tell which of the possible poles is meant positively or negatively in the dream-thoughts'.[6]

I must stress that this fact has not met with any understanding at all as yet. But it does seem to indicate an important feature of unconscious thinking, which in all probability lacks any process comparable to 'judging'. In the place of a negative judgement, what one finds in the unconscious is 'repression'. It is probably right to describe repression as the intermediate stage between defence-reflex and condemnation by the judgement.[7]

All the same, the nonsense, the absurdity that occurs so frequently in dreams and has called down so much undeserved scorn upon it, has never arisen by accident, by just jumbling up ideas [*Vorstellungen*]; rather, it can be shown every time to have been allowed in by the dream-work on purpose, and intended to represent embittered criticism and scornful contradiction within the dream-thoughts. The absurdity of the dream-content, that is, takes the place of the judgement 'that's nonsense' in the dream-thoughts. In my *Interpretation of Dreams* I laid great stress on pointing this out, because I thought this was the most forcible way to combat the error of denying that the dream is a psychical phenomenon at all, barring as it does the way to understanding the unconscious. We have now learned (in solving certain tendentious jokes, pp. 47–9) that nonsense in jokes is put in the service of the same purposes of representation. We also know that a façade of nonsense in a joke is quite particularly suited to raising [*steigern*] the listener's psychical expenditure and so to increasing [*erhöhen*] the amount [of energy] freed for its release by laughter. But besides that, let us not forget that nonsense in a joke is an end in itself, since the intention of regaining the old pleasure in nonsense belongs to the motives of the joke-work. There are other ways of regaining nonsense and deriving pleasure from it; caricature, exaggeration, parody and travesty make use of it, and in this way create 'comic nonsense'. If we subject these forms of expression to an analysis similar to the one we made of jokes, we will find that to explain them, not one gives any occasion for us to enlist unconscious processes as we understand them. We can now understand, too, why the characteristic of 'jokiness' can be added to caricature, exaggeration, parody as an extra garnish; it is the difference in 'scene of action' that makes this possible.[8]

As I see it, moving the joke-work to the unconscious system has become a great deal more valuable to us now that it has opened up the way to understanding the fact that the techniques to which the joke after all is attached are, on the other hand, not its exclusive property. A number of doubts, which we had to set aside during our early investigation into these techniques, now find their fitting solution. So one reservation deserves our consideration all the more: it reminds us that the undeniable presence of the joke's relationship to the unconscious is true only of certain categories of the tendentious joke, whereas we are prepared to extend it to jokes of all species and at all stages of development. We must not evade examining this objection.

The formation of jokes in the unconscious can certainly be assumed when it is a matter of jokes in the service of unconscious intentions [*Tendenzen*], or of intentions reinforced by the unconscious, that is, in most 'cynical' jokes. For then the unconscious intention draws the preconscious thought down towards it into the unconscious in order to reshape it there – our study of the psychology of neuroses is familiar with numerous analogies to the process. However, in tendentious jokes of a different kind, and in innocuous jokes and pleasantries, this downwards force seems to be absent, so the relation of the joke to the unconscious is called into question.

But let us now take the case of a thought, not without value in itself, which comes to the surface in the course of a train of thinking and assumes expression in the form of a joke. For this thought to become a joke, there clearly needs to be a selection of possible forms of expression to find just the one that comes bearing the gain of verbal pleasure. We know from self-observation that it is not conscious attention that makes this selection; but the selection would certainly benefit if the energy-charge of the preconscious thought were reduced to an unconscious one, for in the unconscious the connecting pathways leading from words are treated, as we have learned from the dream-work, in the same way as connections between things. The unconscious charge offers far more favourable conditions for selecting the expression. Besides, we can assume without hesitation that the possible form of expression containing the amount of verbal pleasure gained will have a downwards pull on the still undecided wording of the preconscious thought similar to that effected by the unconscious tendency in the earlier case. In the simpler case of the pleasantry, we may imagine that an intention, always alert to attain a yield of verbal pleasure, seizes the occasion found where else but in the preconscious to draw the process of charging, again according to the familiar model, down into the unconscious.

I could wish it were possible for me on the one hand to present my view of the joke more clearly on this one point, and on the other to reinforce it with compelling arguments. But actually, this is not a question of a twofold failure, but of one and the same. I am unable to give a clearer exposition because I have no further proof for my view. This developed out of my study of joke-technique and from the comparison with the dream-work, in fact only under this one aspect, which allows me to see that on the whole it is quite excellently fitted to the distinctive characteristics of the joke. So this view is one that has been inferred; in drawing such an inference, if one reaches a field that is not familiar, but strange, new to one's thinking, one calls this inference a 'hypothesis', and – rightly – one does not let the relation of the hypothesis to the material from which it is inferred count as 'proof'. It will count as 'proven' only if one has also reached it along a different path and can demonstrate that it is the junction-point for other interconnections as well. But a proof of this kind – for our knowledge of unconscious processes has scarcely begun – is not to be had. Knowing that we are standing on ground as yet utterly untrodden, let us be content with pushing one single, narrow, unsteady spar out into the unfathomed.

There is not very much we can build on this foundation. If we relate the various stages of the joke to the temper of mind favourable to them, we might say something like this: a *pleasantry* arises from a cheerful mood, which seems to be characterized by an inclination to lower the psychical charge. It already employs all the characteristic techniques of the joke and already fulfils its basic condition in selecting verbal material or thought-connections of a kind that will satisfy both the demand for obtaining pleasure and the claims of rational criticism. We shall conclude that the descent of the thought's energy-charge to the unconscious level, eased along by the cheerful mood, already applies to the pleasantry. This help from the mood is not required for a *joke* that is *innocuous* but still linked with the expression of a valuable thought; in this case we need to assume a particular *personal aptitude*, expressed in the ease with which the preconscious charge is dropped and momentarily exchanged for the unconscious one. In this process, an ever-watchful intention to renew the original gain in pleasure from the joke has a downward effect on the still-unsettled preconscious expression of the thought. In a cheerful mood, most people are, I suppose, capable of pleasantries; the aptitude for making jokes independently of mood is present only in a few. Finally, the most powerful stimulus to the joke-work is the presence of strong tendencies, reaching into the unconscious, which represent a special aptitude for producing jokes and may explain why the subjective conditions for making jokes are so frequently fulfilled in neurotic persons. Under the influence of strong tendencies, even those who are otherwise ill-equipped may become witty.

However, with this last contribution to an explanation, though still hypothetical, of the joke-work in the first person, our interest in the joke is, strictly speaking, at an end. All that remains is for us to make a brief comparison of the joke with the better-known dream, premised on the expectation that two such disparate functions of the psyche will – apart from the one correspondence already discussed – reveal only differences. The most important difference lies in their social behaviour. The dream is a completely asocial product of the psyche; it has nothing to communicate to anyone else; arising in one person as a compromise between the conflicting forces within it, it remains unintelligible to the dreamer himself and so for that reason is completely uninteresting to anyone else. The dream not only has no need to place any value on intelligibility, it must even guard against being understood, for otherwise it would be destroyed; it can only exist in disguise. That is why it may employ the mechanism that governs unconscious thought-processes unimpeded, to the point of irremediable distortion. The joke on the other hand is the most social of all the psyche's functions that aim to obtain pleasure. It frequently needs three persons, and to be consummated it requires someone else to participate in the psychical processes it has set going. So it has to commit itself to the condition of intelligibility; it may not make use of the distortion from condensation and displacement that is possible in the unconscious to any further extent than can be redressed by the third person's understanding. For the rest, the two – joke and dream – have grown up in quite different regions of the inner life, and they are to be located in parts of the psychological system far away from each other. The dream is always a wish, however unrecognizable this has been made; the joke is developed play. Despite all its practical nullity, the dream maintains a relation to our great vital interests; it attempts to fulfil our needs by the regressive roundabout route of hallucination, and it owes its admission to the one need that is active during the night – the need to sleep. The joke on the other hand attempts to draw a small amount of pleasure from the sheer activity, free of all needs, of our psychical apparatus; later to catch it as a by-product of the activity of that apparatus. In this way it arrives *secondarily* at certain not unimportant functions turned towards the outside world. The dream predominantly serves to spare ourselves unpleasure, the joke to gain pleasure; but in these two aims, all our psychical activities meet.

Notes

1. I have been able to demonstrate that condensation is a regular and important process elsewhere, besides in the dream-work and joke-technique: in the mechanism of normal (not purposeful) *forgetting*. Distinctive impressions put difficulties in the way of forgetting; other impressions somehow analogous to these are forgotten by being subject to condensation at one of the points of overlap. Mixing up analogous impressions is one of the preliminary stages of forgetting.

2. Many of my neurotic patients under psychoanalytic treatment habitually confirm it with a laugh when [the analysis] has succeeded in revealing faithfully what had been hidden and unconscious to their conscious perception; and they also laugh even if the content of what has been disclosed would certainly not justify it – though the condition for this, of course, is that they have come close enough to what was unconscious to grasp it after the physician has guessed it and presented them with it.

3. In doing so we should not forget to take into account the distortion caused by the censorship, which is still active, even in psychosis.

4. *The Interpretation of Dreams* [VII.E].

5. The characteristic of comedy described as 'dryness' also relies on the separation between speech and accompanying gestures (in the widest sense).

6. *The Interpretation of Dreams* [VI.C].

7. This most remarkable and still insufficiently recognized behaviour in the relations between opposites in the unconscious is probably not without some value for understanding 'negativism' in neurotics and the mentally ill. (Cf. the two most recent works on the subject: Bleuler, 'Über die negative Suggestibilität', *Psych. Neurol. Wochenschrift*, 1904, and Otto Gross, 'Zur Differentialdiagnostik negativistischer Phänomene', ibid.; further, my paper on the 'Antithetical Meaning of Primal Words', *Jahrbuch der Psychoanalyse* II, 1910.)

8. An expression of G. Th. Fechner's which has become very important for my theory.

VII *The Joke and the Varieties of the Comic*

[A]

We have approached the problems of the comic in an unusual way. It seemed to us that the joke, which is otherwise regarded as a subspecies of comedy, offers sufficient distinctive features to be attacked directly, and so we have avoided considering its relation to the more comprehensive category of the comic for as long as possible, though not without picking up a few useful hints towards the comic on the way. We had no difficulty in discovering that socially the comic behaves differently from the joke. It can be content with only two persons, the first, who *finds* what is comic, and the second, in whom it is found. The third person, to whom what is comic is told, reinforces the comic process, but does not add anything new to it. In the joke, this third person is indispensable to consummating the process of bringing pleasure; on the other hand, the second person can be dropped in cases where it is not a question of a tendentious, aggressive joke. The joke is made, comedy is found – in persons above all, and only by extension in objects, situations and the like. With respect to the joke, we know that the sources of pleasure it wants to promote lie not in other persons, but in our own thinking-processes. We have learned further that the joke can sometimes open up again sources of comedy which have become inaccessible, and that the comic frequently serves the joke as a façade, taking the place of the fore-pleasure which, as we know, the joke-technique is otherwise meant to produce (p. 149). None of this exactly indicates very simple relations between the joke and comedy. On the other hand, the problems of the comic have shown themselves to be so complicated, so successful in defying all the efforts of the philosophers to solve them to date, that we cannot expect to master them in a surprise attack, as it were, by approaching them from the angle of the joke. In investigating the joke, we also brought along an instrument which others had not used before: our knowledge of the dream-work; inquiring into the comic, we have no similar advantage at our command, and so we may expect that we will learn nothing more about the nature of comedy than what the joke has already shown us, in so far as it belongs to the [category of the] comic and carries some of its features either unchanged or modified in its own nature.

The genre of the comic closest to the joke is the *naïve*. Like the comic in general, the naïve is found, and not, like the joke, made; in fact, the naïve cannot be made at all, whereas in [the category of] the purely comic, there is also making someone comic, calling the comedy up, to consider. The naïve has to emerge without any contribution from us in the speech and actions of other people, who take the place of the *second* person in the comic or in the joke. The naïve arises when someone is completely unaffected by an inhibition because it is simply not present in him, that is, when he seems to overcome it without any effort. It is a condition for the naïve to make its effect that we know the person does not have this inhibition, otherwise we do not call him naïve, but cheeky, and do not laugh at him, but get indignant. The naïve has an effect which is irresistible and which seems simple to our understanding: on hearing the naïve remark, an expenditure we habitually make on inhibition suddenly becomes unusable and is released by laughter; in the process, our attention does not need to be distracted, probably because the inhibition is lifted directly and not through the mediation of some operation that has been set going. In this we are behaving rather like the third person of the joke, who has the saving in inhibition given him as a gift without any effort of his own.

After our insights into the origins of inhibitions, acquired when we were pursuing the development from play to joke, we shall not be surprised that the naïve is most of all to be found in children, and by extension in uncultivated adults, whom we may think of as childish as far as their intellectual development is concerned. Naïve remarks are naturally better suited for comparison with jokes than naïve actions, for speech, not action, is the usual form of expression for a joke. It is telling that we can without any strain also call remarks such as children make 'naïve jokes'. Some examples will make it easy for us to see the correspondence and the reasons for the difference between jokes and naïvety.

A little girl, three-and-a-half years old, warns her brother: 'Don't eat so much of that pudding, else you'll get ill and you'll have to have some bubicine.' 'Bubicine?' asks her mother. 'What's that?' 'When I was ill,' the child explains, 'I had to take medicine too.' The child thinks that the remedy prescribed by the doctor is called 'medi-cine' [*Mädi*, 'little girl'] when it is meant for little girls, and concludes that it will be called 'bubi-cine' [*Bubi*, 'little boy'] if it is to be taken by the little boy. Now this is composed like a verbal joke working with the technique of similarity of sound, and it could even have been made as a proper joke, in which case we would, half against our will, have given it a smile. As an example of naïvety it seems excellent and makes us laugh out loud. But where does the difference lie here between the joke and the naïve? Obviously it is not in the wording or the technique, which are the same in both possibilities, but in a factor which at first glance seems pretty remote from both. It is only a question of whether we assume that the speaker has intended to make a joke, or wanted – the child – in good faith to draw a serious conclusion on the basis of her uncorrected ignorance. Only the latter case is one of naïvety. We note here for the first time that the other person has put himself into [*Sichhinein-versetzen*] the psychical process going on in the person producing the remark.

An examination of a second example will confirm this view. A brother and sister, a twelve-year-old girl and a ten-year-old boy are performing a drama they have composed themselves before an audience of uncles and aunts. The scene represents a hut on the sea coast. In the first act, the two playwright-performers, a poor fisherman and his good wife, lament the hard times and poor living. The husband decides to sail the wide seas in his boat to seek his fortune elsewhere, and after a tender farewell between the two, the curtain is drawn. The second act takes place a few years later. The fisherman has returned a rich man with a big bag of money and tells his wife, whom he encounters waiting outside the hut, what good fortune he has had in foreign parts. The wife interrupts him proudly: 'Meantime I too have not been idle,' and opens up the hut to his gaze, where twelve large dolls, representing children, are to be seen sleeping on the floor . . . At this point in the drama the actors were interrupted by a storm of laughter from the spectators, which they could not understand. They stared in puzzlement at their nearest and dearest, who up until then had been behaving themselves properly and listening with great attention. The premiss explaining this laughter is the spectators' assumption that the young dramatists were still ignorant of the requirements for the origin of children and so could believe that a wife would boast of the progeny born during her husband's long absence, and that a husband would join her in rejoicing. But what our playwrights produced on the basis of such ignorance could be described as nonsense, as absurdity.

A third example will show us another technique that we have met in jokes being used in the service of the naïve. A 'Frenchwoman' was employed as a governess for a little girl, but did not meet with her approval. The newly engaged governess had scarcely left the room when the little girl gave voice to her criticism: 'That's supposed to be a Frenchwoman! Perhaps that's what she calls herself because she was lying next to a Frenchman once!' This might almost be a passable joke – *double entendre* with ambiguity or ambiguous allusion – if the child had had an inkling of the possibility of a *double entendre*. In reality she was only transferring to the stranger she disliked a bantering contention, which she had often heard, that something was sham ('That's supposed to be genuine gold? Perhaps it was lying next to gold once!'). On account of this ignorance on the part of the child, which so thoroughly alters the psychical process going on in the sophisticated listeners, what she says becomes naïve. However, because of this condition, there is also such a thing as a misleading naïvety; it is possible to assume in a child an ignorance which no longer exists, and children often pretend to be naïve to exploit a freedom which they would not otherwise be granted.

These examples make it possible to clarify the position of the naïve between the joke and the comic. The naïve (in speech) coincides with the joke in wording and content, it brings about misuse of words, nonsense or obscenity. But the psychological process going on in the first person, who produces it, which in jokes offered so much to interest and puzzle us, is entirely absent here. The naïve person imagines he has been using language and logic normally and simply without any ulterior intent; nor does he draw any gain in pleasure from producing what is naïve. All the characteristics of the naïve exist only in the perception of the person listening, who is identical with the third person in the joke. Also, the persons who produce it do so without any effort; the complicated technique intended in the joke to paralyse the inhibition created by rational criticism is absent in them because they do not yet possess this inhibition, and so can utter nonsense or obscenity directly and without compromise. To that extent the naïve represents a borderline case of joking which comes about when, in the formula for joke-formation, the quantity of this censorship is reduced to zero.

Whereas it was a condition for a joke to work that both persons should have more or less the same inhibitions or internal resistances, we recognize that it is a condition for the naïve that the one person should possess inhibitions which the other lacks. The perception of what is naïve is found in the person with inhibitions, no one but he experiences the gain in pleasure that it brings about, and we are close to guessing that this pleasure arises from the lifting of inhibitions. As the pleasure of a joke has the same origin – a kernel of pleasure from words and nonsense and a shell of pleasure from lifting and relief – this relation, similar to inhibition, is what accounts for the inner affinity between the naïve and the joke. In both the pleasure arises from lifting an internal inhibition. But in the case of the naïve, the psychical process going on in the recipient – which in the naïve invariably coincides with our self, whereas in the joke we are also able to put ourselves in the position of the person producing it

– is more complicated to the same degree as the process going on in the person producing it is more simplified, in comparison with the joke. The naïve [remark] the recipient has heard must on the one hand have the effect on him of a joke – as witness our particular examples – for, as in the joke, it has enabled the censorship to be lifted by the mere effort of listening. But only a part of the pleasure created by the naïve admits of this explanation, indeed, even this part might be endangered in other instances of the naïve, for example, on hearing a naïve obscenity. One could react to naïve smut with the same prompt indignation that might perhaps arise towards a real obscenity, if another factor did not spare us this indignation and at the same time provide us with the more significant share of pleasure we get from the naïve.

This other factor is given by the condition just mentioned: in order to recognize the naïve, we should know that the person producing it is without internal inhibition. Only when we are sure of this, will we laugh instead of being indignant. That is, we take the psychical state of the person producing it into account, put ourselves into it, try to understand it by comparing it with our own. From such transpositions and comparisons, a saving in expenditure results, which we release by laughter.

One might possibly prefer the simpler account: if we consider that the person does not need to overcome any inhibition, our indignation becomes superfluous; and then our laughter would occur at the cost of the indignation saved. To keep this generally misleading view at bay, I will make a sharper distinction between two cases which I treated as one in the above account. The naïve as it appears before us can have the nature either of a joke, as it did in our examples, or of an obscenity, indeed, of what is generally offensive – which would happen particularly if it were expressed not in speech but in action. This latter case is really misleading; one might assume of it that our pleasure arose from the indignation that has been saved and transformed. But the former case does throw light on the problem. The naïve remark about 'bubicine', for example, can actually work as a little joke, and give no cause for indignation; this is certainly the less-frequent case, but it is more pure and far more instructive. Once we think that the child has seriously and without ulterior intent taken the syllables 'medi' in 'medicine' to be identical with her own name, 'Mädi', our pleasure in what we have heard sustains an intensification that no longer has anything to do with the pleasure we take in a joke. We now look at what she has said from two different points of view, once in the way it was produced in the child, and once as it would be produced in ourselves, and in this comparison we find that the child has discovered an identity [between words] and that she has overcome a barrier that exists for us, and so our thoughts go on as if we were to say to ourselves: if you want to understand what you have heard, you can save yourself the effort of keeping up the barrier. The expenditure set free in such a comparison is the source of our pleasure in the naïve and is released by laughter; though it is, of course, the same expenditure that we would otherwise have transformed into indignation, if that were not precluded by our understanding of the person who produced the naïve [remark] and in this instance also by the nature of what she said. But if we take the case of the naïve joke as the model for the other case of the naïve – the naïvely offensive – we shall see that here too the saving in inhibition can proceed directly from the comparison, that it is not necessary for us to assume a starting and stifling of indignation, and that this indignation corresponds only to putting the liberated expenditure to some other use, whereas in the joke complicated protective arrangements were required.

This comparison, this saving of expenditure in putting oneself into the internal processes of the person producing, can only be important for the naïve if it does not apply to the naïve alone. In fact, we begin to suspect that this mechanism, which is entirely alien to the joke, is a part – perhaps the essential part – of the comic. From this point of view – it is certainly the most important aspect of the naïve – the naïve presents itself, then, as a species of the comic. In our examples of naïve remarks, what is added to the pleasure of the joke is 'comic' pleasure. We might be generally inclined to assume of this comic pleasure that it arose by saving the effort of comparing someone else's remarks with our own. But as we are standing on the brink of far-reaching thoughts here, let us first bring our discussion of the naïve to a close. The naïve, then, is a species of the comic, in so far as its pleasure comes from the difference [in quantity] of expenditure arising in the course of trying to understand the other, and it approaches the joke on account of the condition that the expenditure saved in the course of comparing must be an expenditure of inhibition.[1]

Let us go on quickly to establish some points of agreement and difference between the concepts we have just arrived at, and those that have long been identified in the psychology of comedy. Putting oneself in the other's frame of mind, wanting to understand – this is evidently no more than the 'comic lending'[2] that has played a part in the analysis of the comic ever since Jean Paul; 'comparing' the psychical processes in the other person with one's own corresponds to the psychological contrast, which we can at last accommodate here, after we could not do anything with it in our study of jokes. But in our explanation of comic pleasure we part company with several authorities who argue that the pleasure is supposed to arise from the wavering of attention to and fro between the contrasting ideas [*Vorstellungen*]. We would have no way of understanding a pleasure-mechanism of this kind, though we do point out that in comparing the contrasts, there emerges a difference in [quantity of] expenditure which – as long as it is not put to any other use – becomes capable of release and in this way becomes a source of pleasure.[3]

It is only with some timidity that we dare approach the problem of the comic itself. It would be presumptuous to expect our efforts to contribute anything decisive to its solution, when the works of a great number of very fine thinkers have not been able to yield a generally satisfying explanation. We really do not intend to do anything more than take up those aspects that have proved valuable in understanding the joke and pursue them some way further into the field of the comic.

The comic turns out first of all to be something unintended we find in human social relations. It is found in persons, in their movements, forms, actions and traits of character – originally perhaps only in physical characteristics, and later in mental [*seelisch*] ones as well – and in their respective ways of expressing them. Then, in a commonly used kind of personification, animals and inanimate objects become comic too. However, the comic is capable of being detached from persons if the circumstance that makes a person appear comical is recognized. This is how 'the comic of situation' arises, and this knowledge brings the possibility of making a person comic at will, by placing him in situations where these conditions for the comic attach to his actions. The discovery that one has it in one's power to make someone else comical opens up access to an undreamed-of gain in comic pleasure, and is the origin of a highly developed technique. One can also make oneself comic just as easily as one can anyone else. The devices for making someone comic are: putting them in comical situations, imitation, disguise, unmasking, caricature, parody, travesty, etc. It almost goes without saying that these techniques can also serve hostile and aggressive tendencies. One can make a person comical in order to make him contemptible and rob him of any claim on dignity or authority. But even if such an intention invariably underlay making someone comic, this need not be the meaning of what is comic of its own accord.

From this secondary survey of the incidence of the comic, one can already see that it has to be credited with a very extensive field of origin, and that specialized conditions such as we find applying to the naïve, for example, are not to be expected in this case. In order to track down the condition that holds good for the comic, the most important thing is our choice of instance to start from; we shall select the comedy of movement, because we recall that the most primitive theatrical performance, mime, makes use of this resource to make us laugh. Our answer to the question as to why we laugh at the movements of a clown would run: because they appear disproportionate and impracticable. We are laughing at an over-great expenditure. Let us now look for this condition outside the comedy that has been artificially contrived, that is, where it can be found unintended. The movements of children do not appear comical to us, although they wriggle and squirm. On the other hand it is comical when a child is learning to write and stretches out his tongue to follow the movements of the pen; in these accompanying motions we see an unnecessary expenditure of movement which we would spare ourselves if we were doing the same thing. Likewise, we find other accompanying movements or even merely expressive gestures comic in adults too. Quite pure instances of this kind of comedy are the movements made by a skittle-player after he has thrown the bowl, following its course as if he could still control it in retrospect; all grimaces are comical too, when they exaggerate the normal expressions of emotion, even when they happen involuntarily, as in those suffering from St Vitus's dance (*chorea St Viti*); and the passionate movements of a modern conductor will appear comic to someone unmusical who does not understand their necessity. Indeed, the comic in physical shapes and facial features branches off from this comedy of movement, when they are perceived as if they were the result of some extravagant and pointless movement. Eyes popping, nose hooked down to the mouth, ears sticking out, humped back – it is probable that all these only have a comic effect because we are imagining the movements that might have been necessary to bring these features about, whereby nose, ears and other parts of the body appear to be more movable to the imagination than they are in reality. It is surely comical when someone can 'waggle their ears', and quite certainly it would be even more comical if he could move his nose up and down. A good deal of the comic effect animals make on us comes from perceiving certain movements of theirs that we are unable to imitate.

But how do we arrive at laughter when we have recognized someone else's movements as disproportionate and impracticable? By making a comparison, I think, between the movement I observe in the other person and the one I would have performed myself in their place. The two things compared, of course, must be measured by the same standard, and this standard is my own expenditure of innervation as it is connected with imagining the respective movements. This assertion needs to be explained and developed further.

What we are bringing into relation here is the psychical effort spent in the act of imagining [*vorstellen*] something on the one hand, and the actual content of the thing that is being imagined

[*Vorstellungsinhalt*] on the other. We maintain that the former is not in general and in principle independent of the latter, that is, of the content of the idea imagined [*Vorstellung*]; in particular we maintain that imagining something large requires a greater effort than imagining something small. As long as it is only a question of imagining movements of a different scale, we should not have any difficulty in providing a theoretical basis for our thesis nor in demonstrating it empirically. We shall see that in this instance one characteristic of the imagined idea does in fact coincide with one characteristic of the thing imagined, although psychology usually warns us against mistaking the one for the other.

I have acquired the imagined idea of a certain-sized movement by performing or imitating the movement myself, and by this action I have learned a standard for this movement in my innervatory sensations.[4]

Now when I perceive a similar, larger or smaller movement in someone else, the surest path to understanding it – to its appercep- tion – is to perform it in imitation myself, and then I can decide by comparing them on which movement my expenditure was the greater. An urge to imitate such as this certainly appears in our perception of movements. But I do not perform the imitation in reality, just as I no longer spell out the letters when I have learned to read in this way. Instead of imitating the movement with my muscles, I imagine it through the traces left in my memory by expenditures made on similar movements. Imagining or 'thinking' is distinguished from acting or performing above all because it displaces far smaller energy-charges and holds back the main expen- diture from being released. But how is the quantitative factor – the greater or smaller size – of the perceived movement given expression in the imagined idea? And if a representation of quantity is absent from the idea – which has been imagined as composed of qualities – how can I distinguish between imagined ideas of movements with differing dimensions, and how can I make the comparison that is at issue here?

This is where physiology shows us the way by teaching us that in the course of imagining too, innervations travel to the muscles, though they do, it is true, correspond to a very modest expenditure. But it now seems very reasonable to assume that the innervatory expenditure that accompanies imagining is used to represent the factor of quantity in the idea imagined, and that it will be larger when a large movement is imagined than if it were a question of a small movement. The imagined idea of the larger movement, then, would really be the larger idea, that is, accompanied by a larger expenditure [of energy].

Direct observation shows us that people habitually express dimensions of large and small in their imagined contents by means of varying expenditure in a kind of *mimicry of the imagination*.

If a child, or a man of the people, or a member of certain races is recounting or describing something, it is easy to see that it is not enough for him to make his idea apparent to his listener by choosing clear words; rather he also represents its content in his expressive gestures; he combines representation by mime with representation in words. He describes both quantities and intensities at the same time. 'A high mountain' – as he describes it, he lifts his hand above his head; 'a little dwarf' – and he holds it close to the ground. If he has given up the habit of using his hands for illustration, he will still do so with his voice, and if he is in control of himself in that respect too, I am willing to bet that when describing something large he will open his eyes wide, and when describing something small he will squeeze them shut. It is not his affects that he is expressing in this way, but actually the content of what he has imagined.

Are we to assume, then, that this need for mimicry is roused only when communication is required, even though much of this mode of representation will escape the listener's attention altogether? I believe rather that this mimicry does exist, though less vigorously, quite apart from any communication, and that it also comes about when a person is imagining to himself, thinking of something vividly; and that he is then expressing the dimensions of large and small in his body, just as he does when speaking, at least by means of alterations in the innervation of his facial features and sensory organs. Indeed, I rather think that the physical innervation corresponding to the content of what is imagined was the beginning and origin of the mimicry employed for communicating; indeed, all it needed was to be intensified and made noticeable to others to serve this purpose. Although I am putting forward the view that to the 'expression of emotions', familiar to us as a physical side-effect of processes within the psyche, we should add this 'expression of the content as imagined', it is quite clear to me that my remarks on the category of large and small do not exhaust the topic. There is an array of things I could add myself before reaching the manifestations of tension by which someone indicates in their body the concentration of their attention and the level of abstraction at which they are thinking at the moment. I think the subject is very important, and I believe that to follow up the mimicry of the imagination could be as useful in other fields of aesthetics as it has been here in understanding the comic.

To return to the comedy of movement, I repeat: with the perception of a particular movement, there comes an impulse to imagine it by making a certain expenditure [of energy]. That is, when 'trying to understand' this movement, in apperceiving it, I make a certain expenditure [of energy], behaving in this part of the psychical process entirely as if I were putting myself in the position of the person I am observing. But, probably at the same time, I have an eye on what this movement is aiming at, and from past experience I am able to estimate the quantity of expenditure required to attain it. In doing so, I leave the person I am observing out of account and behave as if I myself wanted to attain that end. These two possibilities in my imagination amount to a comparison between the observed movement and my own. If the other person's movement is disproportionate and impracticable, the surplus energy I expend to understand it is inhibited *in statu nascendi*, as it is being mobilized, so to speak, and declared to be superfluous; it is free to be used elsewhere, possibly for release in laughter. This would be the kind of course taken as our pleasure in a comical movement arises – as long as other circumstances are favourable: an innervatory expenditure turning into an unusable surplus as I compare the comical movement with my own.

We note now that we shall have to continue our discussions in two different directions, first in order to establish the conditions for the release of the surplus, and then to examine whether other instances of the comic can be conceived in similar terms to the comic of movement.

We shall turn to the latter task first and after the comic of movement or action we shall consider the comic that is found in the intellectual performance and character traits of other persons.

We can take the comic nonsense produced by ignorant candidates in an examination as the model for the genre, though it may be more difficult to give a simple example of character traits. We need not be put off that nonsense and foolishness, which so frequently have a comic effect, are not perceived as comic in every instance, just as the same character who makes us laugh at him at one moment for being comical, may appear contemptible or hateful at another. However, this fact, which we should keep in mind, only indicates that for comic effect other relations besides the familiar one of comparison come into consideration, conditions which we may be able to trace in another context.

The comic quality that is found in someone else's intellectual or mental characteristics is again evidently the outcome of comparing him with my [own] self, but oddly it is a comparison that usually produces the opposite outcome to the one resulting from a comic movement or action. In this latter case, it was comic when the other person went to far greater lengths in his expenditure [of energy] than I thought I would need [myself]; in the case of mental [*seelisch*] performance, by contrast, it becomes comic if the other person has economized on expenditure which I regard as indispensable – for nonsense and stupidity are of course examples of under-performance. In the first instance I laugh because the other person has made things too hard for himself, in the second because he has made things too easy. The comic effect, then, depends apparently only on the difference between the two expenditures of energy, that of the 'empathy' [*Einfühlungsaufwand*[5]] and that of our self [*Ich*] – and not on the one who has the advantage from this difference. But this oddity, confusing to our judgement at first, disappears if we consider that it is in keeping with the course of our personal development towards a higher level of culture to limit the labour of our muscles and increase the work of our thoughts. By increasing the effort we spend on thinking we are able to reduce the effort we spend on movement to perform the same function – a cultural achievement to which our machines are witness.[6]

It adds up to a consistent explanation, then, that a person should appear comical to us if he expends too much [energy] on the feats performed by his body and too little on those of his mind [*seelisch*] in comparison with ourselves; and in both cases our laughter is undeniably the expression of our pleasure in the superiority we ascribe to ourselves in relation to him. If the relation is reversed in both cases, and the other person's somatic expenditure is perceived as less and his mental expenditure as greater than our own, then we no longer laugh, but wonder and admire.[7]

The origin of comic pleasure in the comparison of the other person with one's self which we have been discussing here – in the [quantitative] difference between his empathetic expenditure and that of our self – is probably the most significant genetically. But it is certain that it is still not the only one. At some time we have learned to disregard such comparison between someone else and our self and draw the pleasure-bringing difference [in amount] from one side only, whether from the empathy or from the processes going on in our self – which proves that the feeling of superiority is not *essentially* related to comic pleasure. A comparison is [, it is true,] indispensable for this pleasure to arise; we find that this comparison takes place between two expenditure-charges following rapidly one after the other and applying to the same function; either we produce them in ourselves by way of empathizing with someone else, or, without this relation, we discover them in our own internal processes. The first case – in which, that is, the other person still plays a part, though not in a comparison with our own self – arises when the pleasure-bringing difference between the expenditure-charges is brought about by external influences which we can sum up as a 'situation' – which is why this species of comedy is called *comedy of situation*. The characteristics of the person providing the comic are not the main thing under consideration; we laugh, even though we have to tell ourselves that in the same situation we would have been bound to do the same thing. We are deriving the comedy here from the relation of human beings to the often overwhelming power of the external world; to a human being's mental [*seelisch*] processes this is also represented by the conventions and necessary demands of society, indeed even by his own bodily needs. A typical example of this last kind is when someone is suddenly disturbed in an activity demanding all his mental powers by some pain, or by excremental need. The contrast, which as we empathize provides us with the comic difference, is between the great interest before the disturbance and the minimal interest the person still has left for his mental activity after the disturbance has occurred. The person who provides us with this difference again becomes comical in our eyes as an inferior figure; but he is only inferior in comparison with his earlier self and not in comparison with us, for we know that in the same situation we could not behave any differently. But it is worth noting that we are only able to find this humiliation of a human being comical in the case of empathy, that is, in someone else, while we ourselves, in these or similar awkward situations, are only conscious of feelings of embarrassment. It is probably only by distancing the feelings of distress from ourselves in this way that we are able to take enjoyable pleasure in the difference between the varying charges that arises from the comparison.

The other source of the comic, which we find in the transformations of our own [energy-]charges, lies in our relations to what is to come in the future, which we are accustomed to anticipate with our imagined expectations. I assume that a certain quantity of expenditure always underlies every imagined expectation, and hence that if an expectation were disappointed, the expenditure would be reduced by a certain amount – here again I refer to my earlier remarks on the 'mimicry of the imagination'. But it seems to me to be easier to demonstrate a real mobilization in the expenditure of energy-charge in the cases of expectation. In a number of instances it is quite evident that preparatory movements are the expression of expectation, first in all cases where the expected event makes demands on my capacity for movement; these preparations can without hesitation be quantitatively determined. If I am expecting to catch a ball thrown to me, I put my body under certain tensions which are meant to help it withstand the impact of the ball, and the superfluous movements I make if the ball I catch turns out to be too light, make me comical in the eyes of the spectators. I have let myself be misled by expecting an excessive expenditure of movement. Similarly, for example, if I pick out of a basket a fruit which I take to be heavy but – deluding me – is hollow, an imitation made of wax: the quick upward jerk of my hand reveals that I had put an innervation at the ready which was too great for its purpose, and so I am laughed at. Indeed, there is at least one case in which the expenditure on expectation can be shown in a physiological experiment on animals to be directly measurable. In Pavlov's[8] experiments on the secretion of saliva, dogs that have been fitted with a saliva fistula are shown various kinds of food, and the various amounts of saliva fluctuate according to whether the conditions set up in the experiment reinforce or disappoint the dog's expectations of being fed what it has been shown.

But even when what I expect merely makes demands on my sensory organs and not on my capacity for movement, I may assume that the expectation is expressed in a certain motor outlay [*Verausgabung*] towards alerting my senses and warding off other impressions that are not expected; and I may in general conceive the attitude of attention as a motor function equivalent to a certain expenditure [of energy]. I may further assume that the preparatory activity of expectation will not be independent of the scale of the expected impression, but rather that I shall represent its size, large or small, by mimicry, by a larger or smaller preparatory expenditure, as I did in the case of communication, and in the case of thinking where there is no expectation. The effort expended on expectation is made up of several components, it is true, and a variety of factors will apply even to my disappointment, not only whether what happened was on a larger or smaller scale than I had expected, but also whether it was worth the great interest I had invested in expecting it. In this way, apart from my expenditure on representing the scale of large and small (mimicry of the imagination), I might also be led to take into account my expenditure on alerting attention (expenditure on expectation), and in other cases my expenditure on abstraction besides. But these other kinds of expenditure can be traced back to expenditure on large and small, for what is more interesting, more sublime, or even more abstract, are after all only specialized instances of what is larger. If we add that according to Lipps and others it is the *quantitative* and not the qualitative contrast that is regarded first and foremost as the source of comic pleasure, then we shall on the whole be pleased that we chose the comic of movement as the starting-point of our investigation.

In elaborating on Kant's statement that 'the comic is an expectation that has vanished away into nothing', Lipps attempted – in the book I have quoted so often – to derive comic pleasure generally from expectation. However, despite the many instructive and valuable results brought to light by this attempt, I should like to add my voice to the criticism put by other authorities that Lipps has conceived the field of origin for the comic much too narrowly, and has not been able to submit its manifestations to his formula without forcing them.

[B]

Human beings have not been content to enjoy the comic where they happen to come upon it in their experience of life; they have also attempted to create it intentionally, and we shall learn more about its nature if we study the means employed to make [someone or something] comic. First of all one can conjure up the comic in oneself to amuse other people – by pretending to be clumsy or stupid, for example. Doing this, one is creating the comedy just as if one were really clumsy or stupid, by fulfilling the condition of the comparison that leads to the difference in expenditures. But one does not make oneself ridiculous or contemptible by doing this – on occasion one can even win admiration. The feeling of superiority does not arise in the other person if he knows that one has been just pretending, and this offers good fresh evidence in principle for the independence of comedy from the feeling of superiority.

The main means of making someone else comic is to put them into situations in which they become comic as a consequence of human dependence on external circumstances, particularly on social factors. Putting someone in a comic situation in this way can be done in reality (a practical joke [Freud's English]) by tripping him up so that he falls down like a clumsy person, or by making him appear stupid by exploiting his credulity, persuading him of something absurd, and so on; or it can be feigned in speech or play. It is a great help to aggression, which habitually takes advantage of making someone comic, that comic pleasure is independent of the reality of the comic situation, so that actually everyone is defenceless and vulnerable to being made comic.

But there are also other means of making someone comic which are worth special consideration, and in part also reveal fresh origins of comic pleasure. This is where *imitation*, for example, belongs; it gives the listener a quite extraordinary pleasure and makes its object comical even if it is still a long way from exaggerated caricature. It is much easier to find the reasons for the comic effect of *caricature* than it is of mere imitation. Caricature, parody and travesty, just like their counterpart in real life, unmasking, are aimed at persons and things with a claim on authority and respect, and in some sense '*sublime*'. They are methods of degrading [*Herabsetzung*], as the happy German expression has it.[9] The sublime is something on a large scale in a metaphorical, transferred psychological sense, and I would like to make, or rather repeat, the hypothesis that this too, like that which is large somatically, is represented by an extra expenditure [of energy]. It takes little observation to establish that when I am speaking of what is sublime, I innervate my voice in a different way and try to bring my body-language into harmony as it were with the dignity of what I am imagining. I put on a solemn constraint, not unlike my behaviour if I were to come into the presence of some noble personage, a monarch or a prince of science. I shall hardly be mistaken in assuming that the different innervation involved in this mimicry by my imagination corresponds to extra expenditure. I daresay I shall find the third instance of this kind of extra expenditure when I think along abstract lines of thought instead of in ordinary concrete and visualizable images [*Vorstellungen*]. Now if the methods we have just discussed of degrading the sublime let me imagine it as something everyday where I do not have to stand to attention, and in whose imagined presence I can put myself 'at ease', as the military formula has it, then it saves me expending extra effort on solemn constraint; and the comparison between that way of imagining, set going by empathy, with my usual one, which is simultaneously trying to re-establish itself 'as you were' [*sich herstellen*: another military term], again creates the difference in expenditure, which can be discharged by laughter.

Caricature, as we know, degrades by highlighting one single intrinsically comical trait out of the sublime object's expressive features as a whole [*Gesamtausdruck*]; the kind of trait, that is, which was bound to be overlooked as long as it could only be perceived within the total picture. By isolating it a comic effect can be achieved, extending in our memory to the whole – provided, that is, that the presence of the sublime object itself does not hold us fast in an attitude of veneration. Where an overlooked comic trait of this kind is absent, caricature will go ahead and create one by exaggerating one that is not in itself comic. Again, it is indicative of the origin of comic pleasure that the effectiveness of caricature is not fundamentally damaged by such distortion of reality.

Parody and *travesty* bring about the degradation of the sublime in a different way, by destroying the unity existing between the public character of a personage and his words and actions, replacing either the sublime personage or his utterences with low substitutes. This is how they are distinguished from caricature, not, however, by the mechanism that produces comic pleasure. The same mechanism also applies to *unmasking*, which is involved only where someone has seized dignity and authority for himself by deception, and these have to be taken from him in reality. We have already met the comic effect of unmasking in some examples of the joke, for example, in the one about the noble lady who called out in her early labour pains: 'Ah mon Dieu,' but was refused any help by her physician until the stage when she cried 'Ai waih' (p. 70). Now that we have got to know what characterizes the comic, we can no longer dispute that this story is actually an example of comic unmasking and has no justified claim to be called a joke. It recalls jokes merely by the way it is set up, and by the technical device of 'representation by something small', in this instance by the cry, which is found to be a sufficient indication. All the same, it is still the case that if we appeal to our feeling for language to decide, it has no objection to calling a story of this kind a joke. We may find an explanation for this if we reflect that linguistic usage does not set out from the scientific understanding of the nature of jokes that we have acquired in the course of this laborious investigation. Since it is one of the functions of the joke to make hidden sources of comic pleasure accessible once more (p. 100), any device that brings buried comedy to light, can by loose analogy be called a joke. However, this is particularly true of unmasking, though it also applies to other methods of making someone comic.[10]

'*Unmasking*' can also include those now familiar methods of making someone comic, which degrade the dignity of an individual person by drawing attention to the frailty he shares with all human beings, but especially to the dependency of his mental achievements on bodily needs. The unmasking then becomes the equivalent of the admonition: this or that worthy, admired as a demi-god, is after all only a human being like you and me. In addition it includes all those efforts to lay bare the monotonous psychical automatism lying behind the wealth and apparent freedom of our mental achievements. We have met examples of this kind of 'unmasking' in the marriage-broker jokes, and we might well have felt doubtful at the time whether we were right to regard these stories as jokes. We are now able to decide with greater certainty that the anecdote of the echo – who underlines every statement the marriage-broker makes and finally reinforces his admission that the bride is hump-backed with the cry: 'But such a hump!' [p. 55] – is essentially a comic anecdote, an example of the unmasking of psychical automatism. All the same, the comic story is functioning here only as a façade; for anyone with an ear for the hidden meaning of the marriage-broker anecdotes, the entire story is still a splendidly dramatized joke. Anyone who does not go so deeply into it will stop short at the comic anecdote. Something similar applies to the other joke about the marriage-broker who tries to refute an objection, but finally, crying 'But I ask you, who would lend these people anything!' [p. 55], admits the truth; a comic unmasking as the façade for a joke. But its character as a joke is far more evident here, for the broker's remark is also an instance of representation by the opposite. At the same time as he is trying to show that these people are rich, he is also showing that they are not rich but, on the contrary, very poor. Joke and comedy converge here, teaching us that the same statement can be both joking and comic at the same time.

We are glad to seize the opportunity to return from the comedy of unmasking to jokes, for of course our actual task is to clarify the relationship between the joke and what is comic, not to define the nature of the comic. So alongside the case that revealed psychical automatism – and where our sense of whether something was comic or was a joke left us in the lurch – we shall add another, in which joke and comedy are likewise confused, the case of nonsense jokes. But our investigation will show us in the end that in this second case the convergence of the joke and what is comic can be deduced theoretically.

When we were discussing joke-techniques, we found that giving free rein to ways of thought that are usual in the unconscious and can only be judged as being 'faulty logic' in conscious [mental activity] constitutes the technical means in very many jokes. But we then went on to have doubts as to whether these did have the character of jokes, so that we were inclined to classify them simply as comic stories. We could not come to any decision about our doubts, at first because we had no knowledge of the essential nature of jokes. Later, by way of analogy to the dream-work, we discovered it in the functioning of the joke-work as a compromise between the demands of rational criticism and the impulse not to give up the old pleasure in verbal play and nonsense. What came about in this way as a compromise – when the preconscious prompting of the thought was momentarily given over to unconscious revision – satisfied both claims in all cases, but was still open to criticism in various forms and had to accommodate the variety of its judgements. On one

VII The Joke and the Varieties of the Comic

occasion a joke would succeed in surreptitiously taking the form of a trivial but at least admissible statement; on another it would smuggle itself in under the expression of a worthwhile thought; but in borderline cases of compromise, it would give up satisfying the critical judgement and come before it as sheer nonsense, defiantly insisting on the sources of pleasure at its disposal and not even afraid of rousing its opposition, because it could rely on the listener to put right any distortions unconscious revision had made in its expression, and so give it back its meaning.

In what cases, then, will a joke appear before the judgement of criticism to be nonsense? Especially when it makes use of those modes of thought that are usual in the unconscious and prohibited in conscious thinking, – faulty logic, that is. For certain unconscious modes of thought have been preserved in conscious thinking too, for example, some kinds of indirect representation, allusion and so on, even though their conscious use is subject to quite strong limitations. Using these techniques, a joke will provoke little or no objection from criticism; that response will make an appearance only if the joke also takes for its technique those means that conscious thinking no longer wants to have anything to do with. A joke can still avoid provoking objection, if it glosses over the flaw in thinking it has been employing, disguises it with the appearance of logic – as in the stories of the pastry and the liqueur (p. 51), or of the salmon mayonnaise [pp. 41–2], and such. But if it presents the flaw in thinking without disguise, criticism is certain to protest.

In this case, there is something else that will come in useful for the joke. As unconscious modes of thought, the faulty reasoning used by the joke in its technique will seem – though not invariably so – comic to our critical reason. Giving free rein consciously to unconscious modes of thought which are rejected as being faulty is one means of producing comic pleasure; and this is easily understandable, for it certainly needs a far greater expenditure to create a preconscious charge of energy than it does to give free rein to an unconscious charge. As we listen to a thought framed as if it had been formed in the unconscious and compare this with our correction of it, what ensues for us is the difference in expenditure that gives rise to comic pleasure. In this way, a joke using this kind of faulty reasoning for its technique and thus appearing to be nonsense can at the same time have a comic effect. If we do not get the joke, what we are left with again is only the comic story, the 'merry tale'.

The story of the borrowed kettle – the one that on return had a hole in it, whereupon the borrower swore first that he hadn't borrowed any kettle at all, then that it had had a hole in it already when he borrowed it, and finally that he had given it back undamaged, without a hole in it at all (p. 53) – is an excellent example of a purely comic effect made by giving free rein to unconscious modes of thinking. For it is the very logic by which several thoughts, each one in itself soundly motivated, will cancel one another out that is absent in the unconscious. The dream, in which the unconscious modes of thinking do indeed become manifest, accordingly knows no 'either/or',[11] only a simultaneous 'side by side'. In the example of a dream I chose for my *Interpretation of Dream*, despite its complications, to be the model for the work of interpretation,[12] I am trying to exonerate myself from the charge that in treating a patient's psyche I have not made her pains disappear. My reasons run: 1. it is her own fault that she is ill, because she does not want to accept my solution; 2. her pains have an organic origin, so they are no concern of mine; 3. her pains are related to the fact that she is a widow, which is not my fault; 4. her pains are caused by an injection from a dirty syringe given to her by someone else. All of these reasons stand side by side, as if they did not exclude one another. Instead of the 'and' in my dream, I should have put an 'either/or', if I wanted to avoid being accused of nonsense.

The one about the blacksmith in a Hungarian village would, similarly, be a comic story. He was guilty of a crime carrying the death penalty, but the Mayor decided to punish not the blacksmith, but a tailor instead, for, he said, there were two tailors settled in the village, but not another blacksmith, and *someone* had to expiate the crime. Such a displacement from the guilty person on to someone else naturally contradicts all the laws of logic, but not in the least the mode of thinking of the unconscious. I have no hesitation in calling this one a comic story – and yet I put the one about the kettle under the heading of jokes. Now I admit that the latter, too, is much more rightly described as being 'comic' than as being a joke. But now I understand how it happens that my feeling, in other instances so secure, can leave me in doubt as to whether it is a comic story or a joke. A case where I am unable to decide by my feeling occurs, that is, when the comedy arises from uncovering the mode of thinking belonging exclusively to the unconscious. An anecdote of this kind can be a comic story and a joke at the same time; but it will make the impression of being a joke, even when it is merely comic, because its use of the strategies of faulty logic characteristic of the unconscious reminds me of a joke, just as previously (p. 197) the measures taken to bring hidden comedy to light also did.

I am bound to set great store on clarifying this issue, which is the trickiest point in my discussion – the relation of the joke to comedy, that is – so I shall amplify what I have said with some negative propositions. First I can draw attention to the point that the instance of the convergence of joke and comedy dealt with here is not identical with the earlier one (p. 198). This is a rather fine distinction, but it can be made with certainty. In the earlier case, the comedy derived from the uncovering of psychical automatism. Now this is by no means peculiar to the unconscious alone, nor does it play any noticeable part among the joke-techniques. Unmasking is related to the joke only fortuitously, when it serves some other joke-technique – for example, representation by the opposite. In the case where unconscious modes of thought are given free rein, however, the convergence of joke and comedy is a necessary one, because the same technique that is used here by the first person of the joke as a means for releasing pleasure by its very nature produces comic pleasure in the third person.

One might be tempted to generalize this last case and look for the relation of the joke to what is comic in the theory that the effect of the joke on the third person happens according to the mechanism of comic pleasure. Not in the least. Contact with the comic certainly does not apply to all jokes, nor even to the majority; on the contrary, in most cases the joke and what is comic are to be sharply distinguished. Whenever a joke or witticism successfully avoids the appearance of absurdity – that is, in most jokes based on double meaning or allusion – nothing resembling a *comic* effect can be seen in the listener. One can try this out on the examples I have given earlier, or on some new ones quoted here.

Telegram congratulating a gambler on his seventieth birthday: '*Trente et quarante.*' (Division of words with allusion.)

Hevesi once described the process of tobacco manufacture: 'The light yellow leaves were *sauced in this pickle* and *pickled in this sauce.*' (Multiple use of the same material.)

Madame de *Maintenon* was called Madame de *Maintenant*. (Modification of the name.)

Professor Kästner says to a Prince who is standing in front of a telescope: 'Prince, I am fully aware you are "Durch *läuchtig* [Your Highness]", but you are not "durch*sichtig* [transparent]".'

Count Andrassy was called the *Minister of the Fine Exterior*.

In addition, one might also believe that all jokes with a façade of nonsense are bound to appear comic and have a comic effect. However, let us remind ourselves at this point that jokes of this kind very often have a different effect on the listener, and may provoke bafflement or an inclination to reject them (see pp. 135–6, note 13). So it obviously depends on whether the nonsense in the joke appears to be comic nonsense or just ordinary plain nonsense – and we have not yet inquired into the conditions for this. Accordingly, we shall stick to the conclusion that the joke is by its nature to be distinguished from what is comic and converges with it on the one hand only in certain special cases, and on the other in its tendency to obtain pleasure from intellectual sources.

In the course of these investigations into the relations between joke and comedy we have had revealed to us the distinction which, we must stress, is the most significant one, and which at the same time points towards an important psychological characteristic of comedy. We had to remove the source of pleasure in jokes to the unconscious; we have no occasion to make the same localization for the comic. Rather, all our analyses so far indicate that the source of comic pleasure is the comparison of two expenditures, both of which we have to assign to the preconscious. Jokes and the comic are above all distinguished by their localization in the psyche: *the joke is as it were the contribution made to the comic from the realm of the unconscious.*

[C]

We have no need to accuse ourselves of digressing, for after all it was the relationship of the joke to what is comic that made us investigate the comic in the first place. But it is high time we returned to the topic we were discussing before, which dealt with the means employed to make someone or something comic. We opened our discussion with caricature and unmasking, because they could both provide some linkage for our analysis of the comedy of *imitation*. Imitation is, I suppose, shot through and through with caricature, the exaggeration of traits that are otherwise unremarkable, and it also has a degrading function. But these do not seem to exhaust its nature; undeniably, it represents an extraordinarily rich source of comic pleasure in itself, for it is the very faithfulness of the imitation that we laugh at. It is not easy to give a satisfying explanation for this, unless one adopts Bergson's view,[13] which makes the comedy of imitation approach the comedy that uncovers psychical automatism. As Bergson sees it, everything about a living person that makes us think of an inanimate mechanism has a comic effect. His formula for this runs: 'mécanisation de la vie [mechanization of life]'. He explains the comedy of imitation by taking up a problem raised by Pascal in his *Pensées*: why do we laugh when we compare two faces that are alike, though neither of them separately has a comic effect? 'What is living should, in our expectation, never be repeated in forms that are exactly alike. Where we find such a repetition, we always presume there is some mechanism hiding behind the living [creature].' If we see two faces that are too much alike, we think of two copies pressed from the same mould, or of some similar method of mechanical production. In short, the cause of laughter in these cases would be the divergence of the living from the lifeless (loc. cit., p. 35). If we accept this persuasive argument of Bergson's, it will not, by the way, be difficult for us to accommodate his view under our own formula. Having learned from experience that every living thing is different and requires us to make some sort of effort to understand it, we are disappointed if a perfect resemblance or a deceptive imitation makes any further effort unnecessary. But we are disappointed in the sense of relieved, and the effort we spent on expectation – now become superfluous – is released in laughter. The same formula would also cover all the cases of comic rigidity (*raideur*) that Bergson considers – professional habits, fixed ideas, set phrases repeated at every opportunity. All these cases would come down to a comparison between the effort spent on expectation and the expenditure of effort required for understanding what has stayed the same – in which the greater effort spent on expectation is based on our observation of the individual variety and malleability of living forms. So in imitation, the source of comic pleasure would not be the comedy of situation, but of expectation.

Since we are deriving comic pleasure generally from making a comparison, we are obliged to examine the comic of comparison as well, for of course it is used to make persons or things comic. Our interest in this question will be increased if we recall that in the case of metaphor too, our 'feeling' whether something should be called a joke or merely comic often left us in the lurch (see above, pp. 70–71).

The topic would certainly deserve greater attention than we can pay it from the angle of our own interests. The main feature we look for in a metaphor is whether it is apt, i.e., whether it makes us notice a correspondence that is really present between two different objects. The original pleasure in discovering similarity (Groos, p. 103) is not the only motive favouring the use of comparisons; in addition, metaphor is capable of a use that also brings relief to intellectual work, when, that is, we compare the less familiar with the more familiar, as we mostly do, or the abstract with the concrete, and use the comparison to explain the item that is more difficult and unfamiliar. All comparisons of this kind, particularly comparisons of the abstract with matters of fact, involve some degradation and some saving in the effort spent on abstraction (in the sense of mimicry of the imagination), but of course this is not sufficient to bring out the comic character clearly. It does not surface suddenly, but gradually, from the pleasurable relief brought by the comparison; there are plenty of cases that merely touch on the comic, where we might doubt whether they do display that character. There is no question that a comparison becomes comic when the difference in level of expenditure on abstraction between the two poles of the comparison is increased, when something serious and unfamiliar, particularly if it is of a moral or intellectual nature, is drawn into comparison with something low or trivial. The preceding pleasure from relief and the contribution made by the conditions for mimicry of the imagination may perhaps explain the gradual transition as determined by quantitative considerations from pleasure at large to the comic pleasure taking place in the course of making the comparison. I shall probably avoid misunderstandings if I emphasize that I am deriving the comic pleasure we take in metaphor not from the contrast between the two poles of the comparison but from the difference between the two amounts of effort spent on abstraction. What is unfamiliar and difficult to grasp, abstract – intellectually sublime, in fact – is unmasked by its alleged congruence with some low familiar thing as being just as low itself, for when we imagine something low, any effort spent on abstraction no longer applies. So the comic of comparison boils down to an instance of degradation.

Now a comparison, as we saw earlier, can have the character of a joke or witticism without any trace of a comic ingredient, precisely, that is, when it avoids degradation. Thus the comparison of truth with a torch which cannot be carried through a crowd without singeing someone's beard is a witticism pure and simple, because it gives full value to a faded idiom ('the torch of truth'); and it is not comic, because the torch, as an object, is not without a certain grandeur, though it is only a concrete thing. But a metaphor can just as easily be a joke as it can be comic – the one independently of the other, in fact – when the comparison becomes an aid to certain joke-techniques, e.g., unification or allusion. Thus Nestroy's comparison of memory with a 'storeroom' (p. 74) is both comic and a joke, the first on account of the extraordinary degradation that the psychological concept has to put up with in being compared to a 'storeroom', and the second because the person using the metaphor is a shop-assistant, who sets up a quite unexpected unification in this comparison between his psychology and his job. Heine's lines – 'Finally burst all the buttons/ On the breeches of my patience' [p. 74] – at first appear to be a splendid example of a comic, belittling metaphor; but on closer consideration it has to be conceded the character of a joke as well, for the metaphor, used as a means of allusion, touches on the field of the obscene, and thus makes it possible to liberate pleasure in obscenity. By a convergence which is not, it is true, entirely accidental, the same material gives rise to a gain in pleasure deriving from both its comic and its joking qualities; if the conditions of the one also further the emergence of the other, this kind of union has a confusing impact on the 'feeling' which is supposed to tell us whether we are faced with something joking or something comic, and only an attentive examination independent of any disposition towards either kind of pleasure will produce a decision.

However tempting it might be to trace these more intimate determinants of a gain in comic pleasure, the author still has to bear in mind that neither his earlier training nor his daily profession justify him in extending his investigations far beyond the field of jokes, and he has to admit that this topic of comic comparison in particular makes him aware of his incompetence.

So we bow to the reminder that many authorities do not recognize the sharp conceptual and factual distinction we were led to make between the joke and what is comic, and that they simply describe the joke as 'the comedy of speech' or 'of words'.

> With a fork and effort too
> His mother pulled him from the stew [p. 59]

is merely comic; but Heine's statement about the four castes in the population of Göttingen: 'professors, students, philistines and swine' [p. 59] is an exquisite witticism.

For intentional comedy of speech, I shall take Stettenheim's[14]

'Wippchen' as my model. Stettenheim has been called witty because he possesses the skill of conjuring up the comic to an especially high degree. The wit that one 'has', in contrast to the witticism that one 'makes', is indeed precisely defined by this ability. It is undeniable that the Letters from Wippchen, the Correspondent from Bernau, are also witty because they are generously sprinkled with jokes of every kind, some of them seriously clever ('in ceremonial undress' – of a parade of savages); but what gives his productions their distinctive character is not these separate jokes, but the comedy of speech that flows almost too abundantly in them. Originally, Wippchen was certainly meant to be a satirical figure, a variant of Gustav Freytag's Schmock,[15] one of those uneducated figures who take the nation's cultural heritage in vain, but the author's easy enjoyment of the comic effects achieved in presenting the figure has evidently driven his satirical intention gradually into the background. Wippchen's productions are for the most part 'comic nonsense'; the author has – quite justifiably, by the way – made use of the pleasurable mood he has successfully created by the pile-up of such feats to produce, alongside perfectly admissible remarks, all sorts of feeble ones too, which would be insufferable by themselves. Wippchen's nonsense now appears to be of a specific kind, using a particular technique. If we look at these 'jokes' more closely, we are struck by some genres in particular, which stamp his entire performance. Wippchen primarily makes use of combinations (conflations) or modifications of familiar phrases or quotations, replacing banal individual elements in them by more pretentious, highfalutin means of expression. This does approach techniques used by the joke.

The following, for example, are conflations, picked from the Preface and the first pages of the whole series:

'Turkey has money like straw by the sea'; which is a patchwork of the two phrases:

'Money like straw [*Geld wie Heu*]'

'Money like sand by the sea [*Geld wie Sand am Meere*]'. [Both phrases are clichés for vast and random quantity.] Or: 'I have become nothing but a leafless column, bearing witness to vanished splendour,' condensed from 'leafless tree'[16] and 'a column, bearing, etc.'. Or: 'Where is the Ariadne's thread that will lead me out of the Scylla of this Augean stable?', to which three Greek legends have donated one element each.

These modifications and substitutions can be summed up without difficulty; their nature can be seen in the following examples characteristic of Wippchen, in which another, current, mostly trivial wording, one sunk to a commonplace, invariably shimmers through: 'They have hung my paper and ink up higher.' We say: 'hanging someone's bread-basket higher' figuratively for putting them into difficult [financial] circumstances. Why shouldn't we extend this image to other material?

'Battles in which the Russians sometimes drew the shorter, sometimes the longer [straw].' Only the first phrase is in use, as we know; in accordance with its derivation, there would also be some sense in making the other one current.

'Pegasus stirred early in me.' If we replace 'the poet', this is a cliché of autobiography which has already been devalued by frequent use. 'Pegasus' in fact is not suitable to be a substitute for 'poet', but has a certain conceptual relationship to it – and sounds elevated.

'Thus I lived through thorny childhood shoes.'

Nothing but an image instead of a simple word. 'Outgrowing childhood shoes' is one of the images connected with the idea of childhood.

Out of the profusion of Wippchen's other productions, one can pick out several as examples of pure comedy, e.g., of comic anticlimax: 'for hours the battle raged to and fro, and finally it remained undecided'; or of comic unmasking (of ignorance): 'Klio, the Medusa of history'; quotations like 'Habent sua fata morgana [a conflation of *Habent sua fata libelli*: 'Books have their destinies'; and *fata morgana*: 'mirage'].' But our interest is sooner aroused by his conflations and modifications, because they reproduce familiar joke-techniques. Compare Wippchen's modifications, for example, with jokes such as: 'He has a great future behind him' [p. 20]; 'He has an ideal in front of his head' [p. 66]; or to Lichtenberg's modification-witticisms: 'New spas cure well' [p. 65], and the like. Are what

Wippchen produces with the same technique now to be called jokes? If not, what is it that distinguishes them from jokes?

It is certainly not difficult to give an answer. Let us recall that a joke turns two faces towards the listener, forcing him into two different interpretations. In the nonsense jokes, like the ones just mentioned, the one interpretation – which considers only the wording – declares it is nonsense; the other follows the allusions and, taking the route via the unconscious in the reader, discovers the excellent sense. In Wippchen's joke-like productions the one face of the joke is empty, as if atrophied; a Janus-head, but with only one face fully developed. We come upon nothing when we are lured into the unconscious by the technique. The conflations do not lead us to any instance in which the two conflated items really give rise to a new meaning; if we try to analyse them, they fall apart entirely. The modifications and substitutions lead us to a current and familiar wording, as they do in a joke, but the modification or substitution itself says nothing more, and as a rule one cannot even *do* anything with what it *does* say. So in fact only the one interpretation is left to apply to these jokes: nonsense. We can decide one way or another whether we call these productions – which have exempted themselves from one of the most essential characteristics of the joke – 'bad' jokes or deny that they are jokes at all.

There is no doubt that this sort of atrophied joke has a comic effect, which we can explain to ourselves in more than one way. Either the comedy arises from uncovering the modes of thinking of the unconscious, as in instances we looked at earlier, or the pleasure comes from comparison with a fully formed joke. There is nothing to prevent us from assuming that both ways of giving rise to comic pleasure converge here. There is no denying that it is just this inadequate adoption of the form of a joke [*Anlehnung an*] that turns this nonsense into comic nonsense.

For there are other instances easy to see through in which such inadequacy makes the nonsense irresistibly comic by the comparison with what it ought to be doing. The joke's counterpart, the riddle, may perhaps provide us with better examples than the joke itself. For example, a bantering question runs: 'What hangs on the wall that you can dry your hands on?' It would be a stupid riddle if the answer were: 'A hand-towel.' Rather, this answer gets rejected. – No, a herring. – But for heaven's sake, comes the startled protest, a herring doesn't hang on the wall! – But you *could* hang it up there. – But who's going to dry their hands on a herring? – Well, comes the soothing reply, you don't *have* to. – This explanation, given by means of two typical displacements, demonstrates how much is lacking in this question to make it a real riddle, and on account of this absolute inadequacy, it appears senselessly silly instead – irresistibly comic. In this way then – by not observing essential conditions – jokes, riddles, as well as other genres that do not in themselves produce comic pleasure, can be turned into sources of comic pleasure.

There are even fewer difficulties in understanding the case of the involuntary comedy of speech – of which we can find in any amount among the poems of Frederike Kempner,[17] for instance.

> Gegen die Vivisektion
> *Ein unbekanntes Band der Seelen kettet*
> *Den Menschen an das arme Tier.*
> *Das Tier hat einen Willen – ergo Seele –*
> *Wenn auch 'ne kleinere als wir.*

[*Against Vivisection*: An unknown bond connects the souls/ Of poor dumb animals to human powers./ The animal has will – and therefore soul –/ Though more diminutive than ours.]

Or a tender conversation between husband and wife (*Der Kontrast*):

> *'Wie glücklich bin ich,' ruft sie leise,*
> *'Auch ich,' sagt lauter ihr Gemahl.*
> *'Es macht mich deine Art und Weise*
> *Sehr stolz auf meine gute Wahl!'*

[*The Contrast*: 'How happy am I,' in her quiet voice./ She murmurs. 'So am I,' he says – more loud./ 'Your pretty ways make me so proud –/ I'm glad I made so good a choice.']

Now there is nothing here to remind us of a joke. But beyond doubt, it is the inadequacy of these 'poems' that makes them comical – the quite extraordinary clumsiness of their mode of expression, tied as it is to the most commonplace phrases or journalistic clichés, the simplistic limitation of her thoughts, the absence of any trace of poetic thought or language. But for all that, it is not self-evident that we should find Kempner's poems comical; there are many similar productions that we just find pretty dreadful, but we do not laugh at them; they only irritate us. But the very immensity of the distance from what we expect of a poem forces us into a comic reading; if this difference were smaller, we would sooner be inclined to criticism than to laughter. Besides, the comic effect of Kempner's poems is ensured by other secondary circumstances: by the poetess's palpable good intentions, by a certain sincerity of feeling which we can sense behind her inept diction and which disarms our mockery or irritation. This reminds us of a problem which we have postponed addressing. Difference in expenditure of effort is certainly the fundamental condition of comic pleasure, but observation shows us that pleasure does not arise from this difference every time. What further conditions must also be present, or what disturbances must be held at bay for comic pleasure really to arise from the difference in expenditure? But before we turn to answering this question, let us confirm the conclusion to our previous discussion: comedy of speech does not coincide with the joke, so the joke must be something different from comedy of speech.

Now that we are about to propose an answer to our last inquiry about the conditions necessary for comic pleasure to arise from difference in expenditure[s], we may allow ourselves some relief which can only bring us pleasure too. A precise answer to this question would be identical to an exhaustive description of the nature of the comic – for which we can claim neither the ability nor the authority. So once again we shall be content to throw light on the comic only in so far as it stands out clearly from the joke.

All theories of the comic have been taxed by their critics that their definitions overlook what is essential for comedy. 'The comic depends upon a contrast of ideas'; yes – in so far as this contrast has a comic effect, and not a different sort. 'The comic feeling derives from the evaporation of an expectation'; yes – as long as this disappointment is not frankly distressing. The objections are no doubt justified, but we are overestimating them if they lead us to conclude that the essential feature distinguishing the comic has so far eluded our understanding. What detracts from the general validity of those definitions are [certain] conditions that are indispensable for comic pleasure to arise, though we do not have to look to them for the essence of comedy. All the same, we will only be able to refute the charges and clear up the objections to the definitions of the comic with any ease if we have comic pleasure arise from the comparative difference between two expenditures. Comic pleasure and the effect by which it is recognized – laughter – can arise only when this difference becomes unusable and capable of release. We will not obtain any pleasurable effect, at most only a fleeting feeling of pleasure showing none of the characteristics of the comic, if the difference, once recognized, is put to some other use. Just as particular arrangements have to be made in the joke to avoid some other use for the expenditure [that has been] recognized as superfluous, comic pleasure too can arise only under circumstances that fulfil this last condition. Hence the instances in which such differences in expenditure arise in our imaginative life are uncommonly numerous; the instances in which comedy arises from them are, by comparison, very rare.

Two considerations force themselves on the observer who surveys if only briefly the conditions under which comedy arises from difference in expenditure[s]: first, that there are cases in which the comedy arises regularly and as if by necessity and, by contrast, there are others in which it seems entirely dependent on the circumstances of the case and the point of view of the observer; second, however, that unusually large differences very frequently break through unfavourable circumstances, so that the comic feeling arises in spite of them. With reference to the first point, it would be possible to set up two classes – the inevitably comic and the occasionally comic – although one would from the start have to accept that in the first class the inevitability of the comic would not be free of exceptions.

It would be tempting to go in pursuit of the conditions setting the terms for the two classes.

The conditions applying essentially to the second class are some of those which we grouped together as 'isolating' the comic situation. A closer breakdown reveals that the situation is rather as follows:

a) The most favourable condition for comic pleasure to arise comes from the generally cheerful mood in which one is 'disposed to laughter'. In a toxic mood of cheerfulness, almost everything appears comical, probably in comparison with expenditure in a normal state of mind. Indeed, jokes, comedy, and all similar methods of obtaining pleasure from psychical activity, are nothing more than ways of recovering this cheerful mood, euphoria, – if it is not present as a general disposition of the psyche – from one single point.

b) The expectation of comedy, the readiness for comic pleasure, functions in a similar favourable way. Hence, if the intention to make [someone or something] comic is shared by another person, differences of such a minute amount are sufficient that they would probably have been overlooked if they had occurred in experience unintentionally. Anyone about to read something comical or to see a farce in the theatre, has this intention to thank for laughing then at things which in his ordinary life would scarcely have produced an instance of comedy. Ultimately, he laughs at the memory of having laughed, or at the expectation of laughing the moment he sees a comic actor enter the stage before the performer could even attempt to make him laugh. That is why one also admits feeling ashamed after the event at what one was able to laugh at in the theatre.

c) Unfavourable conditions for comedy result from the nature of the mental activity occupying the individual at the moment. Work of the imagination or the intellect in pursuit of serious aims interferes with the capacity of the energy-charges for release, which of course such work needs for its displacements, so that only unexpectedly large differences in expenditure are able to break through to comic pleasure. What is especially unfavourable for comedy are all those modes of the thinking process that have moved sufficiently far away from the concrete to bring mimicry of the imagination to a halt; in abstract reflection there is absolutely no room for comedy, except when this mode of thinking is suddenly interrupted.

d) The opportunity for releasing comic pleasure also vanishes if attention is focused on the actual process of comparing which can give rise to the comedy. Under such circumstances, what is usually most certain to produce a comic effect loses its comic power. It is not possible for a movement or an act of mind to become comic for someone whose interest is bent on comparing it with a standard that he has clearly in his mind's eye. So it is that the examiner does not find anything comic in the nonsense that the examinee in his ignorance produces; he is irritated by it, while the candidate's colleagues, who are far more interested in how he will fare than in how much he knows, will laugh heartily at the same nonsense. A gymnastics instructor or a dancing-master will rarely have an eye for the comedy of movement in his pupils, and the comedy of human weaknesses escapes the clergyman entirely, though the writer of comedies is able to detect it to such great effect. The comic process does not stand up to being too intensely charged with attention, it has to happen entirely unnoticed – in this respect, by the way, very like the joke. But it would go against the terms describing the 'processes of consciousness' which I had good reason to use in *The Interpretation of Dreams* if one were to call it a necessarily *unconscious* process. It belongs rather to the *preconscious*; and processes of the kind that happen in the preconscious and do not have the attention-charge with which consciousness is linked can appropriately be called 'automatic'. The process of comparing the expenditures has to remain automatic if it is to produce comic pleasure.

e) It is extremely disturbing for comedy if the situation from which it is to arise is also the occasion for a powerful liberation of affect. As a rule, release of the effective difference [in expenditures] is then out of the question. The individual's affects, disposition and attitudes in each case make it understandable that the comic can appear or vanish according to the standpoint of the individual person, and that anything absolutely comic will exist only in exceptional cases. That is why the dependent or relative nature of what is comic is far greater than that of the joke: this never just happens, but is habitually *made*, and while it is in the making, the conditions under which it will be received can already be taken into account. However, the development of affect is the most intense of the conditions that will disturb comedy, and no one has misjudged it in this respect.[18] That is why it is said that the comic feeling most readily comes about in quasi-indifferent cases without the involvement of strong feelings or interests. Still, it is possible to see how an especially powerful difference in expenditures gives rise to the automatism of discharge, above all in cases where affect is released. When Colonel Butler answers Octavio's warnings '*laughing bitterly*' with the exclamation:

'*Thanks* from the House of Austria!'[19]

his bitterness has not prevented his laughter, which refers to his memory of the disappointment he believes he has suffered; and on the other hand there is no more impressive way for the poet to portray the immensity of Butler's disappointment than by showing it capable of forcing laughter in the midst of the storm of affects unleashed. I would think that this explanation is applicable to all cases where laughter occurs on occasions which are anything but pleasurable, and in connection with affects of intense distress or tension.

f) If we add that the occurrence of comic pleasure can be furthered by any other pleasurable addition to the situation, as if by a kind of contagion (after the manner of the fore-pleasure principle in tendentious jokes), we shall have discussed the conditions for comic pleasure not completely, it is true, but sufficiently for our purpose. We can now see that no other hypothesis is more adequate to explaining these conditions, as well as the arbitrariness and chanciness of comic pleasure, than the derivation of comic pleasure from the discharge of a difference, which can, under the most varying circumstances, be subject to other uses than that of discharge.

[D]

Sexual and obscene comedy might deserve a more thorough discussion, but we shall only touch on them here with a few remarks. Here too our starting-point would be stripping someone naked. A chance stripping has a comic effect on us, because we are comparing the ease with which we enjoy the sight with the great expenditure which would otherwise be required to attain this end. In this way the case approaches that of the naïve-comic, but it is simpler than this. Whenever a third party makes us the spectator – or the listener in the case of dirty talk – of such undressing, it is equivalent to making the person thus stripped comic. We have learned that it is the task of the joke to take the place of dirty talk, and in this way to open up a lost source of comic pleasure. On the other hand, spying on someone undressing is not comic for the spy, because his own efforts [*Anstrengung*] in doing so nullify the determinant of comic pleasure; all that is left is the sexual pleasure in what is seen. If the spy tells the tale to someone else, the person [*die Person*] spied on becomes comical again, because the predominant view is that she[20] has not expended [*Aufwand*] the care which would properly have hidden her privacy. The field of sexuality and obscenity also offers a wealth of other opportunities for obtaining comic pleasure as well as sexual arousal, in so far as human beings are shown in their dependence on bodily needs ('degradation') or the physical imperative behind romantic [*seelisch*] love is uncovered.

[E]

An invitation to look for an understanding of the comic in its psychological origins has also come, surprisingly, from Bergson's attractive and lively book, *Le Rire*. Bergson, whose formulae for understanding the nature of the comic we have already met – 'mécanisation de la vie' [p. 203], 'substitution quelconque de l'artificiel au naturel [any kind of substitution of the artificial for the natural]' – moves by way of a neighbouring connection of thought from automatism to the automata, and he attempts to trace a number of comic effects back to the faded memory of some childhood toy. In this context, there is one point where he adopts a view – though only to drop it again – in which he tries to derive the comic from the long-term influence of childhood delights. 'Peut-être même devrions-nous pousser la simplification plus loin encore, remonter à nos souvenirs les plus anciens, chercher dans les jeux qui amusèrent l'enfant la première ébauche des combinaisons qui font rire l'homme . . . Trop souvent surtout nous méconnaissons ce qu'il y a d'encore enfantin, pour ainsi dire, dans la plupart de nos émotions joyeuses [Perhaps we should push simplification even further, go back to our oldest memories and look among the games that amused the child for the first draft of the combinations that make the adult laugh . . . Above all, we all too often fail to recognize that there is something childish, as it were, in most of our joyful feelings]' (pp. 68ff.). As we have now traced the joke back to the child's play with words and ideas, which rational criticism has [now] denied us, we cannot but be tempted to go in pursuit of these roots of the comic in childhood too, as Bergson conjectured them.

In fact, we come upon quite a number of connections which look very promising when we investigate the relationship of comedy to children. Children themselves do not appear comical to us at all, although their nature fulfils all the conditions which in comparison with our own produce a comic difference: the disproportionately great expenditure on movement as much as the very slight intellectual expenditure, the domination of mental by bodily functions, and other features as well. Children strike us as comic only when they behave not like children but like serious grown-ups, and then they do so in the same way as other figures who dress up in disguise; but as long as they preserve their childish nature, our perception of them gives us a pure pleasure, perhaps with a touch of the comic. We call them naïve in so far as they display their lack of inhibition, and we call what they say naïvely comic, though from someone else we would have judged it to be an obscenity or a joke.

On the other hand, children have no feeling for comedy. This proposition does not seem to say any more than that the comic feeling only sets in at some time in the course of the child's psychical development – like so much else. And that would not be in the least remarkable, especially when one has to admit that it already makes a distinct appearance at an age which we have to regard as belonging to childhood. All the same, it can still be shown that the statement that children lack a feeling for the comic says more than the obvious. First of all it makes it easy to see that it could not be otherwise, if our theory is correct in deriving the comic feeling from a difference in expenditure which arises in the course of understanding another person. Let us once more choose the comedy of movement for our example. The comparison that provides the difference, formulated consciously, runs: 'that's how he does it' and 'that's how I would do it; that's how I used to do it'. But children lack the yardstick contained in the second sentence; they understand by imitating; they do it in the same way. Their upbringing supplies them with the standard: 'that's how you should do it'. If they use the same standard themselves in comparing, the conclusion is evident: 'he hasn't done it right' and 'I know how to do it better'. In this case they will laugh at the other person, making fun of him in the feeling of their own superiority. There is nothing to prevent us from deriving this laughter too from a difference in expenditure, but, by analogy with the instances of ridicule occurring in grown-ups, we may infer that in the child's superior laughter there is no awareness of the comic feeling. It is a laughter of pure pleasure. In our case, when a clear judgement of our own superiority develops, we merely smile instead of laughing, or if we do laugh we still make a clear distinction between this developing consciousness of our superiority and the comic [event] that makes us laugh.

It is probably right to say that the child laughs for pure pleasure under various circumstances which we [adults] feel are 'comic', though we are unable to identify the motives for our feeling, whereas the child's motives are clear and stateable. For example, if someone slips and falls in the street, we laugh because this impression – why, we do not know – is comical. The child will laugh out of a feeling of superiority or *schadenfreude*: 'You've fallen down – I haven't.' We adults seem to have lost some of the motives for pleasure the child has and, instead, under the same circumstances, we are aware of the 'comic' feeling as a substitute for what we have lost.

If one might generalize, it would appear very tempting to relocate the specific characteristic of the comic that we are looking for to the revival of the child in us, and understand the comic as the 'lost laughter of childhood' regained. We could then say: I always laugh at a difference in expenditure between another person and myself whenever I rediscover the child in the other. Or, more precisely, the full comparison leading to a [feeling for] the comic would run:

That's how he does it – I do it differently –

He does it in the way I used to do it as a child.

This laughter, then, would always apply to the comparison between the self as adult and the self as child. Even the sense of unevenness in the comic difference, so that sometimes the greater expenditure and sometimes the lesser appears comic to me, would be in accord with the determinant of childhood; actually, in this process the comic is always on the childhood side.

It is no contradiction to this that when children themselves are the object of the comparison, they do not make a comic impression on me, but rather a purely pleasurable one; nor that this comparison with what is childish works to comic effect only if another use of the difference is avoided. For this is where the conditions for discharge come into play. Anything involving a psychical process in an interconnection [with others] works against the release of the surplus energy-charge and puts it to some other use; anything isolating a psychical act encourages release. Hence a conscious focus on the child as a figure for comparison makes the release required for comic pleasure impossible; only if the charge is preconscious will something approaching isolation arise – of a kind, by the way, which we may ascribe to psychical processes in children too. So the addendum to our comparison – 'that is how I used to do it as a child' – from which the comic effect arose, would come into consideration only for middle-sized differences, if no other interconnection were able to take the newly freed surplus into its control.

If we remain with our attempt to find the nature of comedy in the preconscious connection with our childhood psyche [*das Infantile*], we shall have to take a step beyond Bergson and admit that the comparison producing the comic does not have to revive the old pleasures and play of childhood, rather that it is enough if it touches on children's nature generally, perhaps even on children's suffering. We are departing from Bergson in this, but we are remaining consistent with our own argument if we refer the comic pleasure not to remembered pleasure but as ever to a comparison. It may be that cases of the first kind to some extent coincide with what is invariably and irresistibly comic. Let us refer here to the scheme of comic possibilities we used earlier. We said the comic difference would be found either

a) by a comparison between another person and our self, or

b) by a comparison wholly within the other person, or

c) by a comparison wholly within our self.

In the first case the other person would appear to me as a child, in the second he would bring himself down to [the level of] a child, in the third I would find the child in myself. The comedy of movement and form, of intellectual performance and of character would belong to the first case; the corresponding aspects of childhood would be the urge to movement and the lesser intellectual and moral development of the child, so that for example a stupid person would become comic in my eyes in so far as he reminded me of a lazy child, or a bad person in so far as he reminded me of a naughty child. One could only talk of childhood pleasure lost to the adult in the one instance where it is a matter of the child's delight in movement.

The second case, in which the comedy relies entirely upon 'empathy', embraces the largest number of possibilities: comedy of situation, of exaggeration (caricature), of imitation, of degradation and of unmasking. It is the case that benefits most from the introduction of the child's point of view. For the comedy of situation is mostly based on embarrassments in which we rediscover the helplessness of the child; the worst of these embarrassments, the disturbance of other activities by the imperious demands of our natural needs, corresponds to the child's still insecure control of bodily functions. Where the comedy of situation operates by means of repetitions, it relies on children's particular pleasure in continual repetition ([of] questions and telling stories) which makes them such a pest to the grown-ups. Exaggeration, which also gives pleasure to adults in so far as it can justify itself to their critical reason, is related to children's peculiar immoderation, to their ignorance of all relations of quantity, which they later learn are in fact qualitative. Restraint, moderation even in permitted impulses, is a late fruit of upbringing and is acquired by the reciprocal inhibition of psychical activities drawn into a combination. Where this combination is weakened – in the unconscious of dreams, in the *idées fixes* of the psychoneuroses – the child's immoderation reappears.

We found the comedy of imitation relatively difficult to understand as long as we paid no attention to the infantile factor. But children's greatest skill is imitation; it is the driving motive for most of their games. Their ambition is aimed far less at being eminent among their peers than at imitating the grown-ups. The comedy of degradation also depends on the relationship of children to adults, for it is the correlate of adults' lowering themselves to their level in children's life. There are few things that give children greater pleasure than if a grown-up gets down to their level, abandons his oppressive superiority and plays with them. The relief that gives the child pure pleasure becomes for the adult a means of making persons and things comic by degradation, and a source of comic pleasure. And as for unmasking, we know that that goes back to degradation.

Establishing a motivation in childhood for the third case, the comedy of expectation, encounters the most difficulties – which probably explains why those authorities who start out from this case in their interpretation of the comic have found no occasion to take account of the infantile factor in it. Comedy of expectation is, I suppose, the most remote from children, the capacity to grasp it is the last to appear in them. In most situations of this kind, which seem comical to the adult, the child will probably feel only disappointment. But we could refer to children's joyful expectancy and credulity to understand how we might think we were being 'childishly' comic if we gave way to a comic disappointment.

Even if this argument were to suggest the likelihood of translating the comic feeling more or less as: 'Komisch ist das, was sich für den Erwachsenen nicht schickt[21] [Comic is what is not proper for the grown-ups]', I still, on account of my entire position on the problem of comedy, do not feel bold enough to defend this last statement as I did the argument that preceded it. I cannot decide whether the degradation to the childish state is only a special case of comic degradation or whether all comedy ultimately relies upon degradation to the childish state.[22]

[F]

An investigation of the comic, however briefly it dealt with it, would be sadly incomplete if it did not have space at least for a few remarks on *humour*. There is so little doubt about the essential affinity between the two that the attempt to explain the comic is bound to contribute at least one component towards our understanding of humour. However many true and heart-lifting observations have been made in the appreciation of humour – which is itself one of the highest psychical achievements and also enjoys the special favour of thinkers – we really cannot get out of attempting to express its nature by some approximation to our formulae for the joke and for comedy.

We have seen that the release of distressing affects is the strongest obstacle to the working of comedy. Once some unintentional movement does harm, some stupidity leads to disaster, some disappointment causes pain, there is an end to the possibility of a comic effect, at least for the person who is vulnerable to such unpleasure, is stricken by it himself or has to share in it, whereas the behaviour of someone uninvolved shows that the situation concerned contains everything needed to make a comic effect. Now humour is a means of obtaining pleasure in spite of the distressing affects that disturb it; it acts as a substitute for this emergence of affect, it takes its place. The condition for it is given if there is a situation in which we are tempted to follow our habitual behaviour and give vent to the distressing affect, and if we are then influenced by certain motives to suppress this affect *in statu nascendi*. In the cases just described, the person affected by the harm, pain, etc., might be able to obtain the pleasure of humour, whereas someone uninvolved will laugh the laugh of comedy. The pleasure of humour arises – there is no other way of putting it – at the cost of this release of affect that did not happen. It comes from *an expenditure of affect saved*.

Humour is the most undemanding of the varieties of the comic; the process is already completed in one single person; another person's participation adds nothing new to it. My enjoyment of the humorous pleasure that arose is something I can keep to myself without feeling any urge to communicate it. It is not easy to say what is going on in the production of humorous pleasure in the one person; but we shall gain a certain insight if we investigate those cases of humour that have been communicated or that have been appreciated sympathetically, in which by my understanding of the humorous person I arrive at the same pleasure. The most crass instance of humour – known as gallows-humour – may be instructive. The rogue who is being led to execution on a Monday exclaims: 'Well, that's a good start to the week.' That is actually a joke, for the observation in itself hits the mark, though it is absurdly misplaced, for there is not going to be anything further happening for him this week. But it takes humour to make a joke like that, i.e., to ignore everything that marks the start of this week above all others, and deny the distinction which could have motivated quite special emotions. It is the same when on the way to execution the rogue asks for a scarf for his bare neck so that he doesn't catch cold – an otherwise praiseworthy precaution, but given the imminent fate of this neck one that is tremendously uncalled-for and irrelevant. I must say, there is something like greatness of spirit hiding in this 'blague', in clinging so fast to his normal nature and disregarding everything that was meant to cast him down and drive him to despair. This kind of grandeur in humour makes an unmistakable appearance in instances where our admiration is not inhibited by the circumstances of the humorous figure.

In Victor Hugo's *Hernani*,[23] the bandit who has become involved in a plot against his King, Charles I, King of Spain, and Charles V, the Holy Roman Emperor, has fallen into the hands of this all-powerful enemy. He can foresee what his fate as a convicted traitor will be: his head will roll. But this foreknowledge does not prevent him from revealing that he is a hereditary Grandee of Spain, nor from declaring that he has no intention of giving up his rights as such. A Grandee of Spain may cover his head in the presence of his royal master. Very well:

Nos têtes on le droit
De tomber couverts devant de toi.

[Our heads have the right to fall before you covered.]

This is humour on the grand scale, and if we do not laugh when we hear it, that is because our admiration offsets the humorous pleasure. In the case of the rogue who does not want to catch cold on the way to the gallows, we laugh wholeheartedly. The situation that is supposed to drive the delinquent to despair could rouse intense pity in us; but this pity is inhibited, because we understand that the one who is affected most closely makes nothing of the situation. On account of this understanding, the expenditure on pity that was already mobilized in us becomes unusable – and we laugh it away. The rogue's own indifference – though we note it has cost his psyche great expense – has, as it were, infected us.

A saving in pity is one of the most frequent sources of humorous pleasure. Mark Twain's humour usually operates with this mechanism. When he tells us tales from the life of his brother, who was employed by a great road-building concern, and of how the premature explosion of a mine sent him flying into the air and landing far away from his place of work, emotions of sympathy for the poor man inevitably awaken in us; we would like to ask whether he wasn't hurt in the accident; but the continuation of the story, in which the brother is docked half a day's pay 'for absenting himself from the place of work' diverts us from pity entirely and makes us almost as hard-hearted as that employer, and just as indifferent to the possible damage to the brother's health. On another occasion Mark Twain gives us his family tree, which he follows back more or less to one of Columbus's companions. But after he has described the character of this ancestor – whose entire luggage consists of several shirts, each with a different laundry-mark – we can only laugh at a cost of savings in the family piety we were prepared to identify with at the beginning of the story. In the process, the mechanism of humorous pleasure is not disturbed by our knowledge that this ancestral story is invented, and that this fiction serves the satirical intention of exposing the embellishments trumpeted in similar stories from other people; it is just as independent of any condition of reality as in the case where he made [his brother] comic. Another story of Twain's tells how his brother built an underground den and furnished it with bed, table and lamp, with a roof made out of a large piece of sailcloth with a hole in the middle; but how one night, when the room was finished, a homeward cow fell down through the opening in the roof and put out the lamp; how his brother patiently helped to coax the beast up and reinstate his furnishings, how he did the same thing when the same disturbance was repeated the next night. This kind of story becomes comic by repetition. But Twain brings it to an end by telling us that finally, on the night when the cow fell in for the forty-sixth time, his brother remarked: 'this is getting monotonous'. And then we cannot restrain our humorous pleasure, for we had long been expecting to hear how this stubborn misfortune had – annoyed the brother. The little humour that we come up with ourselves in life is something that as a rule we produce at the cost of annoyance, instead of getting annoyed.[24]

The varieties of humour are extraordinarily various, in accordance with the nature of the emotion that is saved in favour of humour: pity, annoyance, pain, sympathy, etc. Nor does there seem to be any end to their number, because the realm of humour can be extended further and further if the artist or writer is successful in bringing emotions still unmastered till now under the control of humour, and, by tricks like those in the previous examples, in turning them into a source of humorous pleasure. The cartoonists of *Simplizissimus*, for example, have accomplished extraordinary feats in winning humour at the cost of revulsion and gruesomeness. The manifestations of humour, moreover, are determined by two peculiarities that have to do with the conditions under which it comes into being. First, humour can make its appearance in fusion with a joke or some other species of comedy; in this case it has the task of removing any possibility that an affect might emerge to bar the pleasurable effect. It can nullify this emergence entirely or just partially – which is even the more frequent case, because it is more easily achieved, and produces the various forms of 'broken'[25] humour, the sort that smiles in the midst of tears. It withdraws a part of its energy from the affect, and in its stead gives it the touch of humour.

The humorous pleasure gained from sympathy, as can be seen from the examples above, arises from a special technique comparable to displacement, by which the release of affect already mobilized is disappointed and the charge diverted to other, often unimportant, things. We can see that the recipient of the humour imitates its creator in his psychical processes, but we learn nothing about the forces that make this process possible in the creator.

One can only say that if someone succeeds, for example, in overcoming a painful affect by contrasting the greatness of world interests with his own pettiness, we do not regard it as an achievement of humour but of philosophical thought, nor do we gain any pleasure when we identify with his train of thinking. So under the light of conscious attention, humorous displacement is as impossible as comic comparison; like comic comparison, it is tied to the condition of remaining preconscious or automatic.

We come to learn something about humorous displacement if we look at it in the light of a defensive process. The defensive processes are the psychical correlatives of the defence-reflex and pursue the task of preventing unpleasure from arising from internal sources; in carrying out this task they act as an automatic regulator for what happens in the psyche, though ultimately this process turns out to be harmful and so has to be subjected to control by conscious thought. I have shown that one particular variety of this defence, unsuccessful repression, is the operative mechanism for the psychoneuroses to emerge. Humour can now be regarded as the highest of these defensive functions. Unlike repression, it scorns to withdraw the content of the imagined idea connected to the distressing affect from conscious attention, and this is how it overcomes the automatism of defence; it brings this about by finding a means of withdrawing energy from the release of unpleasure already mobilized, and by discharging it, of transforming it into pleasure. Only when we were children were there intense distressing affects such as the adult would laugh at today, just as he laughs with humour at the present affects that distress him. The elevation of his self, as witnessed by humorous displacement – though its translation would still run: 'I am too big (and too great) for such occasions to distress me' – could, I suppose, be derived from his comparing his present self with himself as a child. This view is to some extent supported by the role given to the infantile in the processes of neurotic repression.

On the whole, humour is closer to the comic than to the joke. It also shares with the comic its psychical location in the preconscious, whereas the joke, we were bound to assume, is formed as a compromise between the unconscious and the preconscious. Instead, it has no share in a peculiar characteristic which the joke and comedy have in common and which perhaps we have not so far emphasized sharply enough. The condition required for comedy to arise is that we should be prompted to use two different ways of imagining for the same idea *simultaneously or in rapid succession*; it is between these that the 'comparing' then takes place, producing the comic difference. Differences in expenditure of this kind arise between what is someone else's and what is my own, what I am used to and what has changed, what I have been expecting and what has happened.[26]

In the joke, the difference between two ways of apprehending things, emerging simultaneously and operating with different expenditures, applies to the process going on in the listener. One of these ways, following hints contained in the joke, takes the path of thought through the unconscious, the other remains on the surface and views the joke like any other form of words that has come from the preconscious and become conscious. It would not perhaps be an unjustified way of putting it if we were to derive our pleasure in a joke we are told from the difference between these two ways of viewing it.[27]

We are saying the same thing about the joke here as we did when we described its Janus-head at a stage when it appeared that the relation between the joke and comedy had not yet been cleared up.[28]

In humour, the characteristic foregrounded here has been effaced. True, we do feel humorous pleasure when an emotion is avoided which we might have expected would usually be appropriate to the occasion, and to that extent humour too comes under the extended concept of comedy of expectation. But in humour it is no longer a matter of two differing ways of imagining the same content; the situation is dominated by the emotion to be avoided, which is characterized by unpleasure – and that puts an end to any comparability in character between the comic and the joke. Humorous displacement is actually a case of putting the liberated expenditure to a different use – which turned out to be so dangerous to the comic effect.

[G]

We have come to the end of our task now that we have reduced the mechanism of humorous pleasure to a formula analogous to those for comic pleasure and for the joke. Pleasure in the joke seemed to come from savings in expenditure on inhibition, comic pleasure from savings in the imagining of ideas (when charged with energy), and humorous pleasure from savings in expenditure on feeling. In all three methods of operation in our psychical apparatus, the pleasure comes from a saving; all three concur in representing methods for regaining from the activity of the psyche a pleasure which in fact was lost only with the development of that activity. For the euphoria that we try to reach along these routes is nothing other than the temper of a time in our life when we were wont to defray the work of our psyche with the slightest of expenditures: the temper of our childhood – when we were ignorant of the comic, incapable of making a joke, and had no need of humour to feel happy in our life.

(1912)

Notes

1. I have been identifying the naïve here in all cases with the naïve that is comic, which is certainly not generally admissible. But it is sufficient for our purposes to study the characteristics of the naïve in the 'naïve joke' and in the 'naïve obscenity'. A further scrutiny would assume that I intended taking this as a starting-point to explain the nature of the comic.

2. [See Jean Paul, I, section VI, 'On the Ridiculous': 'We lend *our* insight and our perspective to his effort and produce through this contradiction the infinite absurdity' (Hale, op. cit., p. 77).]

3. Bergson (*Le Rire*, 1904) employs sound arguments when he too rejects (p. 99) a derivation of this kind for comic pleasure, which has been unmistakably influenced by the effort to create an analogy to the laughter of someone being tickled. – Lipps's explanation of comic pleasure is on an entirely different level, which should be presented in connection with his view of the comic as something 'unexpectedly small'.

4. The memory of this innervatory expenditure will remain the essential part of the imagined idea of this movement, and there will always be modes of thinking in my inner life in which the idea is represented only by this expenditure. In other contexts, indeed, this element may be replaced by others, for example, by imagined visual representations of the object of the movement, or by word-representations; and in certain kinds of abstract thinking, a sign will be sufficient instead of the full content of the thing imagined.

5. [Freud adopts Lipps's term. This is a very literal rendering of a sentence so elliptical as to obscure the argument. Expanded to a quasi-explanation, it might read: '. . . the difference between the effort I assume by empathy is expended by the other person and the effort I would expend myself'.]

6. As the saying goes: 'Use your head to save your heels.'

7. This opposition running throughout the conditions for the comic, in which the source of comic pleasure appears now as a 'too much' and now as a 'too little', has made no small contribution to confusing the problem. Cf. Lipps (loc. cit., p. 47).

8. [Ivan Petrovich Pavlov (1849–1936): Russian physiologist. Freud is referring to his systematic experiments on conditioning responses in dogs and other animals, begun in 1902.]

9. According to A. Bain (*The Emotions and the Will*, 2nd ed., 1865). 'The occasion of the Ludicrous is the degradation of some person or interest,

possessing dignity in circumstances that excite no other strong emotion' (p. 248).

[The 'happy German expression' indicates 'bringing low', including 'bringing low in rank', and, by extension, 'humiliation'.]

10. 'So it is that every conscious and skilful evocation of comedy is in general called a joke, whether it is the comedy of contemplation or of situation. Of course we cannot use even this concept of the joke here either.' Lipps, loc. cit., p. 78.

11. At most this is put in as an interpretation by the teller of the dream.

12. Loc. cit. [II].

13. Bergson, *Le Rire, Essai sur la Signification du Comique*, 3me édition, Paris, 1904.

14. [Julius Stettenheim (1831–1916): Berlin journalist.]

15. [Gustav Freytag (1816–95): social novelist and dramatist. Schmock is a figure in Freytag's highly successful drama *Die Journalisten* (1854). Where Stettenheim's Wippchen is presented genially, Freytag's characterization of Schmock has strong anti-Semitic overtones.]

16. [Schiller, *Wallensteins Tod (Wallenstein's Death)*, III.13.7; Lamport, op. cit., p. 390.]

17. [Frederike Kempner (1836–1901): minor social reformer and major classic of involuntary humour. Her *Gedichte* (1873) went through eight editions in twenty years.]

18. 'It's all very well for you to laugh. You don't have to live with it.'

19. [Schiller, *Wallensteins Tod (Wallenstein's Death)*, II.6; Lamport, op. cit., p. 361.]

20. [*Die Person*, though feminine in grammatical gender, may strictly be used of persons of either sex. The context would seem to require 'she' here. See Translator's Preface, p. xlii.]

21. [Freud's formulation varies a famous line from Goethe's drama *Torquato Tasso*: '... erlaubt ist, was sich ziemt' (II.2.1006); lit: 'Allowed is what is proper.' Glossed by Robert David MacDonald (London, 1990) as 'Do what thou wilt, provided it *is* the law' (p. 39).]

22. The fact that comic pleasure has its source in the 'quantitative contrast', the comparison of small and large, which after all also expresses the essential relation of child to adult, would indeed be a curious coincidence, if the comic did not have anything further to do with the childish.

23. [Victor Hugo (1802–85): French romantic poet and dramatist. The battle over his drama *Hernani* (1830) marked the victory of the young romantics over the literary establishment of the time.]

24. The grand humorous effect of a figure like the fat knight Sir John

Falstaff relies upon savings in contempt and indignation. We do, it is true, recognize that he is a good-for-nothing glutton and swindler, but our condemnation is disarmed by a great number of factors. We understand that he knows himself just as well as we do; he impresses us with his wit and, apart from that, his bodily prodigiousness has the contagious effect [upon us] of making us regard his person comically instead of seriously, as though our demands for morality and honour could not but bounce off so fat a belly. What he gets up to is harmless on the whole and is almost excused by the comic baseness of the figures he cozens. We admit, the poor man has a right to live and enjoy like the next, and we almost feel sorry for him because in the most important situations we discover him as a plaything in the hands of a figure far superior to him. That is why we cannot get angry at him, and why we add all the indignation we save on him to the comic pleasure that he otherwise creates for us. Sir John's own humour actually arises from the superiority of a self which neither his bodily nor his moral defects can rob of its cheerfulness and its security.

The ingenious knight Don Quixote de la Mancha on the other hand is a figure who possesses no humour himself and in his seriousness gives us a pleasure which one could call humorous, although its mechanism shows an important departure from that of humour. Don Quixote is by origin a purely comic figure, a great child, for the fantasies from his books of chivalry have gone to his head. It is well known that in the beginning that is all the poet wanted to do with him, and that his creature gradually grew beyond the intentions of his creator. But once the writer had provided this ridiculous person with the most profound wisdom and the noblest aims, and made him the symbolic representative of idealism, one who believes that his aspirations can be realized, takes his duties seriously and his promises literally, this person ceases to make a comic effect. Just as in other cases humorous pleasure arises from preventing an emotion, in this one it arises by disturbing comic pleasure. But with these examples we are already departing noticeably from the simple cases of humour.

25. A term which is used in a very different sense in the aesthetics of Friedrich Theodor Vischer.

26. If we are not afraid of forcing the concept of expectation slightly, we can follow Lipps and ascribe a very large field of the comic to the comedy of expectation. But the very cases that are probably the most primitive instances of comedy – those arising from comparing someone else's expenditure with one's own – would fit this context least.

27. We can keep this formula without further question, for it does not imply anything that might contradict our earlier discussions. The difference between the two expenditures must essentially boil down to the expenditure on inhibition that has been saved. The lack of this saving on inhibition in the comic and the absence of a quantitative contrast in the joke would determine how the comic feeling differs from the impression made by a joke, for all that they share the characteristic of working with two kinds of imagining for the same view.

28. The peculiar characteristic of the 'double face' has of course not escaped our authorities. Mélinaud, from whom I have taken this expression ('Pourquoi rit-on?', *Revue des deux Mondes*, February, 1895), formulates the condition for laughter as follows: 'Ce qui fait rire, c'est ce qui est à la fois, d'un côté, absurde et de l'autre, familier [What makes us laugh is what is at once, on the one hand, absurd and, on the other hand, familiar].' This formula fits the joke better than comedy, but it does not entirely cover the former either. – Bergson (loc. cit., p. 98) defines the comic situation by the 'interférences des séries': 'Une situation est toujours comique quand elle appartient en même temps à deux séries d'évènements absolument indépendentes, et qu'elle peut s'interpréter à la fois dans deux sens tout différents [A situation is always comic when it belongs at the same time to two series of events which are absolutely independent of each other, and which can be interpreted in two entirely different senses at once].' – For Lipps, comedy is 'the bigness and the smallness of the same thing'.